Stoneover

Stoneover

The Observed Lessons and Unanswered Questions of Cannabis Legalization

Edited by
Nikolay Anguelov and Jeffrey Moyer

LEXINGTON BOOKS
Lanham • Boulder • New York • London

Published by Lexington Books
An imprint of The Rowman & Littlefield Publishing Group, Inc.
4501 Forbes Boulevard, Suite 200, Lanham, Maryland 20706
www.rowman.com

86–90 Paul Street, London EC2A 4NE, United Kingdom

British Library Cataloguing in Publication Information Available

Library of Congress Cataloging-in-Publication Data

Names: Anguelov, Nikolay, editor. | Moyer, Jeffrey, 1990– editor.
Title: Stoneover : the observed lessons and unanswered questions of cannabis legalization / edited by Nikolay Anguelov, Jeffrey Moyer.
Description: Lanham : Lexington Books, [2022] | Summary: "Combining examples of the interplay of the benefits and costs of decriminalization implementation with an honest discussion of the possible negative aspects of recreational legalization and whom it most harms, this book offers policy makers information for future policy designs with a goal to decrease negative externalities and social inequity"—Provided by publisher.
Identifiers: LCCN 2021048351 (print) | LCCN 2021048352 (ebook) | ISBN 9781793651525 (cloth) | ISBN 9781793651532 (epub)
Subjects: LCSH: Marijuana—Law and legislation—United States. | Marijuana—Social aspects—United States. | Drug legalization—United States.
Classification: LCC KF3891.M2 S76 2022 (print) | LCC KF3891.M2 (ebook) | DDC 345.73/0277—dc23/eng/20211105
LC record available at https://lccn.loc.gov/2021048351
LC ebook record available at https://lccn.loc.gov/2021048352

Contents

Introduction vii

1 High Polarization, Low Elite Signaling: Public Opinion and Changes in Support for Cannabis Reform 1
Paul Musgrave and Clyde Wilcox

2 The Cannabis Strain: Marijuana Prohibition in an Era of Police Defunding 21
Robert Hardaway

3 Seeing through the Haze: Using Intersectionality to Reveal Systematic Differences in Support for Marijuana Decriminalization 43
Geoffrey Whitebread

4 The Politics of Marijuana, Immigration, and Latinos 61
Joe R. Tafoya and Melissa R. Michelson

5 Implementing Social Equity: Opportunities and Challenges from Marijuana Legalization in Massachusetts 83
Jeffrey Moyer

6 The Regulation of Medical Cannabis: Bureaucracies and Policy Implementation Challenges 109
Céline Mavrot

7 Consumer Well-Being and Cannabis Spending Habits: Evidence from Massachusetts 131
Steven White, Catharine M. Curran-Kelly, Paul Bacdayan, and Marion McNabb

8 Exaggerated Panic or Valid Concerns? Post-Legalization Youth Drug Use 151
Renee Scherlen and José Antonio Cisneros-Tirado

9 Using Administrative and Survey Data to Evaluate the Impact of Changing Marijuana Laws and Policies on Marijuana Use, Treatment Admissions for Marijuana, and Mortality Related to Marijuana and Other Drug Use 167
Maggie Martin, Rebecca Ivester, Jesse Mishra, Maryam Salihu, Sonja Richard, and Ryan Kling

10 The Unintended Consequences of Marijuana Decriminalization on Illegal Commerce and the Opioid Crisis 187
Nikolay Anguelov, Michael P. McCarthy, and Thalia Valkanos

Index 213

About the Editors 215

About the Contributors 217

Introduction

In 2013, noted drug policy scholars Jonathan Caulkins, Beau Kilmer, and the late Mark Kleiman began their concluding chapter to "Marijuana Legalization—What everyone needs to know" with the short but effective statement "We don't necessarily agree, and none of us is sure." Nearly a decade has passed since that writing and when voters in the states of Colorado and Washington charted a new path forward for drug policy in the United States. Over the years, further developments have come at a regular and deliberate pace. According to estimates from the National Conference of State Legislators (NCSL), at least two in five Americans now live in a state with recreational cannabis sales.[1] Data on public opinion on the issue indicate that three in five Americans say that cannabis should be legal for both medical and recreational use.

The voice of the public on the issue has direct political impact on the introduction and diffusion of marijuana reform through the use of direct democracy legislative tools. Generally referred to as "ballot initiatives," cannabis reforms have been passed through the use of ballot measures in two steps of the legislative process. The first is the proposal stage, where enough signatures from citizens are needed to actually appear on ballot, along with other proposed legislation on which citizens vote. The next is the formal vote. Formalized as a legislative tool in state constitutions, ballot initiatives are utilized in 26 states and the District of Columbia.[2] This volume tracks how it was those states in which marijuana decriminalization reforms proliferated. In the context of policy diffusion, even states without direct democracy measures are beginning to successfully introduce and pass cannabis reforms via the formal legislative channels.[3]

Such legislation is nuanced, different in kind and in type, and increasingly cautious. The chapters in his volume offer a chronological account of the national trend of reform with examples of specific issue foci that explain why, even with the general favorable national attitudes for marijuana legalization, messages of caution are entering the discussion. Elected officials in many states, even more liberal ones that do not have ballot measure provisions, have been more cautious in enacting cannabis liberalization measures (Kamin, 2015) with concerns[4] about a stimulus effect on illegal drug commerce and increases in teen and young adult use—a social reality that no decriminalization law addresses (Anguelov, 2018).

Cannabis reforms in their three main incarnations: (1) decriminalization of the possession (and use) of "small amounts,"[5] (2) medical marijuana laws (MMLs), and (3) legal adult recreational use, only impact citizens 21 years of age and older. Yet, the main cannabis consumer in the United States is and has always been the American teenager. Teen consumption is the topic of analysis in several of the chapters in this book, with national and local sample analyses that evaluate the links between the social support for marijuana use among adults (voting age Americans, as captured by the passing of reforms via formal political channels) and teenagers. Even with such hesitation, the political winds have clearly shifted in favor of legal cannabis sales, with legislators in Virginia, New York, Connecticut, New Mexico adopting recreational measures in 2020 alone.

What now are Americans to make of this new reality? As the haze behind the promises of supporters of commercialized cannabis stores rises, the claims seem difficult to fully evaluate. While many states have seen a steady stream of "green" tax revenue, the regulated legal market itself faces an uncertain future when put into competition with the still present unregulated cannabis suppliers.

The unregulated cannabis market poses many challenges, especially in California, where much of the nation's illicit cannabis is grown. This agricultural growth is nearly all unregulated, consuming a great deal of water resources and imposing a significant environmental cost that contributes to extreme climate events. Nationally, the production of cannabis has various shades of legality that flow into an informal distribution network, creating a gray market. The supply dynamics of it undermine tax revenue, public health goals for product purity and safety, as well as "youth diversion," as is the term that has emerged to describe the efforts to educate and prevent increasing teen consumption in states where marijuana commerce is legal to some degree (Saloner, McGinty, & Barry, 2015; Thurstone, Lieberman, & Schmiege, 2011). Officials are still struggling to identify unintended consequences of reform, such as evidence from late 2019 that a chemical used in unregulated vaping products led to increased incidences of a chronic lung disease across the country (U.S. Food and Drug Administration, 2020).

Even in formal legal cannabis markets—those where cultivation for legal sales is under a regulatory state-level structure—there are challenges of social and economic equity for communities impacted by cannabis criminalization. During legalization efforts, equity provisions can sometimes be twisted as linguistic cover for industry-favored frameworks, while the results can disappoint activists from impacted communities. For example, as New Mexico's legislature acted to legalize recreational cannabis in 2021, Hispanic and Native American communities in the state feared legal cannabis producers would take a disproportionate amount of water. Such activists often lack the political access and resources to match industry lobbyists, even with political leaders nominally sympathetic to their cause. The resulting mismatch of economic opportunities flowing to individuals and communities serves to reinforce, rather than disrupt, structural inequalities, making political compromise on further liberalization and harm reduction approaches more difficult.

As the impacts of cannabis decriminalization, and the subsequent market developments, are evaluated in social, political, and medical circles, this text adds to the body of evidence with examples of successes and frustrations. It is still too early to make definitive statements about the increased normalization of cannabis use among the general population. Cannabis is far from being a new substance in medical research. Clinical works on the long-term effects of habitual consumption are entering a new phase, as state-level legality has also enabled more research trials. While much pro-reform rhetoric is based on the long-standing belief of advocates that cannabis is not addictive, has medically beneficial properties, and is not a "gateway" drug that fuels addiction, the clinical works behind these claims are not without their critics. Among the works questioning these assumptions, a vein of literature has emerged that has provided evidence of "cannabis use disorder," as is the phrase, with evidence that it results from heavy use of high-potency strains, consumed in an ever-increasing variety of ways (Ferland & Hurd, 2020; Johnson et al., 2020).

The chapters in this volume offer examples of the interplay of the benefits and costs of decriminalization implementation, with an honest discussion of the possible negative aspects of recreational legalization and whom they befall. It is clear from the two decades (and more) of research covered by the authors in his book that legalization efforts are here to stay. They have reached the federal government in America.[6] This book aims to offer policy makers information for future policy designs with a goal to decrease negative externalities and social inequity.

Nikolay Anguelov, PhD
Jeffrey Moyer, PhD
October 2021

NOTES

1. https://www.ncsl.org/research/civil-and-criminal-justice/marijuana-overview.aspx
2. https://ballotpedia.org/Ballot_initiative

3. https://www.ncsl.org/research/civil-and-criminal-justice/marijuana-overview.aspx

4. https://www.nytimes.com/2019/06/19/nyregion/marijuana-legalization-ny.html

5. a concept discussed throughout the book in its various definitions

6. https://www.latimes.com/politics/story/2021-07-29/what-are-the-chances-senate-will-legalize-pot-marijuana

REFERENCES

Angulov, N. (2018). *From Criminalizing to Decriminalizing Marijuana: The Politics of Social Control.* New York: Lexington.

Caulkins, J., Kilmer, B., & Kleiman, M. (2016). *Marijuana Legalization: What Everyone Needs to Know.* New York: Oxford.

Davis, T. (2021). *State's Water Takes a Hit from Cannabis Farms.* Retrieved from Albuquerque Journal: https://www.abqjournal.com/1406718/states-water-takes-a-hit-from-cannabis-farms.html

Ferland, J. M. N., & Hurd, Y. L. (2020). Deconstructing the neurobiology of cannabis use disorder. *Nature Neuroscience*, *23*(5), 600–610.

Johnson, E. C., Demontis, D., Thorgeirsson, T. E., Walters, R. K., Polimanti, R., Hatoum, A. S., & Wang, J. C. (2020). A large-scale genome-wide association study meta-analysis of cannabis use disorder. *Lancet Psychiatry*, *7*(12), 1032–1045.

Kamin, S. (2015). The battle of the bulge: The surprising last stand against state marijuana legalization. *Publius: The Journal of Federalism*, *45*(3), 427–451.

Rainey, J. (2018). *Why California Won't Necessarily Grow (All) America's Marijuana.* Retrieved from NBC News: https://www.nbcnews.com/news/us-news/why-california-won-t-necessarily-grow-america-s-marijuana-n834466

Saloner, B., McGinty, E. E., & Barry, C. L. (2015). Policy strategies to reduce youth recreational marijuana use. *Pediatrics*, *135*(6), 955–957.

Teehan, S. (2021). *Social Equity Component of CT's New Marijuana Law Could Have Major Impact on Industry's Formation.* Retrieved from Hartford Business Journal: https://www.hartfordbusiness.com/article/social-equity-component-of-cts-new-marijuana-law-could-have-major-impact-on-industrys

Thurstone, C., Lieberman, S. A., & Schmiege, S. J. (2011). Medical marijuana diversion and associated problems in adolescent substance treatment. *Drug and Alcohol Dependence*, *118*(2–3), 489–492.

U.S. Food and Drug Administration. (2020). *Lung Injuries Associated with Use of Vaping Products.* Retrieved from FDA website: https://www.fda.gov/news-events/public-health-focus/lung-injuries-associated-use-vaping-products

Van Green, T. (2021). *Americans Overwhelmingly Say Marijuana Should Be Legal for Recreational or Medical Use.* Retrieved from Pew Research: https://www.pewresearch.org/fact-tank/2021/04/16/americans-overwhelmingly-say-marijuana-should-be-legal-for-recreational-or-medical-use/

Chapter 1

High Polarization, Low Elite Signaling

Public Opinion and Changes in Support for Cannabis Reform

Paul Musgrave and Clyde Wilcox

The politics of marijuana have changed dramatically over the past century. At the beginning of the twentieth century, bureaucratic politics, moral panic, and racism played crucial roles in establishing national prohibition of cannabis (Anguelov, 2018; Lassiter, 2015; Meier, 1994; Michelson & Tafoya, 2014). Consumption of cannabis was originally associated with Mexico and border regions, jazz, and the underclass, and by 1911 a Massachusetts state law regulated cannabis alongside opium and other drugs, soon followed by other states from Maine to California. The increasing restrictions on legally prescribed marijuana drove the drug further into the margins of society, and the federal government criminalized the use of marijuana as early as the 1930s.

By the early 1970s, increasing marijuana use by white, middle-class youth led to a backlash against criminal penalties for marijuana consumption. The changing nature of marijuana consumption disrupted the coalition of bureaucratic entrepreneurs and racially motivated activists who had sustained cannabis prohibition, opening what seemed to be a policy window for legalization or at least decriminalization (Massing, 1998). For a brief moment, it seemed as though marijuana legalization was possible. The high-water mark for support for legalization in the twentieth century was reached in the middle of the 1970s. President Gerald Ford's son Jack publicly discussed his marijuana use and stated his belief that it should be treated no differently than beer and wine ("Ford's Son, 23, Says He Smoked Marijuana," 1975). In 1977, the Carter administration recommended to Congress that marijuana should be decriminalized ("Carter Asks Congress to Decriminalize Marijuana Possession," 1977). During the 1970s, many states moved toward decriminalization, and Alaska's state Supreme Court even discovered a right to privacy that protected an adult's ability to use and possess small amounts of cannabis (Brandeis, 2012).

In the late 1970s and early 1980s, however, the rise of anti-narcotics activists and a series of scandals among prominent decriminalization advocates sparked the Reagan administration's "war on drugs" (Meier, 1994, pp. 49–54; Musgrave & Wilcox, 2014). The backlash was quickly followed by a collapse in support for legalization, which reached its nadir in the late 1980s and 1990s, perhaps best symbolized by Judge Douglas Ginsburg's withdrawing of his nomination to the Supreme Court after news reports of his smoking marijuana emerged (Roberts & Times, 1987)—or by President Bill Clinton's admission as a presidential candidate that he had tried marijuana but "didn't inhale." In 1990, Alaska voters recriminalized marijuana through a voter initiative (Edge & Andrews, 2014).

The pendulum has since swung dramatically toward a pro-legalization stance, especially including the use of marijuana as a form of medical treatment for pain and other conditions with a doctor's prescription—a form of policy innovation that first became law in California in 1996. Since the mid-1990s, increasing numbers of Americans have supported various types of marijuana reform (Galston & Dionne, 2013). As of April 2021, a Pew poll found that 59% of Americans believed that marijuana should be legal for medical and recreational use, while a further 31% reported a belief that it should be legal for medical use only. Only 8% responded that it should not be legal at all (Schaeffer, 2021).

The policy consequences of this attitudinal shift have been real, if uneven. As of this writing, despite continued federal prohibition, about three dozen states have approved cannabis for medicinal uses, while 17 states and the District of Columbia permit recreational consumption (Hartman, 2021). The regulation of the consumption of marijuana by private individuals—much less its cultivation and sale—remain a flashpoint in federal-state relations. The sober Congressional Research Service, a legislative support agency that provides nonpartisan information to members of Congress and its staff regarding policy and legal matters, entitled a report regarding marijuana policy in the states "State Marijuana 'Legalization' and Federal Drug Law," a choice of punctuation that underscores how seriously federal agencies regard the continuing criminalization of marijuana usage, cultivation, and sale.

National policy sends a barrage of mixed messages. Congress has routinely added language to appropriations bills barring the Justice Department from prosecuting medical cannabis operators for noncompliance with federal law if their behavior is legal in the state, which a recent court ruling held does indeed limit the federal government's ability to prosecute violators of certain activities ("Ninth Circuit Clarifies Restrictions On Prosecutions Related To

Medical Marijuana," n.d.). On the other hand, individuals and firms who operate in states that have legal marijuana markets find themselves closed off from most banking operations because their trade is illegal under federal law. Required to operate only in cash, dispensaries and other players in the marijuana markets face not only commercial inconvenience but also risks to safety because the large amounts of cash tempt robbers (Mandelbaum, 2018). On the political level, signals have been similarly mixed, even within the Democratic Party. The Democratic-led House of Representative passed a sweeping reform bill in December 2020 (Edmondson, 2020), but the Biden administration has been slow to embrace reform efforts despite their popularity (Lopez, 2021), even aggressively dismissing staffers who have used marijuana or rescinding job offers for the same reason (Thompson, Fertig, Barrón-López, & Meyer, 2021).

The immense shifts in aggregate public opinion regarding marijuana—and the uneven policy responses that have partly accompanied and partly produced those swings—pose interesting puzzles. Political scientists and legal scholars have grown interested in the political processes related to the mainstreaming of cannabis. Some focus on the issue's implications for federalism (Kamin, 2015; Rose & Bowling, 2015; Shu-Acquaye, 2016) while others examine how marijuana regulation is associated with repressive policing of minority communities (Tate, Taylor, & Sawyer, 2014) and how policy diffusion and other pathways are illuminated by such developments (Anguelov, 2018). Such arguments speak to a broader point: the necessity of understanding the dynamics that created, sustain, and may end marijuana prohibition may matter for issues beyond the regulation of cannabis. Given the inherently political nature of criminalizing, regulating, and liberalizing the use of marijuana, it seems worthwhile to examine what political science can uncover about these broad shifts in society.

To that end, in this chapter, we seek to connect cannabis politics to another debate in political science: political polarization among mass audiences. We examine the puzzle: Why have expressed attitudes toward marijuana changed so much, so quickly? We argue that the evidence proves consonant with a process of opinion formation that involves political polarization but not through the traditional mechanism of elite cues from senior party and political leaders—most of whom have been low-key or hostile to reform efforts even since the 1990s (Musgrave & Wilcox, 2014).

After reviewing the literature in political science about the causes and consequences of polarization, we turn to an analysis of public opinion data to demonstrate quantitatively that since the 1990s public opinion on marijuana reform has become much more associated with party identification. Although the growing popularity of marijuana legalization means that the polarization of this issue is becoming attenuated, striking partisan differences in support for legalization persists, contrary to common assertions that the issue is a rare example of a nonpartisan debate (Franki, 2019; Galston & Dionne, 2013). We argue that top-down models of polarization or sorting cannot explain this outcome, since the conditions asserted to be necessary for such mechanisms to operate have not held. This political account of marijuana attitudes contrasts with social explanations privileging factors such as religious attendance without much evidence. We conclude by outlining implications of our findings and directions for future research.

REVIEWING THE POLARIZATION-SORTING DEBATE

Researchers generally agree that American politics has become more polarized over the past generation, but they debate polarization's cause, extent, and consequences (Hetherington, 2009; Layman, Carsey, & Horowitz, 2006). Some argue that elites have polarized, but most Americans have not (Fiorina, Abrams, & Pope, 2011). Others disagree, favoring an explanation that Americans have not changed their minds about politics, only their affiliation (Levendusky, 2010). In this view, apparent polarization among mass audiences simply reflects that many conservative voters who were once Democrats have moved to a new home in the Republican Party and many liberals who were once Republicans have nested among Democrats (Fiorina & Levendusky, 2006, p. 53). In contrast, scholars such as Abramowitz and Saunders (2008) argue that the mass public's political opinions, affiliations, and even emotional attachments are becoming not only better sorted into parties but also more extreme as voters change their minds to mirror their party's positions (see also Hetherington, Long, & Rudolph, 2016; Mason, 2016; Jacoby, 2014).

Many argue for a central role for elite actors. For instance, Layman and Carsey (2002, p. 788) argue that citizens "receive political cues from party elites," although they contend that only informed citizens will perceive those cues. Such claims resonate with the claims of Carmines and Stimson (1989, p. 6) that "strategic politicians play the most obvious and perhaps most influential role" in issue evolution. Mass sorting and/or polarization would therefore follow, although largely through generational replacement given the stickiness of partisan attachments (Stoker & Jennings, 2008; Zaller, 1992). Levendusky's (2010, p. 35) rejoinder seems to speak for many in asserting the primacy of elite signals and preferences: "Politics, however, is only a peripheral concern for most voters; hence, they need the guidance of elites to make sense of the political world." Such guidance must be sustained: "Because voters pay only sporadic attention to politics, and glean only a basic message from what elites say, they will need to hear repeated messages from elites" (p. 19). And that signal must be clear: "Voters do not deal in subtlety, they deal in simplicity: which party is more liberal, and whether the parties are united or divided on an issue" (p. 19). Extending similar dynamics to positions on particular issues is straightforward: once national leaders—members of Congress, presidents, and candidates for major office—stake out a party's position on a claim, then partisans will either change their beliefs to match or sort themselves into the right category (Carmines & Stimson, 1989).

The implications of a top-down model for marijuana reform political activism would be that, in a polarized society, capturing a party would be essential to carrying out a reform agenda. If voters respond principally to cues from co-partisan elites, then their positions should change most strongly after those cues are given by those elites. If the top-down model described the only mechanism capable of generating changes in voters' beliefs, especially in a highly polarized system, then voters would be essentially unable to discern new, lastingly important opinions of their own.

Others dissent from this top-down model as an explanation for polarization. Lindaman and Haider-Markel (2002) find that elite signaling and polarization are insufficient to shift mass attitudes on "culture war" issues like pornography. Jelen and Wilcox (2003) find remarkable stability in mass attitudes toward abortion despite elite polarization. Lee (2002) argues that the realignments of the civil-rights era, Carmines and Stimson's signature example, resulted not from strategic politicians' efforts but from decades of activism among "non-elite" actors in the black community. Similarly, Feinstein and Schickler (2008) trace the realignment to meso-level activism and entrepreneurship in state parties and networks beyond federal elected officials. Noel (2014) argues that even earlier ideological struggles among journalists and other idea entrepreneurs enabled these coalitional realignments. These critiques suggest how actors other than the policy and political elite could play a role in polarization and sorting—that polarization could be consistent with the operation of bottom-up processes in at least some issue areas. Given the prominence of voter initiatives and ballot referendums in driving marijuana reform efforts over the past quarter-century, there is ample reason to think that these theories might be relevant for marijuana reform politics.

Both elite-driven theories of polarization and sorting, then, agree that polarization (or sorting) require clear signals from party elites (especially candidates and officeholders). The logical contrapositive should be that if national political elites are *not* sending clear signals then polarization should *not* take place. Although elites have shifted over the past few decades, there appears to be no reason to believe that they have sent the kind of consistently pro-reform messages that would be necessary to explain the magnitude of the shifts over the past several decades. Other actors, ranging from activists to popular cultural figures to single-issue mobilizers, however, have been at work on this issue. Accordingly, if we can demonstrate that polarization (or sorting) regarding marijuana mobilization has taken place in the absence of such signals, that would lend credence to those who argue for a more contextualized or contingent view of the processes that cause polarization and issue shifts.

PUZZLE: UNEXPLAINED VARIATION IN SUPPORT FOR MARIJUANA LEGALIZATION

We explore these issues by examining public support for legalization of marijuana. Most accounts of public attitudes on the legalization of marijuana focus on rising levels of support across nearly all social and political groups (Galston & Dionne, 2013). For these authors, attitudes on legal cannabis are conceived of as having similar dynamics to that of support for same-sex marriage, but not that of abortion (Norrander & Wilcox, 1999). In contrast, we demonstrate that rising levels of support across party lines mask a growing partisan polarization on marijuana regulation. In this, we differ from recent studies that have highlighted religious and other related factors in a relatively atheoretical framework (Felson, Adamczyk, & Thomas, 2019). Our wager is that understanding this dynamic will shed light on polarization more generally.

There is little reason to expect that party identification would be associated with support for medical marijuana or for full legalization. Most states have moved toward reform through nonpartisan issue referenda in the absence of strong partisan cues supporting reform. Nor does any major national party "own" marijuana as an issue. Although the 2016 Democratic Party platform committee endorsed the eventual legalization of marijuana, for example, that represented a great (and unexpected) shift from decades during which even Democratic presidents who had used marijuana had distanced themselves from cannabis. Consequently, given that the absence of elite signaling should have resulted in an absence of polarization, marijuana seems like a "most-likely" case for top-down models, which will predict no polarization.

The Null Hypothesis: Growing Support for Cannabis Reflects Generational Shifts

Some scholars have posited that growing support for legalization of marijuana is primarily a function of generational replacement (Galston & Dionne, 2013): that as generations less favorable to legalization have shuffled off the stage, generations more favorable have emerged. To assess competing explanations, we turn to data from the General Social Survey (GSS) (Smith et al.,

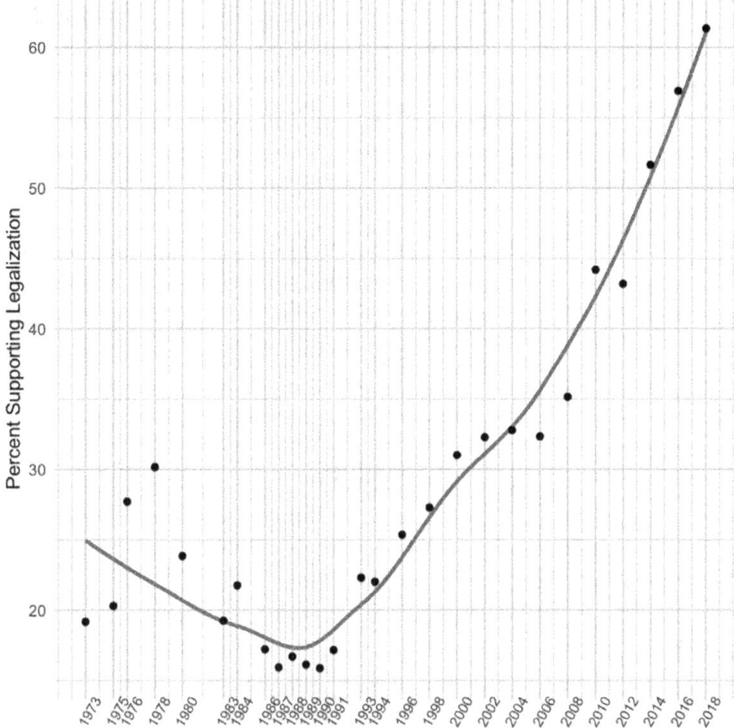

Figure 1.1 Support for Marijuana Legalization, 1973–2018. *Source: General Social Survey.*

2019) to see whether the evolution in mass views has been linear and gradual, as this claim would imply. The GSS question GRASS asks, "Do you think the use of marijuana should be made legal, or not?" Figure 1.1 displays trends in public responses to this question during the past four decades using the GSS data, a consistently measured variable.

Closer investigation of trends by subgroups points toward rejecting, or at least complicating, a generational explanation for these trends. Moderate support for legalization in the late 1970s gave way to a consensus that cannabis should be banned in the 1980s. Attitudes have shifted more recently toward rapidly increasing support for legalization. Generational replacement accounts for some but by no means all of the dynamic changes in abortion attitudes. More important have been period effects. During the late 1970s and throughout 1980s, support for legalization fell sharply among *all* cohorts, resulting in a compression in generational differences by 1990. The magnitude of this change is striking: In the mid-1970s, support for legalization among those born between 1966 and 1975 was nearly three times higher than for those born between 1936 and 1945. By the 1990s, the gap had practically disappeared. In practical terms, by about 1989, the attitudes of the baby boomers (1946–1955) had come to resemble that of their grandparents' restrictive attitude more closely than their own youthful enthusiasm for cannabis. Given the plausibility of arguments that recent policy diffusion at the state level has tracked the views of white baby boomers trying to defend their cultural legacy (Anguelov, 2018, p. 138), it may be surprising to see these shifts in the cohort's views over time. After 1990, younger generations began to evince stronger support for legalization, followed by the baby boomers and trailed by the oldest generations. All cohorts still present in the dataset show sharp increases in support for legalization in the 2000s. In contrast to the expectation of the generational replacement view, support for legalization has been *most* varied among cohorts at the vanguard of changing norms about cannabis usage in the 1970s.

Generational effects may at most explain some variance in *between*-cohort levels of support, but they cannot account for the profound variation *within* cohorts. What explains the residual? Additional descriptive statistics suggest that the importance of politics cannot be neglected. When we divide the data into partisan groups (Republican, Democratic, and Independent), we see something not predicted by a generational or period story. Although all groups have expressed steadily increasing support for marijuana legalization, the increase has been strongest for Democrats and independents, and much weaker for Republicans. (This finding is robust to alternative definitions of party identification.) Over time, moreover, Democrats have become not only as favorable to legalization as have independents, but as of 2018 were even more favorable.

This pattern is so strong, in fact, that it represents prima facie support for an account of growing political polarization despite increasing Republican support. We interpret polarization to include not only precise opposition over an issue but also severe differences between party groups over an issue. The fact that Democrats and independents are nearly twice as likely to favor legalization as Republicans as of 2018—compared with practically identical ratings in 1990 and a gap of fewer than 10 points even in 1978—reflects polarization in itself. To put it another way, a Republican seeking office in a 2018 primary would be campaigning in an electorate that was—at best—evenly divided over legalization, while a Democrat running in a primary in the same year would be campaigning in an electorate in which legalization was almost a fabled 80/20 issue. That both parties' members support legalization more than they did is not grounds to reject polarization. As Hetherington (2009, pp. 430–431) noted about changes in support for marriage equality, differences in rates of change in support for an issue can matter greatly if the issue environment has changed.

REGRESSION ANALYSIS OF SUPPORT FOR LEGALIZATION

We now proceed to test our intuitions using logistic regression. Our chief hypothesis is one predicted by polarization and sorting theories but not predicted by generational, cultural, religious, or other theories: a growing association between party ID and positions on support for legalization.

In the first set of tests, we continue to use GSS data. Our dependent variable remains GRASS, coded 1 for supporting legalization and 0 otherwise. Our chief variable of interest is *Democrat* (1 if the respondent is a Democrat or a Democrat-leaning independent and 0 otherwise). Control variables include *Independent* (1 if the respondent is a "pure" Independent, 0 otherwise) and dummies for *Female, White,* and *College Degree* as well as *Age*, measured in years, and *Income*, as measured by the GSS.[1] We seek to test whether the apparent strengthening relationship between Democratic party identification and support for legalization holds when controlling for other relevant sociodemographic factors.

Using an approach suggested by Gelman and Hill (2007), we calculate separate logit models for each of the 25 GSS surveys to trace the evolution of public opinion. This approach allows us to see if estimated relationships between different factors and our dependent variables are constant or vary over time. We present our results in figure 1.2, showing point estimates of logit coefficients as dots and the 95% confidence intervals for each estimate as lines. We include measurements for standard control variables, including gender, age, education (college degree), white racial identity, household income, religious attendance, and religious affiliation (Catholic, Protestant, and Fundamentalist).[2]

Figure 1.2 suggests that the predictors of support for legalization have changed dramatically over the past five decades. Over time, the association of having attended college with supporting legalization has all but disappeared. Perhaps most important is the emergence of a political split. Democrats have been consistently warmer toward marijuana legalization than Republicans, but this difference was not always statistically significant. After 1990, the coefficients for Democratic party identification have almost always been positive and statistically significant. Furthermore, the trend for those estimates slopes upward, implying that, holding other factors constant, Democrats have grown more supportive of legalization than Republicans.

What do these trends mean in terms of the changing levels and distribution of support in the electorate? Coefficient plots such as those in figure 1.2 may excel in showing trends over time, but they may not immediately demonstrate to most readers the substantive importance of the statistical relationships they describe. To aid in interpretation, we present figure 1.3, which displays

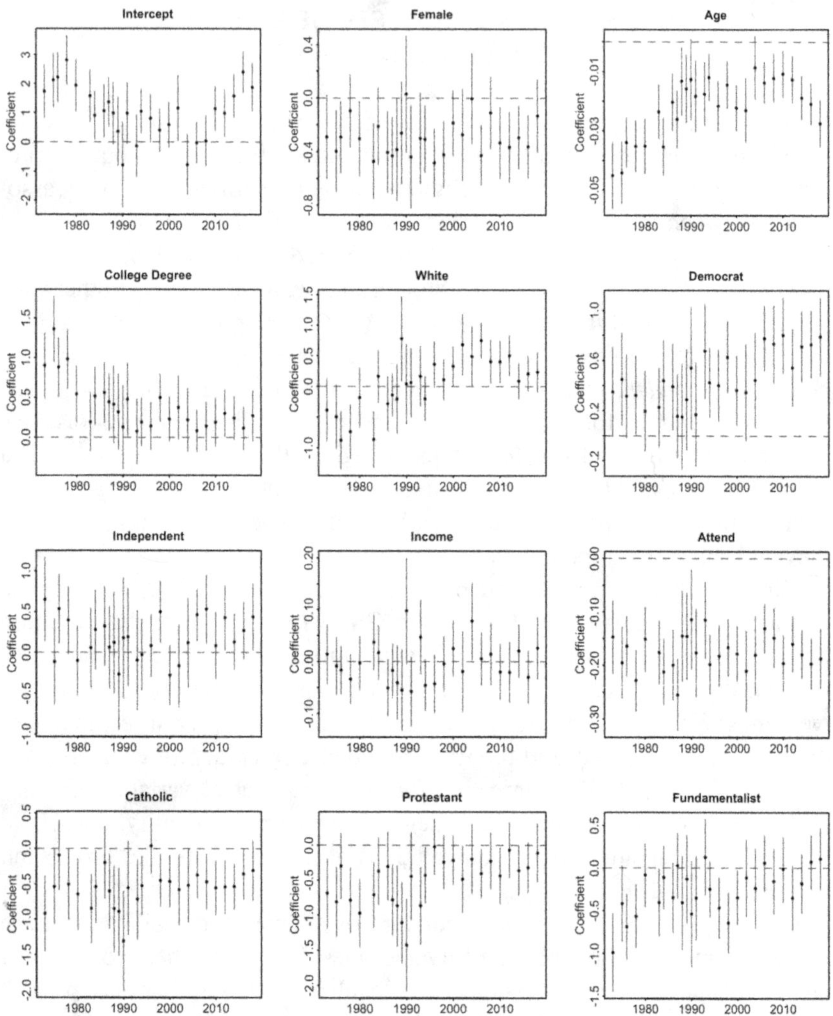

Figure 1.2 Support for Marijuana Legalization by Selected Birth Cohort. Proportion of GSS respondents supporting marijuana legalization by 10-year generational cohort by survey year. *Source: GSS for selected years.*

post-estimation results from the model used in figure 1.2 using GSS data from 1973 to 1975, 1989 to 1990, 2006 to 2008, and 2016 to 2018. We stratify estimates by party and education; all other variables are set at their sample means. In the early 1970s, educated Republicans and Democrats resembled each other in support for legalization. By 1989–1990, college-educated Democrats and Republicans no longer displayed substantial between-party differences. By 2006–2008, between-party differences are readily apparent,

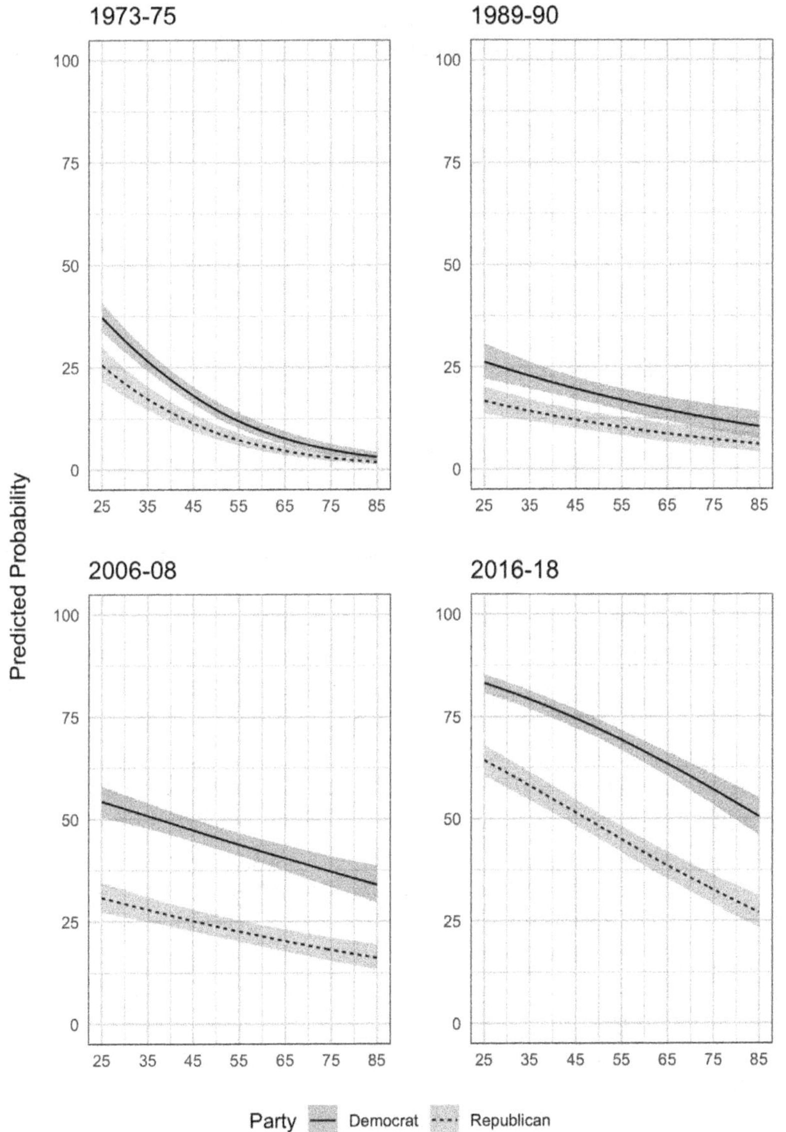

Figure 1.3 Support for Marijuana Legalization by Party, Age, and Year. Percent of GSS respondents supporting marijuana legalization by party identification by survey year. *Source: GSS for selected years.*

and age no longer plays a major role in shaping approval of reform as it had in earlier surveys. In 2006–2008 and 2016–2018, holding other factors constant, *all* Democrats are predicted to support legalization at higher levels than *all* Republicans—and although the model only shows educated partisans, this result holds for Democrats and Republicans regardless of college attainment. To put it another way, in the upper two plots (1973–1975 and 1989–1990), it would be inappropriate to speak of party ID as a major factor; in the lower plots, it would be inappropriate to discuss the issue without putting party ID at the center of the story.

Robustness Checks: Self-Reported Marijuana Usage and Support for Legalization

As useful and as consistent as the GSS data are, they suffer from a major limitation: they do not consistently include a measure of self-reported past marijuana use. Because it is both intuitively obvious (and clear from other analysis of the data) that prior and current users of cannabis may be more likely to support marijuana legalization, it is important to see whether the relationship holds even taking into account variations in prior or current use of marijuana.

To make sure our results are robust to any effect from growing direct familiarity with cannabis, we identify six polls hosted in the ICPSR and Roper databases that have both asked about support for legalization *and* respondents' past marijuana usage. We estimate support for legalization using a model similar to that which produced the estimates in figure 1.2, but omitting religious covariates (which were not measured by these polls). If shifts in identification reflect growing familiarity with cannabis, then the polarization story is unlikely to hold. If, instead, shifts in familiarity with cannabis do not measurably affect the relationship between party ID and support for reform over time, then some explanation involving political factors should be preferred.

We present our results in figure 1.4, displaying coefficient estimates for Democratic Party ID in models of support for legalization including and excluding controls for reported marijuana usage. We omit the presentation of other covariate estimates to focus on comparing the estimated coefficient for party identification for respondents who do, or do not, report having used marijuana. Figure 1.4 demonstrates that, among Democrats, self-reported marijuana use is consistently associated with stronger support for legalization, but including or excluding this factor does not change the estimated coefficient for party identification meaningfully except in a 1997 CBS poll. We repeat the exercise in figure 1.5, switching Republicans for Democrats. This chart reveals almost the precise inverse of figure 1.4. Once again, party identification differs little based upon whether marijuana use

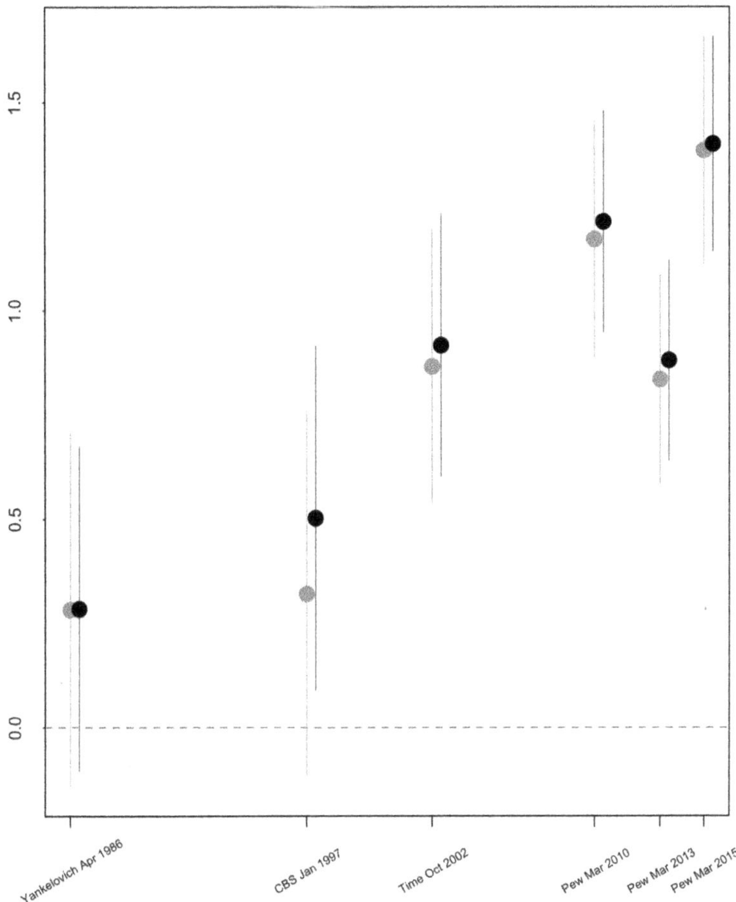

Figure 1.4 Coefficients for Democratic Party ID and Support for Legalization. *Source: GSS for selected years.*

is included in these models—but this time, the relationship between party identification and support for legalization trends sharply downward after the 1987 poll.

To illustrate these findings more completely, we focus on one poll, the March 2015 Pew Research Center survey, and compare predicted support for legalization by party and whether the respondent reports previous cannabis usage (Pew Research Center, 2015). Figure 1.6, based on the March 2015 Pew Research Center national poll, displays a post-estimation plot from a logistic regression model comparing estimated support stratified by party and self-reported marijuana usage. These estimates allow us to compare within-party differences by cannabis usage as well as between-party differences.

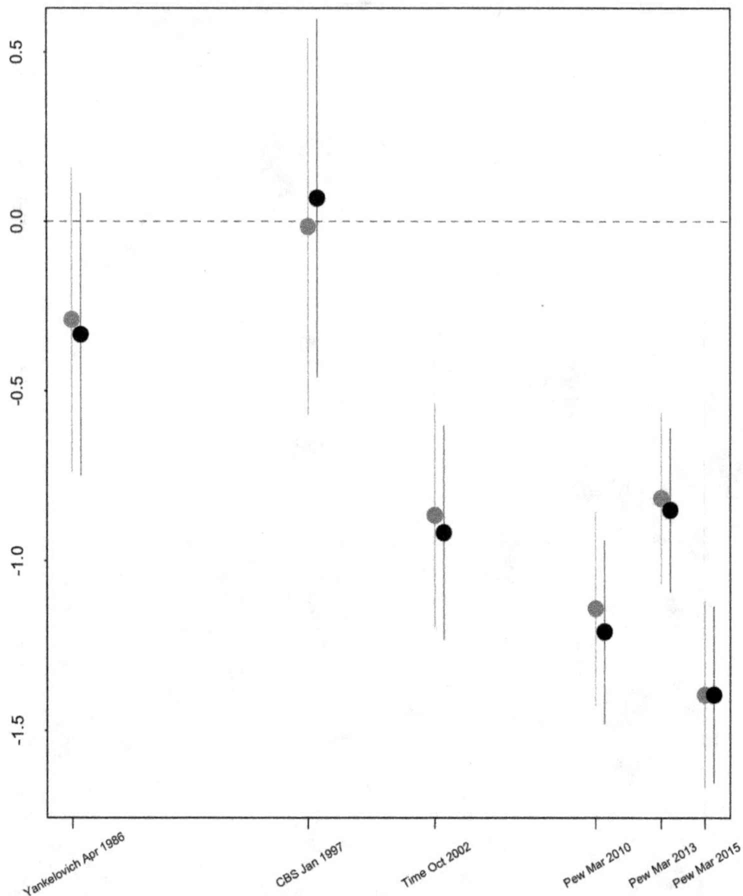

Figure 1.5 Coefficients for Republican Party ID and Support for Legalization. *Source: GSS for selected years.*

Although self-reported marijuana users are more likely than co-partisans to support legalizing marijuana at every age, the substantive impact of party identification is roughly equivalent to that of having been a former (or current) marijuana user: A Democrat who has *not* used marijuana is roughly as likely as a Republican who *has* used to support legalization at any age. This evidence may be taken as a weak signal that sorting is less satisfactory as an explanation than polarization, unless one thinks it is likely that sorting takes place without effecting an underlying propensity to consume cannabis. Taken together, figures 1.4, 1.5, and 1.6 suggest that the association of party with support (opposition) to marijuana legalization is not merely a function

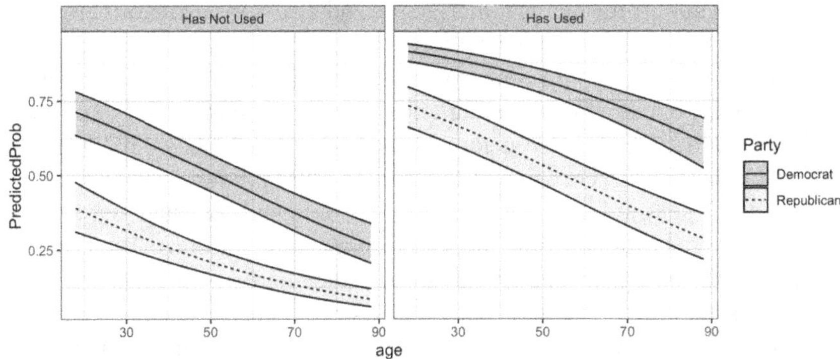

Figure 1.6 Polarization on Marijuana Legalization Between Parties by Self-Reported Marijuana Use. *Source: Polls as indicated retrieved from Roper Center.*

of sorting of cannabis users into one or another party. Rather, party identification in itself has become deeply associated with positions on marijuana legalization.

DISCUSSION: POLARIZATION WITHOUT ELITE SIGNALING?

The partisan gap in support for marijuana legalization has widened over time. This development poses a puzzle, because overt signaling by nationally elected elites has not varied in a way that is immediately apparent to supply a rationale for these differences. Nor, for that matter, have partisan leaders at the national level hastened to support marijuana, even as state-level leaders have turned to the issue—occasionally, as with former New York State Governor Andrew Cuomo's signing of a legalization bill in 2021, as an apparent way to win plaudits with the public during a political crisis (Ferré-Sadurní, 2021).

The signaling of national political elites in both parties has been far from the sustained, clear signal that either sorters (Levendusky, 2010) or polarizers (Abramowitz & Saunders, 2008) assert are most likely taking place. This observation about a lack of elite signaling seems plausibly particularly true for Democrats. Although President Obama hinted at qualified support for some form of decriminalization (Remnick, 2014), Democrats under his administration hardly made it a signature issue. Similarly, in state-level referenda, Democratic officials during this period were often prominent on the anti-legalization side (Blake & Finlaw, 2014, p. 160). Even Republicans have not signaled clearly. Like most Americans, prominent Republicans often voice support for medical marijuana, and also appear rhetorically constrained by the fact that, since most legalization takes place at the state level, opposing it also entails opposing states' rights (Vicens, 2015). It may be the case that Republican elite signaling tends to be more consistently anti-drug than Democratic signaling on the reform side, which may reflect asymmetrical polarization (Grossmann & Hopkins, 2015). Even so, we judge the signals being sent as being far from the unsubtle and repeated signals that top-down models suggest must be sent (Layman et al., 2006). The fact that independents long outpaced members of either party in their support for legalization is consistent with our contention that party leaders long sent negative signals or no signals about their party's position on legalization.

If the top-down models were the only way to produce polarization, then we could not explain why the public is becoming better sorted. And yet it is. How to resolve these discrepant observations? The work of Lee, Feinstein and Schickler, and others suggests that our findings may be comprehensible as part of a process of polarization despite an absence of elite signals if we accept that polarization may take place through less elite-dominated channels, such as activism at the grassroots level, or, alternatively, channels dominated by elites who are not politicians themselves. Although national politicians often refrain from sustained, clear position-taking on state referenda, important *unelected* players in national parties do not, as with the late Republican mega-donor Sheldon Adelson, a Nevada resident who funded 85% of the anti-medical marijuana campaign in Florida (Chokshi, 2014), or liberal billionaire Peter Lewis, donated up to $40 million to advance marijuana reform beginning in the 1980s (Kroll, 2013). The liberal billionaire George Soros may have given even more (Soros, 2010). As students of political parties suggest, intense policy demanders such as activists or wealthy individuals, although not themselves elected officials or office-seekers, may form a part of "extended party networks," and their ability to draw awareness to their favored causes may provide an alternative means of party-based influence on the mass electorate (Bawn et al., 2012; Koger, Masket, & Noel, 2009).

We suggest that the celerity of changes in partisan differences and broad levels of support for marijuana legalization suggests that some form of cue-giving and taking (perhaps even persuasion) is taking place, not just sorting of preexisting beliefs, as Levendusky and others would argue. Such external actors can play a prominent role in helping informed citizens realize what "their" party's position is even if politicians themselves remain silent. These mechanisms might operate even when the forums for deliberating such issues are nominally nonpartisan and elected party elites are silent or mixed on the issue. Similarly, such attempts at changing minds could also help persuade co-partisans' views on this issue once people have sorted themselves into ideologically congruent parties, producing effects like the polarization we see in our statistical analysis of public opinion surveys. We believe that additional work on marijuana reform and related issues could help clarify the mechanisms of polarization and sorting at work not only in these issues but on a deeper theoretical level.

CONCLUSION

Over the past three decades, public opinion regarding the legalization of marijuana has become polarized. Partisanship, once an also-ran in factors predicting members of the public's stance regarding marijuana policy, has become a dominant factor. The growing association of party identification and support for marijuana legalization has occurred largely without the kinds of elite signals or national policy responsiveness that top-down theories would seem to require. The evidence suggests that finding the ultimate cause of this change will have to look not toward the usual suspects of party leaders at the national level and to other surrogates and members of extended party networks.

For political scientists interested in such topics, exploring issues such as marijuana reform presents a potentially rich vein of evidence, theory-generation, and theory-testing to work out how ideological, elite, and mass opinion operates. For activists and others, these findings suggest that substantial movements in public opinion can take place without overtly winning over elites (even if doing so might accelerate mass opinion changes). The continuing gap between public opinion and federal policy change, however, also demonstrates the limits of responsiveness to public opinion.

NOTES

1. Excluding leaning Independents does not substantively change the interpretation presented here.
2. There are too few members of other religions to include them over such a long time period.

REFERENCES

Abramowitz, A. I., & Saunders, K. L. (2008). Is polarization a myth? *Journal of Politics*, *70*(2), 542–555.

Anguelov, N. (2018). *From Criminalizing to Decriminalizing Marijuana: The Politics of Social Control*. Lexington Books.

Bawn, K., Cohen, M., Karol, D., Masket, S., Noel, H., & Zaller, J. (2012). A theory of political parties: Groups, policy demands, and nominations in American politics. *Perspectives on Politics*, *10*(3), 571–597.

Blake, D., & Finlaw, J. (2014). Marijuana legalization in Colorado: Learned lessons. *Harvard Law and Policy Review*, *8*, 359.

Brandeis, J. (2012). The continuing vitality of Ravin v. State: Alaskans still have a constitutional right to possess marijuana in the privacy of their homes. *Alaska Law Review*, *29*, 175–236.

Carmines, E. G., & Stimson, J. A. (1989). *Issue Evolution: Race and the Transformation of American Politics*. Princeton, NJ: Princeton University Press.

Carter Asks Congress to Decriminalize Marijuana Possession. (1977, March 15). *New York Times*. Retrieved from: https://www.nytimes.com/1977/03/15/archives/carter-asks-congress-to-decriminalize-marijuana-possession-cocaine.html

Chokshi, N. (2014, October 10). Casino billionaire Sheldon Adelson is behind 85 percent of Florida's anti-pot campaign. *Washington Post*. Retrieved from: https://www.washingtonpost.com/blogs/govbeat/wp/2014/10/28/casino-billionaire-sheldon-adelson-is-behind-85-percent-of-floridas-anti-pot-campaign/.

Edge, M., & Andrews, L. (2014, April 14). Timeline: Notable moments in 40 years of Alaska's history with marijuana. *Anchorage Daily News*. Retrieved from: https://www.adn.com/cannabis-north/article/alaska-weed-history/2014/04/14/

Edmondson, C. (2020, December 4). House passes landmark bill decriminalizing marijuana. *New York Times*. Retrieved from: https://www.nytimes.com/2020/12/04/us/politics/house-marijuana.html

Feinstein, B. D., & Schickler, E. (2008). Platforms and partners: The civil rights realignment reconsidered. *Studies in American Political Development*, *22*, 1–31. doi: 10.1017/S0898588X08000011

Felson, J., Adamczyk, A., & Thomas, C. (2019). How and why have attitudes about cannabis legalization changed so much? *Social Science Research*, *78*, 12–27.

Ferré-Sadurní, L. (2021, March 31). New York legalizes recreational marijuana, tying move to racial equity. *New York Times*. Retrieved from: https://www.nytimes.com/2021/03/31/nyregion/cuomo-ny-legal-weed.html

Fiorina, M. P., Abrams, S. J., & Pope, J. (2011). *Culture War? The Myth of a Polarized America*. Boston, MA: Longman.

Fiorina, M. P., & Levendusky, M. S. (2006). Disconnected: The political class versus the people. In *Red and Blue Nation? Characteristics, Causes, and Consequences of America's Polarized Politics* (pp. 49–71). Washington, DC: Brookings Institution Press and the Hoover Institution.

Ford's Son, 23, Says He Smoked Marijuana. (1975, October 5). *New York Times*. Retrieved from: https://www.nytimes.com/1975/10/05/archives/fords-son-23-says-he-smoked-marijuana.html

Franki, R. (2019, November 15). *Support for Medical Marijuana Transcends Political Affiliation*. Retrieved May 17, 2021, from MDedge Hematology and Oncology website: https://www.mdedge.com/hematology-oncology/article/212402/oncology/support-medical-marijuana-transcends-political

Galston, W. A., & Dionne Jr, E. J. (2013). The new politics of marijuana legalization: Why opinion is changing. *Governance Studies at Brookings*, 1–17.

Grossmann, M., & Hopkins, D. A. (2015). Ideological republicans and group interest democrats: The asymmetry of American party politics. *Perspectives on Politics, 13*, 119–139. doi: 10.1017/S1537592714003168

Hartman, M. (2021, April 8). *Cannabis Overview*. Retrieved May 17, 2021, from: National Conference of State Legislatures website: https://www.ncsl.org/research/civil-and-criminal-justice/marijuana-overview.aspx

Hetherington, M. J. (2009). Review article: Putting polarization in perspective. *British Journal of Political Science, 39*, 413–448. doi: 10.1017/S0007123408000501

Jelen, T. G., & Wilcox, C. (2003). Causes and consequences of public attitudes toward abortion: A review and research agenda. *Political Research Quarterly, 56*, 489–500. doi: 10.1177/106591290305600410

Kamin, S. (2015). The battle of the bulge: The surprising last stand against state marijuana legalization. *Publius: The Journal of Federalism, 45*, 427–451. doi: 10.1093/publius/pjv026

Koger, G., Masket, S., & Noel, H. (2009). Partisan webs: Information exchange and party networks. *British Journal of Political Science, 39*, 633–653.

Lassiter, M. D. (2015). Impossible criminals: The suburban imperatives of America's war on drugs. *Journal of American History, 102*, 126–140. doi: 10.1093/jahist/jav243

Layman, G. C., Carsey, T. M., & Horowitz, J. M. (2006). Party polarization in American politics: Characteristics, causes, and consequences. *Annual Review of Political Science, 9*, 83–110. doi: 10.1146/annurev.polisci.9.070204.105138

Lee, T. (2002). *Mobilizing Public Opinion: Black Insurgency and Racial Attitudes in the Civil Rights Era*. Chicago: University of Chicago Press.

Levendusky, M. (2010). *The Partisan Sort: How Liberals Became Democrats and Conservatives Became Republicans*. Chicago: University of Chicago Press.

Lindaman, K., & Haider-Markel, D. (2002). Issue evolution, political parties, and the culture wars. *Political Research Quarterly, 55*, 91–110.

Lopez, G. (2021, April 16). Biden's blunt opposition to marijuana legalization. Retrieved April 29, 2021, from Vox website: https://www.vox.com/22387746/biden-marijuana-weed-legalization-schumer-polls

Mandelbaum, R. (2018, January 4). Where pot entrepreneurs go when the banks just say no. *New York Times*. Retrieved from: https://www.nytimes.com/2018/01/04/magazine/where-pot-entrepreneurs-go-when-the-banks-just-say-no.html

Massing, M. (1998). *The Fix*. New York: Simon and Schuster.

Meier, K. J. (1994). *The Politics of Sin: Drugs, Alcohol, and Public Policy*. Armonk, NY: M. E. Sharpe.

Michelson, M. R., & Tafoya, J. (2014). The Latino politics of proposition 19. In K. Tate, J. L. Taylor, & M. Q. Sawyer (Eds.), *Something's in the Air: Race, Crime, and the Legalization of Marijuana* (pp. 115–125). New York: Routledge.

Musgrave, P., & Wilcox, C. (2014). The highs and lows of support for marijuana legalization among white Americans. In K. Tate, J. L. Taylor, & M. Q. Sawyer (Eds.), *Something's in the Air: Race, Crime, and the Legalization of Marijuana* (pp. 79–91). New York: Routledge.

Ninth Circuit Clarifies Restrictions on Prosecutions Related to Medical Marijuana. (n.d.). Retrieved April 29, 2021, from JD Supra website: https://www.jdsupra.com/legalnews/ninth-circuit-clarifies-restrictions-on-87879/

Noel, H. (2014). *Political Ideologies and Political Parties in America.* Cambridge: Cambridge University Press.

Norrander, B., & Wilcox, C. (1999). Public opinion and policymaking in the states: The case of post-Roe abortion policy. *Policy Studies Journal*, *27*(4), 707–722.

Pew Research Center. (2015). *March 2015 Political Survey.* Retrieved November 14, 2021, from Pew Research website: https://www.pewresearch.org/politics/dataset/march-2015-political-survey/

Remnick, D. (2014, January 1). Going the distance. *New Yorker.* Retrieved November 14, 2021, from: http://longform.org/posts/going=the=distance.

Roberts, S. V., & Times, S. T. the N. Y. (1987, November 8). Ginsburg withdraws name as supreme court nominee, citing marijuana "clamor." *New York Times.* Retrieved from: https://www.nytimes.com/1987/11/08/us/ginsburg-withdraws-name-as-supreme-court-nominee-citing-marijuana-clamor.html

Rose, S., & Bowling, C. J. (2015). The state of American Federalism 2014–15: Pathways to policy in an era of party polarization. *Publius: The Journal of Federalism*, *45*, 351–379. doi: 10.1093/publius/pjv028

Schaeffer, K. (2021, April 26). Six facts about Americans and marijuana. Retrieved April 29, 2021, from: Pew Research Center website: https://www.pewresearch.org/fact-tank/2021/04/26/facts-about-marijuana/

Shu-Acquaye, F. (2016). The role of states in shaping the legal debate on medical marijuana. *William Mitchell Law Review*, *42*, 697–791.

Soros, G. (2010, October 10). Why I support legal marijuana. *Wall Street Journal.* Retrieved November 14, 2021, from: http://wsj.com/articles/SB10001424052702303467004575574450703567656.

Stoker, L., & Jennings, M. K. (2008). Of time and the development of partisan polarization. *American Journal of Political Science*, *52*, 619–635.

Thompson, A., Fertig, N., Barrón-López, L., & Meyer, T. (2021, March 30). More potential Biden hires penalized for marijuana use. Retrieved April 29, 2021, from POLITICO website: https://politi.co/3doE65a

Vicens, A. J. (2015, October 10). A blunt guide to how the Republican candidates feel about pot. *Mother Jones.* Retrieved November 14, 2021, from: http://motherjones.com/politics/2015/10/gop=debate=colorado=legal=weed=john=blaze/.

Zaller, J. (1992). *The Nature and Origins of Mass Public Opinion.* Cambridge: Cambridge University Press.

Chapter 2

The Cannabis Strain

Marijuana Prohibition in an Era of Police Defunding

Robert Hardaway

The year 2020 was a year in which several strong societal currents combined to form a perfect storm. A pandemic, the trend toward the decriminalization of marijuana, and outrage over police misconduct converged to lay the foundation for community introspection. The latter in particular has manifested itself in the form of destabilizing civil unrest and demands for solutions to what is perceived as persistent and continuing racial discrimination.

Among the solutions proposed is the defunding of the police as a means of both punishing misconduct and inhibiting police overreach. A number of metropolitan areas across the United States have responded to such demands by implementing this solution. New York City slashed $1 billion from the New York Police Department's 2021 budget (Rubenstein & Mays, 2020), and Los Angeles cut its police force by $150 million (Zahniser, 2020).

Such dramatic reductions have resulted in pushback by those who are convinced that defunding the police will lead to a violent explosion in crime. However, it is unclear that this is the case in practice. For example, New York saw a dramatic 40% rise in shootings in the first three months of 2021 compared to the same period in 2020; this continued increase in gun violence "follows a year where 280 shooting incidents led to murders" (Pereira, 2021). On the other hand, in Chicago, where police budget appropriations have been increasing for four years running (Civic Federation, 2020), there was a 39% jump in murders in June and July 2020, compared to the year before (Andrew, 2020). New York and Chicago's budget appropriations indicate that there is not a direct correlation between increasing police funding and a decrease in criminal activity. It is more complicated than that.

Defunding proponents counter that, in the end, defunding the police would lead to less crime if the city redirected funds for police to social programs that address crime's root causes (Andrew, 2020). They also argue that drastic punitive measures are required to address what they see as systemic racism within the ranks of police across the nation, and have followed up with proposals for "full decarceration of federal [prisons] within 10 years" (Phillips, 2020a). In the aftermath of the violence, defenders attribute the mass exodus of almost a third of a million New Yorkers since the pandemic began to the lockdown rather than the inability or unavailability of police to answer 911 calls (Casiano, 2020).

While police do not deny the existence of some racism within their ranks, it is contended that the internal-affairs departments and local district attorneys rigorously prosecute such officers, and deny any racist agenda or the existence of endemic racism within the police. In support of this contention is data compiled by the Washington Post which shows that during the period 2015–2020 police killed almost twice as many white Americans as black Americans—killing 1,341 black Americans and 2,587 white Americans (Washington Post, 2020).

These raw numbers do not tell the entire story, however, since they fail to take into account the rate of fatal shootings of civilians among black Americans. Analyses of rates reveal that the risk of black men being killed by police—96 black men per 100,000—is more than twice the risk relative to white men (Peeples, 2019). Research suggests that race is a factor in predicting how an officer will police their communities. A study conducted by Texas A&M University also found that white officers were 60% more likely to use physical force than black officers, and that white officers fired their guns twice as often as black officers (Trovall, 2020). Critically, white officers are five times more likely than black officers to use their gun when policing predominantly black neighborhoods (Trovall, 2020).

There is no shortage of analyses of police killings being conducted in the current heated political climate. Public scrutiny of police-involved shootings has increased to an all-time high given heightened racial tensions and the growing prevalence of video cameras. Additionally, given the disproportionate racial biases in these studies' findings, it is difficult to deny that racist tendencies do not play a role in poor policing outcomes.

EFFECTS OF MARIJUANA LAW ON CRIME RATES

It is submitted herein that one of the most destructive assaults on the constitutional rights of black Americans is not to be found in police misconduct—though that must be acknowledged and addressed—but in current drug policy. A monumental study of where the New York City Police Department directs their public safety efforts illustrates the point. From 2002 to 2012, the NYPD spent over 1,000,000 police hours making over 444,000 marijuana possession arrests of mostly young persons of color (Drug Policy Alliance, 2013). Each such arrest by an individual police officer required the expenditure of three to five hours of an individual officer's time, including the arrest itself, booking, the taking of photographs and fingerprints, research of databases and criminal records, transportation to jail, interviews with district attorneys, and subsequent appearances in court (Drug Policy Alliance, 2013).

Such extravagant usage of police manpower and time incurred equally extravagant expenditure of police resources and funding. It is estimated that a single arrest for marijuana possession, including all police resources and court expenses, costs anywhere from $1,500 to over $2,000 (Drug Policy Alliance, 2011). In 2010 alone, New York City spent over $75 million arresting and jailing mostly young people of color for possessing small amounts of marijuana (Drug Policy Alliance, 2011). Over the period 1997–2010, estimates based on data generated by the New York State Division of Criminal Justice Services revealed the total cost to taxpayers of arresting and incarcerating people for possession of marijuana at somewhere between $500 million to over $1 billion (Drug Policy Alliance, 2013). When one considers that during this same time, 8,311 murders took place in New York City (Mitchell, 2008 [data for 1997–1999]; NYPD, 2020 [data for 2000–2010]), the question arises as to whether that $1 billion dollars might have been better directed toward solving murders rather than incarcerating young persons of color for possession of small amounts of marijuana. This question becomes even starker in light of a recent FBI report that found that roughly 40% of the nation's murders went unsolved in 2018 (Jaeger, 2018).

Even those who urge that police funding be directed away from the police toward social services might consider the alternative reform of internally redirecting *current* police funding toward the more immediate task of protecting the lives of black Americans who are now being murdered at a rate many times that of white Americans. In 2018, 7,484 black individuals were murdered, compared to 5,787 white individuals, who represent a much higher percentage of the total population (Statista, 2020). The racial disparity among murder victims is especially concerning in the context of the dramatic increase of homicides in major American cities in 2020 (Calvert & Elinson, 2020).

THE CONSEQUENCES OF CREATING AND ENFORCING LAWS FORBIDDING MARIJUANA USE

A victimless crime is "illegal behavior in which people willingly engage and in which there are no un-willing victims" (University of Minnesota, 2016,

Victimless Crime section, para. 1). Victimless crimes do not have a complainant; the offense is against the state, and law enforcement officers are the ones making the complaint (Bell, 2013). In the case of drug criminalization, the harm to third parties is a by-product of criminalization itself. A Bureau of Justice report, released in 2017, found that between the years of 2007 and 2009, nearly 21% of all sentenced jail inmates committed their offense to get money to spend on drugs (Bureau of Justice, 2017). Additionally, 14% of all sentenced inmates committed violent crimes in order to get money for drugs (Bureau of Justice, 2017). These crimes are pertinent examples of how drug criminalization can turn the otherwise victimless act of personal drug use into potential harm to the rest of society.

A major consequence of enforcing victimless crimes is the mass incarceration of nonviolent offenders. In 1989, toward the peak of the War on Drugs, "drug possessors and traffickers represented roughly 21 percent to 24 percent" of inmates in America's county and municipal jails and "25 percent to 35 percent" of inmates in state and federal prisons (Duke & Gross, 1993, p. 179). In 1989, between 260,000 and 343,000 people were incarcerated in the American penal system for drug crimes (Duke & Gross, 1993). If those convicted of drug-related crimes—crimes to get drug money or murders or assaults arising from the drug business—are included in the calculation, another 150,000 inmates could be included in the tally (Duke & Gross, 1993). Thus, combining these numbers, in 1989, nearly half of the American prison population was composed of people arrested for drug-related offenses (Duke & Gross, 1993).

The legislatures' justification for incarcerating people on such a scale may best be understood through the lens of the Inquisition principle—that a moral higher authority is justified in legislating the actions of the masses, even if those actions are not harming others. By criminalizing drug use, the government is effectively saving the user from harming himself (Barnett, 1994). Even if that is the case, Congress and state legislatures have given far less consideration to the more palpable harm inflicted on innocent people. With such a large percentage of prison space being consumed by drug offenders, "early release programs" have been designed to make room for the influx of drug offenders. Additionally, other crimes are not pursued because police and prosecutors are chasing down drug offenders instead (Barnett, 1994).

A report from Tina Dorsey and Priscilla Middelton revealed that in 1987 drug arrests accounted for 7.4% of all arrests reported to the FBI. By 2007, drug arrests had risen to 13% of all arrests reported to the FBI (Dorsey & Middleton, 2015). Additionally, in 2015, the FBI released their estimates of the number of arrests in the United States during that year. The report revealed that there were nearly 1.5 million arrests for drug-abuse violations (Federal Bureau of Investigation, 2015). Of those 1.5 million drug arrests, 574,640 were for marijuana possession alone (Human Rights Watch, 2016).

This becomes increasingly more concerning when, according to the FBI estimates, there was a total of 505,681 arrests for violent crimes—the FBI has defined violent crimes as murder, non-negligent manslaughter, rape, robbery, and aggravated assault—a number far less than arrests for drug violations (Federal Bureau of Investigation, 2015).

In 2014, black adults represented nearly one-third of those arrested for drug possession despite composing only 14% of those who used drugs in the United States (Human Rights Watch, 2016). Even more, data collected in 2016 revealed that black adults were more than four times as likely to be arrested for marijuana possession compared to white adults (Human Rights Watch, 2016). These statistics suggest an unjustifiable police failure to dedicate sufficient man-hours to protecting black lives in predominantly black communities. One cannot help but wonder how many black lives the police could have saved had they expended more resources toward protecting the lives of the 2,925 black Americans murdered in 2013 (Statista, 2020).

A 2015 Gallup Poll showed that the number of black Americans who wanted *more* police protection in their communities was more than twice as high as the percentage of white Americans who wanted more police in their communities (Mac Donald, 2020). Given that police defunding would result in *less* protection for black Americans who need and want it the most, it is a puzzle as to why some black leaders persist in advocating police defunding as a solution to the disproportionate number of black individuals being murdered in the United States. This puzzle intensifies in light of data showing that this racial disparity is indeed extreme. In 2020, the Huffington Post reported that the murder rate of black Americans is a staggering four times that of the national average (Sugarmann, 2017).

The current high priority given by police to arresting people for possession of small amounts of marijuana, even as 40% of murders go unsolved, is perhaps best understood in the context of a lingering legacy of America's experience with Prohibition. The rationale for that most unfortunate period in the United States' history was that law could be a substitute for social reform; that society should go far beyond simply protecting citizens from the harmful conduct of others and spare no expense in protecting citizens from the consequences of their own behavior. However, by engaging in this process, lawmakers only make matters worse for those whom they are trying to protect.

LAW ENFORCEMENT PRIORITIES

An examination of police priorities at both ends of the law enforcement spectrum illustrates the concerns about the detrimental consequences of marijuana laws. In 2015, Lee Carroll Booker was sentenced to life in prison for marijuana possession after he was caught growing marijuana for his own medicinal use (Walters, 2016). Under Alabama law, former felons convicted for marijuana possession are automatically set to serve life without parole (Walters, 2016). Compare this with a 1994 Indiana murder, where four teenage girls were charged with locking a young woman in a car trunk, sodomizing her with a sharp tire iron, spraying Windex and gasoline on her and then gleefully burning her to death as she pleaded for her life. Even after describing the crime as being "so funny you should have seen it," none of the girls were sentenced to life (Jones, 1994). As of 2019, all four of the murderers have been released (WDRB, 2019).

Booker's life sentence for attempting to alleviate his own health problems is difficult to understand compared to the 60-year sentences in the Indiana murder. However, under the perverse priorities of a society fixated on expending scarce law enforcement resources on tracking down marijuana users, Mr. Booker may have been fortunate to receive only a life sentence without the possibility of parole. In 1989, federal drug czar William Bennett responded to a question about the feasibility of beheading drug offenders by saying, "Morally, I don't have any problem with it" (Moon, 1999, p. 181).

In the 1970s, several states' laws, including Georgia, Louisiana, and Missouri, proscribed the death penalty for youths older than 18 who sold a marijuana cigarette to a youth under 18 (Miller, 1991). In Missouri, the sentence for a second conviction of marijuana possession was life imprisonment without the possibility for parole (Miller, 1991). In California, a first offense for selling a marijuana cigarette carried a life sentence (Miller, 1991).What has been the result of the promulgation of such draconian penalties and the diversion of scarce law enforcement resources to enforcement of marijuana laws in states such as New York City? As Congressman Richard Hobson noted, "[Before criminalization] the narcotic drug addiction problem was a minor medical problem. Today it is a major national health problem, constituting the chief factor threatening public health" (Asbury, 1950, p. 234).

One of the most perverse effects of diverting scarce law enforcement resources away from violent crime to tracking down marijuana offenders is that even modest enforcement successes serve only to intensify the drug problem. As observed by Walter Block, an Austrian economist, in his work *Drug Prohibition: A Legal and Economic Analysis*, "every time a battle is won in the [marijuana war], paradoxically the enemy is strengthened, not weakened. [Interdiction] only succeeds in raising the profit incentives attendant upon production" (Block, 1993, p. 696). This observation holds true even in contemporary society. In 2014, the *Chicago Tribune* released statistics about the average cost of marijuana by state. Those states in which marijuana was fully illegal—meaning neither medical nor recreational use is permitted—had, on average, a higher price per ounce of marijuana than those states where marijuana was legal in at least some capacity (*Chicago Tribune*, 2014). It is not a stretch to conclude that the higher price for marijuana in illicit markets is raising the profit margins of criminals in those markets, whereas criminals in states where marijuana is legal are being undermined by government-regulated marijuana markets.

Nor do the effects of such diversions stop at the borders of America's most drug-ravaged communities. A study by the Drug Abuse Council revealed that for every 10% rise in the price of illegal drugs, overall crime across the United States increased by 2.8% (Silverman et al., 1975). Modern economists argue that this is the case because the demand for illegal drugs is inelastic, meaning that users will pay any price to get their fix. If the supply drops due to increased enforcement, drug dealers are able to increase the price of the drug and sell to addicts to make up for their losses (Wendell, 2016). In Washington DC, this translated into the murder rate doubling after police began to step up and prioritize drug law enforcement (Bandow, 1991). Higher drug prices have another effect on even the most law-abiding, peaceful, and wealthy communities. As reported by the Bureau of Justice, between 2007 and 2009 nearly 40% of state prison inmates arrested for property crimes admitted to committing the crime to obtain money for drugs (Bureau of Justice, 2017).

The exorbitant amount of taxpayer dollars spent on ineffective drug enforcement has yet another collateral and devastating effect on the economy and the states' ability to fund social programs. During the 1980s, at a time when millions of Americans were homeless and desperate, the federal government extracted over $20 billion dollars from hapless taxpayers to fund the "War on Drugs." Drug arrests of Americans doubled during the decade to 825,000. Mass arrests caused the already strained U.S. prison system to parole and grant early release to many murderers, rapists, and child molesters (Barrett, 1998). Domestic wiretaps on American citizens skyrocketed. By 1990, the U.S. State Department reported the results of this mass incarceration of American citizens, predominantly black Americans: production and consumption of illegal drugs climbed to the highest levels in human history (Jehl, 1990). Even faced with the disastrous consequences of diverting scarce resources to the war on marijuana, apologists for the continued criminalization of marijuana possession posited the theory that somehow the expenditure of the country's treasure deterred at least some people from using marijuana and thereby possibly harming their health (Harris & Martin, 2019). However, this is not the case.

Increased drug enforcement only marginally decreases cannabis use at great social expense, while legalization only marginally increases use but is associated with a great increase in tax revenue available for social programs. As was noted earlier, the cost of the War on Drugs was high; however, the results left much to be desired. During the War on Drugs, self-reported cannabis use rose drastically. As was noted in a Gallup study, "before Americans' self-reported experimentation with marijuana leveled off in the 1980s, it surged in the 1970s, rising from 4% in 1969 to 12% in 1973 and 24% in 1977," reaching 33% by 1985 (Saad, 2013). Since 1985, self-reported marijuana use has only risen to 38% (Saad, 2013). Other studies corroborate this research, finding that the prevalence of marijuana use has stayed relatively consistent throughout the end of the 20th century (Miech, 2012). Therefore, increased enforcement does not correlate to a decrease in cannabis use.

While there is no general consensus regarding the effect of marijuana legalization on cannabis use, more recent studies are showing that legalization correlates with a marginal increase in cannabis use among all ages. As researchers discovered in a California case study,

> the proportion of respondents aged 12 to 17 years reporting cannabis use disorder increased from 2.18% to 2.72%, while the proportion of respondents 26 years or older reporting frequent marijuana use increased from 2.13% to 2.62% and those with cannabis use disorder, from 0.90% to 1.23%. (Cerda, 2019, p. 166)

The marginal increase in use is not a simple one-to-one correlation with legalization. Instead, researchers have observed that the social environment surrounding marijuana is often more determinative of other factors. Cohorts born during periods of increased criminalization were less likely to use cannabis than cohorts that were born during periods of relaxed criminalization (Paschall, 2020). The social environment surrounding marijuana can be shaped and mitigated through education and awareness programs, which would be feasible with the increased social spending that is accessible following legalization.

The financial benefits of marijuana far outweigh a minor increase in marijuana use among the population. Since legalizing the sale of marijuana in 2014, Colorado has collected $1.63 billion in tax revenue (Booth, 2021). With this excess funding, Colorado has been able to vastly increase its education spending, enhancing the lives of all individuals enrolled in the state's public school system. Similar results have been found in other states that have legalized the recreational use of marijuana, such as Washington and Oregon, where tax revenue from marijuana in 2020 was $450 million and $133 million, respectively (Bieber, 2021). Oregon has outlined the funds for educational, health, and safety departments, (Oregon Dept. of Revenue, 2021), while Washington focuses on establishing a basic health fund, which, according to the Office of Financial Management, "[provides] basic health care services to working persons and others who lack coverage" (Washington

State Treasurer's Office, 2020). Marijuana tax revenues enrich the lives of their communities, rather than tearing them apart.

THE HARM OF MARIJUANA USE COMPARED TO LIQUOR AND TOBACCO

While some studies have shown less-than healthy effects on recreational marijuana users (Memedovich et al., 2018), they pale in comparison to the adverse effects of other legal drugs and substances. For example, cigarette smoking causes about one in every five deaths in the United States each year, accounting for more than 480,000 deaths annually (U.S., 2015). From 2011 to 2015, excessive alcohol use was responsible for 261 deaths per day, adding up to more than 95,000 deaths each year (Esser et al., 2015). Similarly, in 2019, 70,630 drug overdose deaths occurred in the United States, with deaths involving prescription opioids more than quadrupling since 1999 (Mattson et al., 2019). Furthermore, alcohol has consistently been a major factor in crimes throughout the United States, being involved in roughly 15% of robberies, 37% of sexual assaults and rapes, 27% of aggravated assaults, and 40% of homicide offenses (Galbicsek, 2021).

Conversely, while some marijuana users may experience uncomfortable side effects when consuming products with high levels of THC, as of 2019, there have been no reports of teens or adults dying from a marijuana overdose (National Institute on Drug Abuse [NIDA], 2019). Given these comparisons, it is puzzling why, of the three most commonly used substances—tobacco, alcohol, and marijuana—the federal government has elected to only criminalize marijuana and label it as a Schedule 1 drug. This is the case despite the catastrophic harm that such criminalization inflicts on society and, in particular, on black Americans.

THE RACIST ORIGINS OF ALCOHOL AND MARIJUANA PROHIBITION LAWS

The answer to the mystery of why American laws single out marijuana may lie in the past. Historians can best solve this puzzle by resorting to the history of America's notorious experiment with Prohibition that began with the lightning passage of the Eighteenth Amendment and the Volstead Act in 1919. Like the racist origins of the later prohibition of marijuana by the Federal Government in 1938, Prohibition too can trace its origins to racist attitudes, and to a lesser extent, religious dogma. Unfortunately, lawmakers have paid little attention to the example set by Prohibition. Instead, the racist origins of marijuana regulation live on today and wreak havoc for Americans in minority populations.

As early as 1908, the popular *Collier's* magazine expressed society's racist rationale for Prohibition in an article claiming that liquor inflamed the sexual passions of black Americans: "The primitive [African American] field hand, a web of strong, sudden impulses . . . sits in the road at the height of his debauch, looking at the [picture] of a white woman on the label, drinking in the invitation which it carries. And then comes—opportunity" (*Collier's*, 1908). In League with the Temperance Movement, Protestant denominations in particular viewed alcohol consumption as "undermining Christianity's most powerful incentive to self-discipline and social morality" (Washington, 1903–1919). The result was wretched homes, pauperism, crime, disease and vice, and a general lowering of the moral tone of society. Reformers invoked biblical scripture, citing Ephesians 5:18—"Be ye not drunk with wine" (Washington, 1903–1919).

Whatever the predominant motivation for Prohibition, the tragic results of its imposition became the exemplar for unintended consequences. Production of alcohol doubled from the beginning of Prohibition in 1919 to the height of Prohibition in 1926 (Feldman, 1930). With illicit production left unregulated, death rates from alcoholism and alcohol poisoning quadrupled during the same period (Feldman, 1930). By 1930, the nation's exploding prisons were allocating over a third of its prison space to those convicted of Prohibition offenses, thereby necessitating the parole or early release of murderers, robbers, and rapists (Feldman, 1930).

A blockbuster report to the Wickersham Prohibition Commission in 1929 concluded with much embarrassment, "crime has increased by 50% as a result of Prohibition" ("Records," 1929–1931). Worse still, another official report revealed that "the increase in juvenile delinquency is the direct result of the disrespect for law . . . in the disrespect for the law of Prohibition for liquor and the consequent fear and contempt of the righteous sheriff or policeman" ("Records," 1929–1931). Despite this, a desperate Congress, unwilling to admit the horrors it had unleashed, doubled down in 1929 with the passage of the Jones Act, which created yet another wave of new felonies such as "having knowledge of a speakeasy without reporting it to the authorities" (Clark, 1985, p. 195).

Meanwhile, the politicians who had inflicted this experiment upon a hapless and demoralized nation were reluctant even to consider the possibility of repeal. Senator Morris Sheppard of Texas smugly asserted, "There is as much chance of repealing the Eighteenth Amendment as there is for a hummingbird to fly to the planet Mars with the Washington Monument tied to its tail" (Asbury, 1950, p. 316). In the end, the repeal of the Eighteenth Amendment had less to do with a rejection of the racist and religious attitudes upon which it had been based, but more to do with the desperate need for liquor tax revenue by a Depression-ravaged government (Klein, 2013).

While it is always comforting to believe that policy makers will heed the lessons of history so as not to be doomed to repeat it, such did not prove to be the case when, beginning in 1932, Congress decided to believe its own propaganda and criminalize the importation and use of marijuana—beginning with the Uniform Drug Narcotic Act that culminated in the Marijuana Tax Act (Bonnie, 1980). Earlier state legislation laid the groundwork for establishing a racial premise for a federal law criminalizing marijuana. In 1929, Colorado passed a draconian marijuana law after the *Denver Post* headlined a story about a Mexican who killed his stepdaughter because "his supply of weed had become exhausted for several days before the killing and his nerves were unstrung" (Bonnie & Whitebread, 1970, p. 1014).

Some present-day scholars point to a growing list of studies suggesting a link between marijuana, psychosis, and, consequently, violence. For example, Colorado, Washington, Alaska, and Oregon saw a 37% increase from 450 murders and 30,300 aggravated assaults in 2013 to 620 murders and 38,000 assaults in 2018 after legalizing recreational marijuana (Berenson, 2019). Though these figures may show a correlation between marijuana use and violence, other studies have definitively shown a much stronger link between alcohol use and violence (Galbicsek, 2021). Some may argue that not enough research has been performed on marijuana use to compare its consequences with those of alcohol use. Yet the fact remains that despite a considerable connection between alcohol and crime, alcohol use has remained legal since Prohibition. Meanwhile, marijuana possession and use remain illegal under federal law even though the connection between marijuana use and violence is less convincing.

The failed Prohibition experiment, along with marijuana legislation enacted by Congress and the Colorado legislature, proved to have significant social consequences. It is clear today that policy makers upholding marijuana prohibition have not learned from the mistakes committed by these earlier attempts to eradicate supposed social evils. Indeed, their legacy continues in the current climate of racism demonstrated by the modern-day marijuana regulatory scheme.

MARIJUANA LAW AND RACISM

Since 1990, the United States has arrested 40 million people on drug-related charges, spent over 1 trillion dollars, consumed law enforcement resources that it would otherwise have spent preventing violent crimes, and devastated the lives of millions of people, particularly black Americans (ACLU, 2013). By comparison, 71,000 Americans died from a drug overdose in 2019 (CDC, 2021). A just society should attempt to stop any death that can be prevented.

However, while millions die outright from tobacco and alcohol, the concentration on drug law enforcement remains based on the dubious pretext of preventing 71,000 people from possibly jeopardizing their health with other illicit drugs.

By 2016, the majority of Americans supported the legalization of marijuana. By the end of that year, 49% of Americans had tried marijuana, including a former president and former vice president of the United States, and a former speaker of the House, and 24.6 million Americans had used illegal drugs in the past month (Geiger, 2016; Greene, 1991; Schaeffer, 2021). Yet the impact of selective enforcement has fallen disproportionately on black Americans. Even though black and white Americans use marijuana at similar rates,

> A Black person is 3.73 times more likely to be arrested for marijuana possession than a white person—a disparity that increased by 32.7% between 2001 and 2010. . . . In the worst offending counties, Black Americans were on average 10, or even 30 times more likely to be arrested than white residents in the same county. (ACLU, 2013, p. 9)

In Washington DC, 91% of marijuana arrests were of black individuals; in Mississippi, 69%; in Georgia, 64% (ACLU, 2013).

Given that between 1990 and 2010, the United States had spent over a trillion dollars enforcing drug laws, increased the number of people in state prisons by 52%, and increased marijuana arrests by 188%, an accounting must be made of the results (ACLU, 2013). The answer is that from 2002 to 2010, the number of people using marijuana skyrocketed from 14.5 million people to nearly 18 million. The 2010 National Survey on Drug Use and Health reported that 39.26% have used marijuana, and 17.4 million Americans had used it in the past month (U.S. Department of Health and Human Services, 2011).

Since police find marijuana arrests to be the easiest to make, and far less risky than making arrests for assault or robbery, it is not surprising that police favor making arrests for marijuana possession in order to pad their "record of arrests." Federal subsidies to state and local police to enforce drug laws also create incentives for local police to generate high raw numbers of drug arrests, including arrests for possession of small amounts of marijuana. The greater the federal funding, the greater the incentive for state and local police to make drug arrests (Eisen, 2021). The National Commission recognized these incentives as early as 1973, when it warned that federal funding

> is so structured that it responds only when "bodies" can be produced or counted. Such a structure penalizes a reduction in the body count, while it rewards any increase in incidence figures and arrest statistics with more money. Those

receiving funds have a vested interest in increasing or maintaining those figures. (Andreas & Greenhill, 2010, p. 42)

Nevertheless, those perverse federal funding incentives continue to intensify racial disparities in marijuana enforcement impact. That a funding priority provision buried in a little-known legislative action implemented under the radar of public scrutiny could have such enormous racial impact is indicative of how discrimination can take place without intent.

This is where the issue of collateral consequences of incarceration became especially devastating. The collateral consequences of incarceration are the secondary negative effects of imprisonment, specifically drug convictions. Imprisonment not only constrains an individual's current liberties but damages relationships, increases the cost of living, and leaves a dark shadow looming over future opportunities (The Office of Civil Rights Evaluation, 2019). The collateral consequences of incarceration create a chain of repercussions that affect innocent family members and communities. For example, children with an incarcerated parent are more likely to drop out of school, develop learning disabilities, or even suffer major health problems (Morsey, 2016).

In the United States, black children are six times more likely to have an incarcerated parent (Morsey, 2016). Since black Americans are incarcerated at a higher rate than any other racial ethnic group, collateral consequences more directly affect the lives of black Americans and their families. When a black man is arrested and incarcerated, children are left without a father, mothers are reduced to poverty and reliance on welfare, and the children raised in these devastated communities find few opportunities for economic survival beyond the criminal culture of drug dealing (Morsey, 2016). Therefore, mass incarceration has needlessly disenfranchised the lives of thousands of black Americans for generations.

BLACK LIVES MATTER SOLUTIONS: POLICE DEFUNDING VERSUS MARIJUANA REFORM

The perfect storm of the 2020 presidential election highlighted the Black Lives Matter movement and civil unrest in cities around the nation. "Defund the Police" became the rallying cry of those convinced that diverting police resources to social services would address the disproportionate killing of black individuals by police (Russonello, 2020). Aware that most black Americans needed and wanted more—not less—police protection at a time when black individuals were being murdered at four times the rate of the national average, some Democratic leaders have tried to walk back the defunding mantra and argued that the phrase should not be taken literally (Kapur, 2020).

However, other high-profile Democratic leaders have made it clear that "police defunding" means exactly that. When the New York City Council and Mayor Bill de Blasio cut a billion dollars from the NYPD's budget in June 2020, including cutting the entire July class of 1,163 cadets and cutting $350 million in overtimes pay, Alexandria Ocasio-Cortez, on behalf of the Black Lives Matter movement, proclaimed, "defunding police means defunding police. It does not mean budget tricks or funny math . . . no budget musical chairs" (Phillips, 2020b). This extreme approach has met backlash from law enforcement. Alarmed by both the cuts and the claims by prominent leaders that defunding should in fact be taken literally, the president of the Police Benevolent Association lamented that

> shootings more than doubled again last week. . . . Even now, the NYPD doesn't have enough manpower to shift cops to one neighborhood without making another neighborhood less safe. We will say it again: the mayor and the City Council have surrendered the city to lawlessness. (McGoldrick, 2020)

Data already shows that a disproportionate percentage of murder victims are black. However, this does not explain why black lives should matter more when a white person is involved. Nor does it support the assumption that if police funding is diverted to social services, those services would be better equipped than trained police to prevent, investigate, and apprehend murderers, robbers, and rapists while 911 calls go unanswered.

While politicians debate the meaning and impact of "defunding," we must ask a fundamental question: Are more black lives saved by crippling the police and taking away the resources needed to protect them; or is the better solution to retain current levels of police funding while internally diverting resources from marijuana prosecutions to the investigation, apprehension, and prosecution of violent criminals who murder black individuals at four times the rate of the national average?

If the answer is the latter, it is submitted that the disproportionate attention and publicity paid to the former fatally distracts, compromises, and complicates any police efforts to implement the latter.

CONCLUSION

This disproportionate expenditure of police resources on the enforcement of marijuana laws leaves insufficient resources for the investigation and prosecution of the most violent crimes against black Americans. As long as black Americans are being murdered at four times the rate of the national average, and 40% of murders are unsolved, the expenditure of exorbitant funds to prosecute marijuana cases cannot be morally or financially justified. The fact that a person growing marijuana for their own medicinal use can be imprisoned for life without the possibility of parole, while the perpetrator of torture murder is granted a lenient "give away" plea bargain creates an overall distrust of the entire legal system.

The rationality of this system is further called into question when the use of tobacco and alcohol, which together are responsible for an disproportionate number of fatalities each year, is decriminalized while the use of marijuana can carry a life sentence—despite the fact that "not a single death from a marijuana overdose has ever been established" (NIDA, 2019).

The following are necessary to address the de facto racial discrimination endemic to current drug and marijuana policy:

1. State decriminalization of the recreational use of marijuana by adults:

    This would free law enforcement to concentrate their enforcement efforts on prosecuting the use of marijuana only in situations where its use threatens the safety of others—such as driving under its influence. It would also bring marijuana regulation into line with enforcement of laws against driving under the influence of alcohol.

2. Federal decriminalization of recreational use of marijuana:

    As states act to decriminalize the recreational use of marijuana, federal laws continue to create an irreconcilable conflict between state and federal law. As federal Attorneys General flip-flop on whether they would enforce federal marijuana laws in states that have decriminalized the recreational use of marijuana, the uncertainty of enforcement leaves banks and other financial institutions in limbo as to how to handle marijuana-related transactions. This causes many banks to refuse to process marijuana-related transactions, which in turn leaves many otherwise legal commercial activities subject to the ravages of theft and violence.

3. Redirection of police resources to solving violent crimes such as murder and rape in states that persist in criminalizing marijuana:

    The expenditure of millions of person-hours and trillions of dollars enforcing drug laws: (i) detracts from the government's ability to solve, apprehend, and prosecute violent offenders; (ii) fills scarce and expensive prison space requiring the release of violent offenders; (iii) increases the prices users must pay for marijuana, thus increasing the profits of organized crime and the incentive to produce ever more drugs, and motivates addicts to commit ever more crimes upon innocent victims in order to feed their habit; and (iv) destabilizes and corrupts local governments and police departments by providing incentives for bribery and protection.

4. Treat drug addicts at risk of harming themselves the same way as society treats alcohol or nicotine addicts—as a disease:

   Addiction is a disease that should be treated with mental health resources. The focus of these social programs should be rehabilitation rather than incarceration.

5. Redistribute excessive police funding to social programs:

   The cost of providing treatment and rehabilitation services to those at risk of harming themselves with drugs—both prescribed and non-prescribed—would be miniscule compared to the trillions currently spent in the current policy which serves primarily to increase the number of addicts while discriminating against black Americans, devastating their families and communities, and is a major reason why black Americans are murdered at four times the national average.

REFERENCES

American Civil Liberties Union. (2013). The war on marijuana in black and white. Retrieved from: https://www.aclu.org/report/report-war-marijuana-black-and-white

Andrew, S. (2020, July 14). Crime is surging in U.S. cities. Some say defunding the police will actually make it fall. *CNN*. Retrieved from: https://www.cnn.com/2020/07/14/us/police-violence-defund-debate-trnd/index.html

Asbury, H. (1950). *The Great Illusion: An Informal History of Prohibition*. Garden City, NY: Doubelday.

Bandow, D., (1991). War on drugs or war on America. *Stanford Law and Policy Review*, *3*, 242–260.

Barnett, R. (1994). Bad trip: Drug prohibition and the weakness of public policy. [Review of the publication *America's Longest War: Rethinking Our Tragic Crusade against Drugs* by S. Duke & A. Gross]. *Yale Law Journal*, *103*, 2593–2630.

Barrett, P. (1998, August). Strategic muddle: Federal war on drugs is scattershot affair, with dubious progress. *Wall Street Journal*, p. A1.

Bell, K. (2013). Victimless crime definition. *Sociology Dictionary*. Retrieved from: https://sociologydictionary.org/victimless-crime/

Berenson, A. (2019). Marijuana, mental illness, and violence. *Missouri Medicine*, *116*(6), 446–449.

Bieber, C. (2021, March 29). Marijuana tax revenue: A state-by-state breakdown. *Motley Fool*. Retrieved from: https://www.fool.com/research/marijuana-tax-revenue-by-state/

Block, W. (1993). Drug prohibition: A legal and economic analysis. *Journal of Business Ethics, 12*(1), 696.

Bonnie, R. J. (1980). *Marijuana Use and Criminal Sanctions: Essays on the Theory and Practice of Decriminalization.* Charlottesville, VA: Michie Company.

Booth, M. (2021, February 9). $10 billion in recreational marijuana has now been sold in Colorado, fueled by strong 2020 sales. *Colorado Sun.* Retrieved from: https://coloradosun.com/2021/02/09/colorado-marijuana-sales-pass-10-billion/

Borden, T., & Fellow, A. N. (2016, October 12). Every 25 seconds: The human toll of criminalizing drug use in the United States. *Human Rights Watch.* Retrieved from: https://www.hrw.org/report/2016/10/12/every-25-seconds/human-toll-criminalizing-drug-use-united-states#_ftn70

Bowers v. Hardwick, 478 U.S. 186, 189 (1986), overruled by *Lawrence v. Texas*, 539 U.S. 558 (2003).

Bronson, J., Stroop, J., Zimmer, S., & Berzofsky, M. (2017, June). *Drug use, dependence, and abuse among state prisoners and jail inmates, 2007–2009* (NCJ No. 250546). Retrieved from Bureau of Justice Statistics website: https://bjs.ojp.gov/library/publications/drug-use-dependence-and-abuse-among-state-prisoners-and-jail-inmates-2007-2009

Calvert, S., & Elinson, Z. (2020, December 26). Police are solving fewer murders during the Covid-19 pandemic. *Wall Street Journal.* Retrieved from: https://www.wsj.com/articles/police-are-solving-fewer-murders-during-covid-19-pandemic-11608994800

Casiano, L. (2020, November 22). Subway shoving, flamethrowers, shootings in NYC blamed on "perfect storm" of police reform, pandemic. *Fox News.* Retrieved from: https://www.foxnews.com/us/subway-shovings-flamethrowers-nyc-descends-into-anarchy

Centers for Disease Control and Prevention. (n.d.). Smoking and tobacco use fast facts and fact sheets. Retrieved from: https://www.cdc.gov/tobacco/data_statistics/fact_sheets/index.htm

Cerdá, M., Mauro, C., Hamilton, A., Levy, N. S., Santaella-Tenorio, J., Hasin, D., & Martins, S. S. (2019). Association between recreational marijuana legalization in the United States and changes in marijuana use and cannabis use disorder from 2008 to 2016. *JAMA Psychiatry, 77*(2), 165–171. doi: 10.1001/jamapsychiatry.2019.3254

Civic Federation. (2020, June 23). What is the Chicago police department's budget? *Civic Federation.* Retrieved from: https://www.civicfed.org/civic-federation/blog/what-chicago-police-department-budget

Clark, N. H. (1985). *Deliver Us from Evil: An Interpretation of American Prohibition.* New York: Norton.

Comstock Act, 18 U.S.C. § 1461; 19 U.S.C. § 1462 (1971).

Dorsey, T., & Middleton, P. (2015). Drug and crime facts (NCJ No. 165148). Retrieved from Bureau of Justice Statistics website: https://bjs.ojp.gov/content/pub/pdf/dcf.pdf

Drug Policy Alliance (2011, March). *$75 Million a Year: The Cost of New York City's Marijuana Possession Arrests*. Retrieved from: http://marijuana-arrests.com/docs/75-Million-A-Year.pdf

Duke, S. B., & Gross, A. C. (1993). *America's Longest War: Rethinking Our Tragic Crusade Against Drugs*. New York: G. P. Putnam's Sons.

Eisen, L. (2021, June 07). The federal funding that fuels mass incarceration. *Brennan Center for Justice*. Retrieved from: https://www.brennancenter.org/our-work/analysis-opinion/federal-funding-fuels-mass-incarceration

Eisenstadt v. Baird, 405 U.S. 438 (1972).

Esser, M. B., Sherk A., Liu, Y., Stockwell, T., Stahre, M., Kanny, D., & Brewer, R. (2020, October 2). *Deaths and Years of Potential Life Lost From Excessive Alcohol Use—United States, 2011–2015* (Morbidity and Mortality Weekly Report Vol. 69 No. 39). Retrieved from the Center for Disease Control and Prevention website: https://www.cdc.gov/mmwr/volumes/69/wr/mm6939a6.htm#suggestedcitation

Federal Bureau of Investigation. (2016, July 21). *Estimated Number of Arrests: United States 2015* [Uniform Crime Reporting Dataset]. Retrieved from: https://ucr.fbi.gov/crime-in-the-u.s/2015/crime-in-the-u.s.-2015/tables/table-29

Feldman, H. (1930). *Prohibition: Its Economic and Industrial Aspects*. London: D. Appleton.

Geiger, A. W. (2016, October 12). Support for marijuana legalization continues to rise. *Pew Research Center*. Retrieved from: https://www.pewresearch.org/fact-tank/2016/10/12/support-for-marijuana-legalization-continues-to-rise/

Greene, R. (1991). Toward a policy of mercy: Addiction in the 1990s. *Stanford Law and Policy Review, 3*(227). Retrieved from: http://journals.law.stanford.edu/stanford-law-policy-review/print/volume-3/issue-1-health-care/towards-policy-mercy-addiction-1990s

Group for Advancement of Psychiatry. (1971). *Drug Misuse: A Psychiatric View of a Dilemma*. New York: Scribner's.

Hall, W., & Lynskey, M. (2016). Evaluating the public health impacts of legalizing recreational cannabis use in the United States. *Addiction, 111*: 1764–1773. doi: 10.1111/add.13428

Hardaway, R. M. (2003). *No Price Too High: Victimless Crimes and the Ninth Amendment*. Westport, CT: Praeger.

Hardaway, R. M. (2018). *Marijuana Politics: Uncovering the Troublesome History and Societal Costs of Criminalization*. Santa Barbara, CA: ABC-CLIO.

Harmelin v. Michigan, 501 U.S. 957 (1991).

Harris, K. & Martin, W. (2019). *The Case for Marijuana Decriminalization* (Baker Institute Report 04.16.19). Houston, TX: Rice University's Baker Institute for Public Policy. Retrieved from: https://www.bakerinstitute.org/media/files/files/b4b661ec/bi-report-041619-drug-mjdecrim.pdf

Jaeger, M. (2018, September 25). A shocking number of U.S. murders went unsolved last year. *New York Post*. Retrieved from: https://nypost.com/2018/09/25/a-shocking-number-of-us-murders-went-unsolved-last-year/

Jehl, D. (1990, March). U.S. estimate of word cocaine output up 94%. *Los Angeles Times*, pp. A12.

Jones, A. (1994). *Cruel Sacrifice*. New York: Pinnacle Books.

Kapur, S. (2020, June 8). Democratic leaders clash with Black Lives Matter activists over "Defund the Police." *NBC News*. Retrieved from: https://www.nbcnews.com/politics/politics-news/democratic-leaders-clash-black-lives-m atter-activists-over-defund-police-n1227671

Klein, C. (2018, December 10). The end of prohibition. *History*. Retrieved from: https://www.history.com/news/the-night-prohibition-ended

Le Foll, B., & Matheson, J. (2020). Cannabis legalization and acute harm from high potency cannabis products: A narrative review and recommendations for public health. *Front Psychiatry, 11*. doi: 10.3389/fpsyt.2020.59197

Levine, H., Siegel, L., & Sayegh, G. (2013, March 18). One million police hours: Making 440,000 marijuana possession arrests in New York City, 2002–2012. *Drug Policy Alliance*. Retrieved from: https://drugpolicy.org/resource/one-million-police-hours

MacDonald, H. (2020, July 3). There is no epidemic of fatal police shootings against unarmed black Americans. *USA Today*. Retrieved from: https://www.usatoday.com/story/opinion/2020/07/03/police-black-killings-homicide-rates-race-injustice-column/3235072001/

Mattson, C. L., Tanz, L. J., Quinn, K., Kariisa, M., Patel, P., & Davis, N. L. (2019). *Trends and Geographic Patterns in Drug and Synthetic Opioid Overdose Deaths—United States, 2013–2019* (Morbidity and Mortality Weekly Report Vol. 70 No. 6). Retrieved from the Center for Disease Control and Prevention website: https://www.cdc.gov/mmwr/volumes/70/wr/mm7006a4.htm?s_cid=mm7006a4_w

McGoldrick, M. (2020, June 30). Nobody likes it: Billion-dollar NYPD defunding criticized by protestors and police supporters. *AM New York Metro*. Retrieved from: https://www.amny.com/new-york/nobody-likes-it-billion-dollar-nypd-defunding-criticized-by-protesters-and-police-supporters/

Memedovich, K. A., Dowsett, L. E., Spackman, E., Noseworthy, T., & Clement F. (2018). The adverse health effects and harms related to marijuana use: an overview review. *CMAJ Open. 6*(3), 339—346. doi: 10.9778/cmjao.20180023

Miech, R., & Koester, S. (2012). Trends in U.S., past-year marijuana use from 1985 to 2009: An age-period-cohort analysis. *Drug and Alcohol Dependence, 124*(3), 259–267. doi: 10.1016/j.drugalcdep.2012.01.020

Miller, R. L. (1991). *The Case for Legalizing Drugs*. Westport, CT: Praeger.

Mitchell, C. (2008, January 4). The killing of murder. *New York Magazine*. Retrieved from: https://nymag.com/news/features/crime/2008/42603/index5.html

Moon, J. D. (1999). Drugs and democracy. In P. De Greiff (Ed.), *Drugs and the Limits of Liberalism: Moral and Legal Issues* (pp. 133–155). Ithaca, NY: Cornell University Press.

Morsey, L., & Rothstein, R. (2016, December 15). Mass incarceration and children's outcomes. *Economic Policy Institute*. Retrieved from: https://www.epi.org/publication/mass-incarceration-and-childrens-outcomes/

Musto, D. F. (1973). *The American Disease: Origins of Narcotic Control*. New Haven, CT: Yale University Press.

National Institute on Drug Abuse. (2019, December 24). *Marijuana Drug Facts.* Retrieved from: https://www.drugabuse.gov/publications/drugfacts/marijuana

Office of Civil Rights Evaluation. (2019, June). Collateral consequences: The crossroads of punishment, redemption, and the effects on communities. *U.S. Commission on Civil Rights*, 1–2. Retrieved from: https://www.usccr.gov/pubs/2019/06-13-Collateral-Consequences.pdf

Oregon Department of Revenue. (2021). Oregon marijuana tax statistics. *Oregon.gov*. Retrieved from: https://www.oregon.gov/dor/programs/gov-research/pages/research-marijuana.aspx

Ostrowski, J. (1989, May 25). *Thinking about Drug Legalization* (Policy Analysis No. 121). Retrieved from Cato Institute website: https://www.cato.org/sites/cato.org/files/pubs/pdf/pa121.pdf

Paschall, M., Garcia-Ramírez, G., & Grube, J. (2021, February 15). Recreational marijuana legalization and use among California adolescents: Findings from a statewide survey. *Journal of Studies on Alcohol and Drugs*, *82*(1), 103–111.

Peeples, L. (2019, September 4). What the data says about police shootings. *Nature.* Retrieved from: https://www.nature.com/articles/d41586-019-02601-9

Pereira, S. (2021, March 26). After a painfully violent 2020, NYC shootings continue to spike. *Gothamist.* Retrieved from: https://gothamist.com/news/after-painfully-violent-2020-nyc-shootings-continue-spike

Phillips, M. (2020, November 20). BLM pressures democrats to embrace bill described as "roadmap for prison abolition." *Fox News*. Retrieved from: https://www.foxnews.com/politics/blm-pressures-democrats-breathe-act-prison-abolition

Phillips, M. (2020, June 30). AOC says proposed $1B budget cut to NYPD isn't enough: "Defunding police means defunding police." *Fox News*. Retrieved from: https://www.foxnews.com/politics/alexandria-ocasio-cortez-slams-1b-nypd-budget-cut-defunding-police-means-defunding-police

Records of the Wickersham Commission on Law Observance and Enforcement. (1929–31). Retrieved from: http://www.lexisnexis.com/academic/2upa/Aj/WickershamComm.htm

Rubenstein, D., & Mays, J. C. (2020, July 1). Nearly $1 billion is shifted from police budget that pleases no one. *New York Times*. Retrieved from: https://www.nytimes.com/2020/06/30/nyregion/nypd-budget.html

Russonello, G. (2020, July 3). Have Americans warmed to calls to "defund the police"? *New York Times*. Retrieved from: https://www.nytimes.com/2020/07/03/us/politics/polling-defund-the-police.html

Saad, L. (2013, August 2). In U.S., 38% have tried marijuana, little changed since 80s. *Gallup*. Retrieved from: https://news.gallup.com/poll/163835/tried-marijuana-little-changed-80s.aspx

Schaeffer, K. (2021, April 26). Six facts about Americans and marijuana. *Pew Research Center*. Retrieved from: http://www.pewresearch.org/fact-tank/2015/04/14/6-facts-about-marijuana

Schmoke, K. L. (1990). An argument in favor of decriminalization. *Hofstra Law Review*, *18*, 501–525.

Silverman, L., Spruill, N., & Levine, D. (1975). *Urban Crime and Heroin Availability*. Arlington County, VA: Public Research Institute.

Statista. (2020, September). Number of murder victims in the United States in 2019, by race/ethnicity and gender. Retrieved from: https://www.statista.com/statistics/251877/murder-victims-in-the-us-by-race-ethnicity-and-gender/

Sugarmann, J. (2017, December 6). Murder rate for black americans is four times the national average. *HuffPost*. Retrieved from: https://www.huffpost.com/entry/murder-rate-for-black-ame_b_4702228

Theis, C. F., & Register, C. A. (1993). Decriminalization of marijuana and the demand for alcohol, marijuana, and cocaine. *Social Science Journal*, *30*(4), 385–399.

Trovall, E. (2020, July 13). Report: White police officers are twice as likely to fire their guns than black officers. *Houston Public Media*. Retrieved from: https://www.houstonpublicmedia.org/articles/news/criminal-justice/2020/07/13/377726/report-white-police-are-twice-as-likely-to-fire-their-guns-than-black-officers/

University of Minnesota. (2016, April 8). 7.3 crime and criminals. *Sociology by University of Minnesota*. Retrieved from: https://open.lib.umn.edu/sociology/chapter/7-3-crime-and-criminals/#:~:text=Victimless%20crime%20is%20illegal%20behavior,prostitution%2C%20pornography%2C%20and%20gambling

U.S. Department of Health and Human Services. (2011, September). *Results from the 2010 National Survey on Drug Use and Health: Summary of National Findings*. Retrieved from: https://www.samhsa.gov/data/sites/default/files/NSDUHresults2010/NSDUHresults2010.pdf

U.S. Department of Health and Human Services. (2014). *The Health Consequences of Smoking: 50 Years of Progress*. Retrieved from: https://www.ncbi.nlm.nih.gov/books/NBK179276/pdf/Bookshelf_NBK179276.pdf

Walters, J. (2016, April 15). Supreme court considers taking case of man given life in prison for growing pot. *Guardian*. Retrieved from: https://www.theguardian.com/society/2016/apr/15/lee-carroll-brooker-alabama-marijuana-sentence

Washington, E. (1901–1919). Correspondence. The reverend Eli Washington John Lindesmith Papers (ACUA 024), Special Collections of the University Libraries at the Catholic University of America, Washington DC.

Washington Post (2020, December 22). Fatal force. *Washington Post*. Retrieved from: https://www.washingtonpost.com/graphics/investigations/police-shootings-database/

Washington State Treasurer's Office. (2020). *Washington Marijuana Revenues and Health*. Retrieved from: https://tre.wa.gov/portfolio-item/washington-state-marijuana-revenues-and-health/

WDRB. (2019, September 5). Melinda Loveless, mastermind of 1992 murder of Shanda Sharer, released from prison. *WDRB Media*. Retrieved from: https://www.wdrb.com/news/melinda-loveless-mastermind-of-1992-murder-of-shanda-sharer-released-from-prison/article_994b41c4-d00e-11e9-8e56-9b9b497efced.html

Wendell, T., Geert, D., & Curtis, R. (2016, November 18). Cheaper drugs, and thus less crime: the crime drop's "Philosopher Stone"? *Dialectical Anthropology*,

40(4), 385–393. Retrieved from: https://link-springer-com.du.idm.oclc.org/article/10.1007/s10624-016-9442-5

Zahniser, D., Smith, D., & Reyes, E. A. (2020, July 1). Los Angeles cuts LAPD spending, taking police staffing to its lowest in its lowest level in 12 years. *Los Angeles Times*. Retrieved from: https://www.latimes.com/california/story/2020-07-01/lapd-budget-cuts-protesters-police-brutality

Chapter 3

Seeing through the Haze

Using Intersectionality to Reveal Systematic Differences in Support for Marijuana Decriminalization

Geoffrey Whitebread

INTRODUCTION

In an era of #BlackLivesMatter and #MeToo movements, identities have renewed importance in assessing support for policies and the impact of policies on society. These identities shape how many people report their experience with inequality or discrimination, using these experiences as calls to make society fairer. Within these movements, there is an increasing awareness of stereotypes—an acknowledgment that not all members of a race, gender, sexual orientation, or disability have shared thoughts or experiences. In academic circles, this trend is indicative of "intersectionality," or understanding how multiple identities have an interlocking effect in creating policy preferences distinct from others with a single shared social identity (Crenshaw, 1991; Hancock, 2007a). I discuss this at length later in the chapter.

The specific question for this chapter is, *Is there evidence of intersectionality in attitudes toward marijuana decriminalization?* Using the marijuana decriminalization debate in the United States from 2012 to 2016, evidence suggests that there are substantial differences between black men, black women, white men, and white women in support for marijuana decriminalization. Of particular interest is the fact that women have a distinct perspective toward marijuana decriminalization.

Marijuana is a useful context for studying intersectionality for several reasons. The first is that attitudes toward marijuana decriminalization have changed significantly and those who are opposed to decriminalization are decidedly in the minority (Daniller, 2019). As a result of this rather sudden shift, marijuana decriminalization is now a fast-moving policy issue, where states are rapidly adopting new marijuana-friendly policies (Hartman, 2021). Historically, marijuana was largely favored by whites (Angeuelov & McCarthy, 2018; Bonnie & Whitebread, 1999), although this gap has closed in recent years and current prevalence rates show that blacks and whites use marijuana equally (Compton et al., 2004; Hasin et al., 2015; Keyes et al., 2017; Tate, 2013). The change in attitudes toward decriminalization, and the resulting policy shifts, is driven by Americans' rapidly evolving perceptions of marijuana. Many Americans no longer see marijuana as a dangerous substance or as a gateway drug (Jones, 2019). Rather, an increasing number of Americans now view marijuana as a relatively harmless recreational drug akin to alcohol (Politico & Harvard, 2019).

States have pressed ahead with a variety of tactics to decriminalize marijuana, from outright legalization, to reducing penalties for possession to a small fine, to legalizing marijuana for medical use. Some states are even adopting policies to regulate the sale of marijuana to the public (Hartman, 2021). The result was the United States had a patchwork of marijuana policies across the country, with the federal government arguing that their prohibition should remain in place (Hartman, 2021). Differences between state and federal drug policy meant that in jurisdictions where medical marijuana was legal, research was often stymied due to federal prohibitions (Lovett, 2014; Phillips, 2014). In states where recreational marijuana was legalized, states were expecting a tax bonanza on marijuana sales, but emerging marijuana dispensaries were often unable to get loans from major banks (Kovaleski & Apuzzo, 2014). While states are moving relatively quickly to adopt new marijuana laws, the federal government is (as of this writing) not changing marijuana's status as a Schedule 1 drug, making it subject to enhanced federal penalties for possession and distribution.

The media during the 2012–2016 time period portrayed marijuana legalization as a largely partisan issue, with conservatives opposing marijuana decriminalization and liberals supporting it. Republican opposition in the state legislature was credited with scuttling New York State's early effort to decriminalize marijuana (Kaplan & Eligon, 2012). By 2014, pundits were suggesting that the degree of the partisan divide on the issue had started to erode. Survey measures indicating conservative voters were undergoing a change of opinion when states led by libertarian Republicans began to consider decriminalization (Kopicki, 2014; Lyman & Sussman, 2014).

A second reason why marijuana decriminalization is an interesting issue area to study is the high disparity in arrest rates and prison sentences for black and white Americans (Gase et al., 2016). The "war on drugs" is widely blamed for causing widespread racial inequity in arrest and imprisonment rates (Edwards et al., 2013; Mauer, 2009). Yet, liberalizing drug laws going forward does little to address past racism. Thus, marijuana provides a rich opportunity to study a controversial policy within a rapidly changing social and legal landscape. Black men are much more likely to be arrested for possession of marijuana and, once convicted of possession, are more likely to serve longer prison sentences (Edwards et al., 2013; Rehavi & Starr, 2014). This creates an interesting context to study the policy preferences of men and women of different races. How will these two forces shape the policy preferences of black women, black men, white women, and white men?

INTERSECTIONALITY

Intersectionality is an approach to thinking about people and society that invites scholars to wrestle with the "complexity" of identities, systems, and society. Collins and Bilge (2016) define intersectionality as:

> a way of understanding and analyzing the complexity in the world, in people, and in human experiences. The events and conditions of social and political life can seldom be understood as shaped by one factor. They are generally shaped by many factors in diverse and mutually influencing ways. When it comes to social inequity, people's lives and the organization of power in a given society are better understood as being shaped not by a single axis of social division, be it race or gender or class, but by many axes that work together and influence each other. Intersectionality as an analytic tool gives people better access to the complexity of the world and of themselves. (p. 2)

In the context of marijuana decriminalization, focusing on the intersectional attitudes allows us to think in a more complete way about the differences that exist by race and gender. The intersectional framework holds that individuals experience privilege and oppression based on their social identities. Society privileges favored identities and oppresses non-favored identities. Another key component of the intersectional approach is that identities are interdependent and interlocking, and not independent units for analysis (Bowleg, 2008; Hancock, 2007a). The experience of being a black woman, for example, is more than a simple mathematical combination of black + woman (Bowleg, 2008).

The idea of intersectionality comes from black women who were exploring and challenging the double oppressions they faced because of their race and gender since before the civil war (Richardson, 1987). Over time, intersectionality has become more influential and is changing the understanding of the relationships between identities and society generally (Else-Quest

& Hyde, 2016a). The more generalized approach to intersectionality is the source of some contention, since the generalized approach shifts the focus away from the experiences of black women (Alexander-Floyd, 2012; J. S. Jordan-Zachery, 2018; Nash, 2008). More recently, the generalized approach to the study of intersectionality has entered the quantitative realm, as scholars incorporate this new understanding in their respective fields. The quantitative study of identity has traditionally used race and gender as stand-alone identities that impacted various social or political phenomena. Intersectionality is the study of the connections within and between these identities. For example, a scholar looking at an intersectional analysis of race and gender would focus on how the combinations of races and genders impact various political phenomena by looking at black men, black women, white men, white women, and so forth.

While the application of intersectionality to social sciences is relatively new, the importance of the connection between identity and social structures, such as discussed earlier, has been important to political science. The intersectional political-science literature examines the complexity of examining intersectionality in the gay rights movement (Lindsay, 2013; Wadsworth, 2011) and the importance of having diverse representation in political organizations (Hardy-Fanta, 2006; Mansbridge, 1999; Minta, 2012; Simien, 2007; Strolovitch, 2006; Uhlaner, 2012). Other sections of the political-science literature are devoted to the study of how race and gender impact political preferences. Scholars have studied the role of race or gender in vote choice (Clayton & Stallings, 2000; Dawson, 1995; Huddy & Terkildsen, 1993; Kahn, 1994; Philpot & Walton, 2021; Sanbonmatsu, 2002) and the role of race or gender in determining the political preferences (Conover, 1988; Gay & Tate, 1998; Simien & Clawson, 2004). Much of the literature on how race impacts decriminalization preferences is centered on the unequal imprisonment rates resulting from the war on drugs (Bobo & Johnson, 2004; Koch et al., 2016; Nunn, 2002; Schoenfeld, 2012), including some work on the unequal arrest rates faced by black women specifically (Bush-Baskette, 1998). Tate (2013) in her study of black opinion toward marijuana decriminalization, theorizes that black opposition to marijuana decriminalization comes from two separate mechanisms. The first is that blacks having a negative affect toward other blacks are more likely to oppose decriminalization. The second is that members of the black community use a racial utility heuristic, within which blacks think about policy support in terms of the collective benefit to the black community.

Evidence for how gender may generally influence preferences comes from the renewed interest in the gender gap, which describes how women hold politically distinct attitudes. These studies show that gender influences political preference by women having higher levels of empathy and concern for others, manifested in women having higher levels of egalitarian attitudes (Barnes & Cassese, 2017; Bittner & Goodyear-Grant, 2017; Blinder & Rolfe, 2018). Tate (2013) explained that women may be more opposed to marijuana decriminalization because their socialized role as caregivers may make women more concerned about the negative impacts of decriminalization on communities.

An intersectional analysis requires scholars to embrace several assumptions in their analytical approach. The quantitative intersectionality framework posits three major assumptions (Else-Quest & Hyde, 2016a, 2016b). The first assumption of intersectionality posits that identities are necessarily connected to structures of power (Else-Quest & Hyde, 2016a; Hancock, 2007b). Different genders and races have different connections with power. In a traditional hierarchy of American social power, whites have more power than people of color and men have more power than women (Crenshaw, 1991). Thus, a typical, but simplified hierarchy of power in America has white men with the most power, followed by white women, then black men, and last black women. In the context of public opinion, the different experiences identities have with power then shape policy preferences.

The second assumption of intersectionality is that identities are fluid and dynamic (Else-Quest & Hyde, 2016a; MacKinnon, 2013). This dynamism can affect the salience of identities in a given context. Identity salience is affected by the research questions or the political context. For example, in a study of LGBT+ support for policy issues, the intersection of race, gender, sexual orientation, and gender identity may be important. In a more general study of a population, however, a scholar may find the intersection of race, gender, and class may be relevant to their research question. Because salience is context-driven, however, scholars need to identify salient identities for analysis and may not be able to rely on a core set of identities for all research questions. Dhamoon (2001) discusses the complexity of intersectionality, in particular, the highly contextualized nature of humanities-based inquiry where much intersectionality work has been done to date. In this context, it can seem daunting to include a wide range of identities to understand an individual's perspective in a given situation. In dealing with populations, scholars do not need to fear an "infinite" number of identities being salient at once. Rather, scholars should determine which identities are appropriate for a given context (MacKinnon, 2013).

Third, and perhaps as a result of the social power structure, intersectional theorists argue that the effects of race and gender are interconnected and operate simultaneously. In other words, they are interdependent. Intersectional scholars argue that scholars cannot separate the effects of race and gender (Bowleg, 2008; Hancock, 2007a). A white man cannot separate his experiences in whiteness from his experiences in maleness. How an individual experiences one identity affects how they experience another identity. In the context of the salient identities of this chapter, *the effects of race and gender cannot be disaggregated.*

Selection of Quantitative Methods

As intersectionality finds a footing in quantitative scholarship, it is important that scholars pay attention to the methods used. This is particularly important because intersectionality holds very specific assumptions about the relationships between salient identities. Quantitative methods have their own assumptions about the relationships between observations which practitioners must satisfy, and these assumptions need to be compatible with the assumptions of intersectionality.

A common quantitative analysis tools used in quantitative intersectionality is linear regression. Linear regression has four assumptions: linearity, homoscedasticity, independence, and normality. For this discussion, I will focus on the independence assumption because it is the most relevant. The independence assumption requires that observations be independent of each other (Fox, 1997). That is, observations cannot be related. For example, in a linear regression model, a scholar might include race and age in their model. These satisfy the independence assumption because racial identity is independent of age. In that same tradition, practitioners often include race and gender in a linear regression model. A linear regression model then assumes that race and gender are completely independent of each other. But recall the assumptions of intersectionality, which hold that race and gender are interdependent and interlocking. It follows, conceptually, that the relationship between race and gender violates the independence assumption.

Furthermore, when treating race and gender as separate and unconnected identities, scholars mask what happens at the intersection of these two identities. Model outputs report coefficients for races, ethnicities, and gender. These results do not allow us to infer what the implications are for different women of color, since the gender variable includes women of all races and ethnicities. By masking what happens at the intersection, this approach continues the exclusion of black women from scholarship (Jordan Zachary, 2013).

A second approach is to use multiplicative terms (Scott & Siltanen, 2017). Multiplicative terms, or interaction terms, are a way scholars can combine two variables to look for patterns. This approach allows scholars to determine how much impact the interaction between two variables has on the dependent variable. While this approach is useful in many contexts, I suggest that it is not useful in the study of intersectionality. Following the assumptions of intersectionality discussed earlier, scholars cannot disaggregate the effects of "race" or "gender" because they are interlocking. Thus, even when using multiplicative terms, the interaction between race and gender still violates the independence assumption. In choosing a method for intersectional analysis, scholars must remember that salient identities are interdependent, and are part of a larger—and inseparable—whole.

In my view, the best approach is to treat race and gender as a combined variable (e.g., black men, black women, etc.). This approach is consistent with the assumptions of intersectionality theory and linear regression. By using this approach, scholars account for the interdependence of race and gender by treating the two previously separated identities and interlocking. This approach recognizes that a relationship between them exists and is a "black box" that cannot be disaggregated further. In doing so, this approach avoids violating the independence assumption of linear regression by not including two independent but related variables.

Data and Methods

The data for this analysis comes from the 2012 and 2016 American National Election Studies (ANES) (American National Election Study, 2013, 2017). The ANES is generally conducted every four years during presidential election years in the United States. The 2012 ANES has 5,466 respondents and the 2016 ANES has 4,270 respondents. I selected the ANES because they have larger sample sizes which are important in conducting intersectional research. The 2012 and 2016 ANES surveys asked about marijuana policy preferences. The unit of analysis in this survey is the individual responder. Categories used for dependent and independent variables are categories available in the ANES data.

Dependent Variable: Support for decriminalization is measured with a dichotomous dependent variable. In both the 2012 and 2016 ANES, the question asked is "Should Marijuana be legal?" Answers are coded as 1 for support for decriminalization and 0 for not supporting. Table 3.1 reports the question wording for each survey.

Independent Variables of Interest: I code race and gender as categorical variables for black men, black women, white men, and white women following the intersectional assumption that it is not possible to disaggregate the effects of race and gender in this context.

Controls: I also include age, education, ideology as control variables. Higher values correlate with higher levels of age, education, and income. Ideology is measured on a 7-point scale with higher values correlating with more liberal views.

I report the logistic regression coefficients model with marginal effects and margins plot to estimate support for marijuana decriminalization across

Table 3.1 Support for Marijuana Decriminalization in the United States

	ANES 2012	*ANES 2016*
Black Men	0.68***	0.35
	(0.16)	(0.26)
White Women	0.42***	0.45***
	(0.10)	(0.14)
White Men	0.84***	0.79***
	(0.10)	(0.14)
Other	0.44***	0.12
	(0.16)	(0.20)
Ideology	−0.54***	0.31***
	(0.03)	(0.02)
Age	−0.02***	−0.04***
	(0.00)	(0.00)
Education	0.02***	0.02
	(0.02)	(0.02)
Constant	2.6***	0.34
	(0.23)	(0.27)
Wald Test for Difference of Parameters		
White Women and White Men	20.92***	10.86***
White Men and Black Men	1.02	3.06*
Observations	3,609	2,608

Source: Logistic regression using data from ANES 2012 Time Series Study (2013) and ANES 2016 Times Series Study (2017).

ideology. I use Wald Tests for difference of parameters to test for significance between independent variables of interest in the model. The baseline for all models is black women.

HYPOTHESES

The literature has two general frameworks for how race and gender affect marijuana preferences that I will examine. The first framework comes from the gender gap. The gender gap supposes that women, as a single analytic category, will feel one way about a policy issue relative to men generally. I expect that women will be less likely to support decriminalization relative to men.

A second body of literature suggests that race and gender are interconnected and interlocking, and that combinations of race and gender comprise a new identity altogether. The intersectionality framework suggests that black women will have distinct attitudes relative to black men and white women.

In the case of marijuana, because of Tate's (2013) work, I expect that black women will be more opposed to decriminalization relative to each of the groups mentioned earlier.

RESULTS

The results from the logistic regressions using ANES data are displayed in table 3.2. The baseline identity is black women. In 2012, black men, white men, white women, and other races/ethnicities are more likely to support marijuana decriminalization at the 0.01 level relative to black women. To test for significant differences between black men, white men, and white women, I use Wald Tests for the difference of between groups. White men are more likely to support decriminalization relative to white women at the 0.01 level. Black men and white men do not have statistically distinct attitudes in 2012.

In 2016, black men are not more likely than black women to support decriminalization. White men and white women are more likely to support decriminalization relative to the black women at the 0.01 level. Looking to the results of the Wald Tests, white men remain more supportive of decriminalization relative to white women. In 2016, white men are more likely to support decriminalization relative to black men at the 0.1 level. The results of this Wald test, combined with the loss of significant difference in in support for marijuana decriminalization between black men and women, suggests that in the four years between 2012 and 2016, that we see some convergence of attitudes between black women and black men.

In sum, this evidence is consistent with the intersectional hypothesis. Black women have statistically distinct attitudes relative to all other groups, except black men in 2016 when there seems to be some convergence in policy preferences. The Wald Tests for 2012 and 2016 further show that white men and women have statistically distinct preferences.

To show the importance of intersectional analysis, figure 3.1 includes both a traditional use of logistic regression correlating white, black, and women separately and the intersectional approach to highlight the importance of considering the intersection of race and gender. The left graph in figure 3.1 shows the traditional analysis using black, white, and gender. Whites are more supportive of decriminalization relative to blacks. The effect of gender is quite dramatic, with women being substantially less likely to support decriminalization than blacks or whites. This supports the gender hypothesis.

The graph on the right shows systematic differences by race and gender across ideology. White men are the most likely to support decriminalization, followed by black men, and then white women. All three groups are more likely to support decriminalization relative to the baseline of black women.

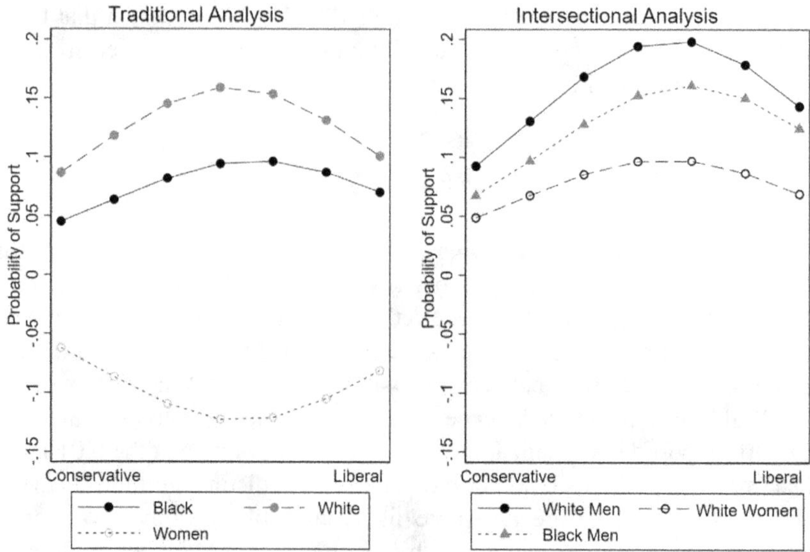

Figure 3.1 Support for Decriminalization by Race and Gender in 2012. *Source: ANES 2012 Time Series Study (2013).*

The right graphs show that women of a given race are less likely to support decriminalization than their male counterparts, supporting the intersectional hypothesis. These results show differences not reflected in the traditional analysis graph on the left, which masks the opposition of black women relative to the other groups. The traditional graph masks the experience of black women who are most opposed to discrimination of the groups discussed in this chapter.

Figure 3.2 shows the same data for 2016. The graph on the left shows the traditional analysis, which suggests that whites are most likely to support marijuana decriminalization, followed by blacks then women. This supports the gender hypothesis that women will be less likely to support decriminalization than men. The graph on the right is the intersectional analysis, which shows that white men are most supportive of decriminalization, followed by white women and black men. As evidenced by the probabilities, black women are the least likely to support discrimination of the four groups discussed in this chapter. I note that the statistical significance in table 3.1 is not significant for the difference between black women and black men in the 2016 model. In general, however, this supports the intersectional hypothesis that there are significant differences by race and gender. Both figures show evidence of sorting along race and gender lines, that is masked in the traditional analysis.

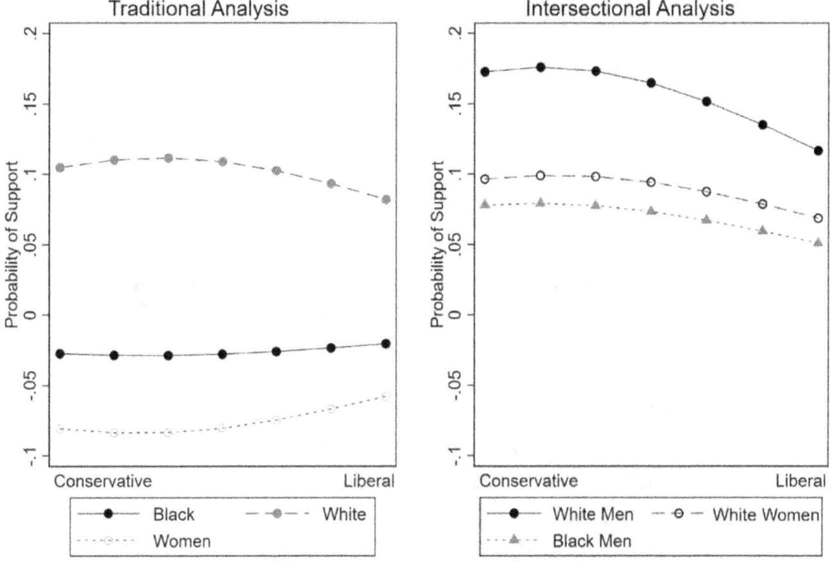

Figure 3.2 Support for Decriminalization by Race and Gender in 2016. *Source: ANES 2016 Time Series Study (2017).*

DISCUSSION

The research question for this chapter was "*Is there evidence of intersectionality in attitudes towards marijuana decriminalization?*" This chapter looked for evidence of intersectionality by testing two hypotheses testing gendered support for decriminalization and then intersectional support for decriminalization. The results above show support for both hypotheses. Women are more likely to oppose decriminalization in both the 2012 and 2016 surveys. Yet there is more information in the intersectional models that shows substantial differences between the groups discussed in this chapter. The traditional models mask the unique opposition to decriminalization of black women. The intersectional graphs show that in 2012, black women are distinct from black men, white women, and white men. In 2016, there remains a significant difference between black women, white men and white women, but the significant difference between black men and black women has disappeared. This raises the question: what are the dynamics affecting black men and black women in such a way that attitudes converged fairly rapidly? Perhaps increased use of marijuana in the black community lead to a convergence of preferences? Or perhaps there is another factor not considered here. More research is needed here to explain what mechanisms affect black women's and black men's preferences.

The effect of partisanship was fairly for all race and gender combinations. In general, attitudes coalesced around certain policy preferences with strong ideological partisans but were more varied with moderates. This is a piece of evidence that suggests—at least in the case of marijuana decriminalization—that ideology seems to operate relatively similar across all groups even if there are different starting points.

This work highlights the importance of revisiting the traditional literature that focuses on race and gender as separate, equal, and unrelated entities. Despite the repeated framing of marijuana as a "race" issue with black men suffering from disparities in arrest and sentencing rates, women are still generally more opposed to decriminalization relative to men of their same race. How does the egalitarian framework operate when women have two competing interests that would benefit from a more egalitarian disposition? Perhaps women—and perhaps especially black women—are more keenly aware of the negative impact of drug use on communities, frequently correlated with declining health, increased poverty, and imprisonment, as suggested by Tate (2013). Another question is, why do scholars generally focus on how women are different? Although this trend is beginning to change, scholars frequently assume that men are the baseline. We have research on the gender gap focusing on how women are distinct, but what are frameworks that motivate men to support or oppose policies? Perhaps some notion of rugged individualism and free choice? Or, perhaps the notion of rugged individualism is a white-centered concept, and other frameworks may differentiate men and women of different races/ethnicities.

This study is limited by the correlational nature of the research design. There was evidence that something affected black support for decriminalization between 2012 and 2016, although that reason is not immediately apparent. Absent a strong theoretical literature on mechanisms that affect black men and black women (together and independently), it is difficult to formulate an explanation beyond conjecture.

Decriminalization is a new, relatively fast-moving policy area that has seen local and state governments move quickly on decriminalization while the federal government has been slower to act relative to the state governments. This new issue area provides interesting opportunities to learn important lessons about quantitative intersectionality generally, as well as for studying marijuana policy in the future. This research highlights the importance of intersectionality in understanding policy support among different groups. Treating race and gender as solitary identities is not sufficient to accurately capture policy support and masks what happens to those at the intersection. And there are some opportunities for understanding how race and gender are interlocking to better ground future research.

On a larger note, this work continues a recent trend of quantitative scholarship that highlights the importance of adopting the intersectional framework as a causal mechanism to explain policy preferences. In some ways, using the intersectionality framework is a counter-trend to the contemporary focus in some fields on experimental analysis. Identities cannot be randomly assigned. In some circumstances, an intersectional approach may reveal new patterns in how stimuli affect outcomes. However, current work in the social sciences on intersectionality is focused largely on understanding how interdependent multiple identities shape policy preferences. More work is needed to understand how race/gender serves as a lens that filters stimuli to affect policy preferences.

REFERENCES

Alexander-Floyd, Ni. (2012). Disappearing acts: Reclaiming intersectionality in the social sciences in a post—Black feminist era. *Feminist Formations*, *24*(1), 1–25.

American National Election Studies, University of Michigan and Stanford University. 2013. *ANES 2012 Time Series Study*. Ann Arbor, MI: Inter-University Consortium for Political and Social Research [distributor]. Available at https://electionstudies.org/data-center/2012-time-series-study/

American National Election Studies, University of Michigan and Stanford University. 2017. *ANES 2016 Time Series Study*. Ann Arbor, MI: Inter-University Consortium for Political and Social Research [distributor]. Available at https://doi.org/10.3886/ICPSR36824.v2

Anguelov, N., & McCarthy, M. P. (2018). *From Criminalizing to Decriminalizing Marijuana: The Politics of Social Control*. Lexington Books.

Barnes, T. D., & Cassese, E. C. (2017). American Party Women: A Look at the Gender Gap within Parties. *Political Research Quarterly*, *70*(1), 127–141.

Bittner, A., & Goodyear-Grant, E. (2017). Digging Deeper into the Gender Gap: Gender Salience as a Moderating Factor in Political Attitudes. *Canadian Journal of Political Science*, *50*(2), 559–578.

Blinder, S., & Rolfe, M. (2018). Rethinking Compassion: Toward a Political Account of the Partisan Gender Gap in the United States: Rethinking Compassion in the Partisan Gender Gap. *Political Psychology*, *39*(4), 889–906.

Bobo, L. D., & Johnson, D. (2004). A Taste for Punishment: Black and White Americans' Views on the Death Penalty and the War on Drugs. *Du Bois Review: Social Science Research on Race*, *1*(1), 151–180.

Bonnie, R. J., & Whitebread, C. (1999). *The Marijuana Conviction*. North Wales Press.

Bowleg, L. (2008). When Black + Lesbian + Woman ≠ Black Lesbian Woman: The Methodological Challenges of Qualitative Research and Quantitative Intersectionality Research. *Sex Roles*, *59*, 312–325.

Bush-Baskette, S., R. (1998). Crime Control and Women: Feminist Implications of Criminal Justice Policy. In *Crime Control and Women: Feminist Implications of Criminal Justice Policy* (pp. 113–129). Sage Publications.

Clayton, D. M., & Stallings, A. M. (2000). Black Women in Congress: Striking the Balance. *Journal of Black Studies*, *30*(4), 574–603.

Compton, W. M., Grant, B. F., Colliver, J. D., Glantz, M. D., & Stinson, F. (2004). Prevalence of Marijuana Use Disorders in the United States: 1991–1992 and 2001–2002. *JAMA*, *29*(17), 2114–2121.

Conover, P. J. (1988). Feminists and the Gender Gap. *Journal of Politics*, *50*(4), 985–1010.

Crenshaw, K. (1991). Mapping the Margins: Intersectionality, Identity Politics, and Violence against Women of Color. *Stanford Law Review*, *43*(6), 1241–1299.

Daniller, A. (2019, November 14). *Two-thirds of Americans Support Marijuana Legalization*. Retrieved from: https://www.pewresearch.org/fact-tank/2019/11/14/americans-support-marijuana-legalization/

Dawson, M. (1995). *Behind the Mule: Race and Class in African American Politics*. Princeton University Press.

Dhamoon, R. K. (2011). Considerations on Mainstreaming Intersectionality. *Political Research Quarterly*, *64*(1), 230–243.

Edwards, E., Bunting, W., & Garcia, L. (2013). *The War on Marijuana in Black and White*. American Civil Liberties Union.

Else-Quest, N. M., & Hyde, J. S. (2016a). Intersectionality in Quantitative Psychological Research: I. Theoretical and Epistemological Issues. *Psychology of Women Quarterly*, *40*(2), 155–170.

Else-Quest, N. M., & Hyde, J. S. (2016b). Intersectionality in Quantitative Psychological Research: II. Methods and Techniques. *Psychology of Women Quarterly*, *40*(3), 319–336.

Fox, J. (1997). *Applied Regression Analysis, Linear Models, and Related Methods*. Sage Publications.

Gase, L. N., Glenn, B., Gomez, L., Kuo, T., Inkelas, M., & Ponce, N. (2016). Understanding Racial and Ethnic Disparities in Arrest: The Role of Individual, Home, School, and Community Characteristics. *Race and Social Probems*, *8*, 296–312.

Gay, C., & Tate, K. (1998). Doubly Bound: The Impact of Gender and Race on the Politics of Black Women. *Political Psychology*, *19*(1), 169–184.

Hancock, A.-M. (2007a). When Multiplication Doesn't Equal Quick Addition: Examining Intersectionality as a Research Paradigm. *Perspectives on Politics*, *5*(1), 63–79.

Hancock, A.-M. (2007b). Intersectionality as a Normative and Empirical Paradigm. *Politics and Gender*, *3*(2), 248–254.

Hardy-Fanta, C. (2006). *Intersectionality and Politics: Recent Research on Gender, Race, and Political Representation in the United States*. Routledge.

Hartman, M. (2021, April 8). *Cannabis Overview*. National Conference of State Legislatures. Retrieved from: https://www.ncsl.org/research/civil-and-criminal-justice/marijuana-overview.aspx

Hasin, D. S., Saha, T. D., Kerridge, B. T., Goldstein, R. B., Chou, S. P., Zhang, H., Jung, J., Pickering, R. P., Ruan, W. J., Smith, S. M., Huang, B., & Grant, B. F. (2015). Prevalence of Marijuana Use Disorders in the United States Between 2001–2002 and 2012–2013. *JAMA Psychiatry*, *72*(12), 1235–1242.

Huddy, L., & Terkildsen, N. (1993). Gender Stereotypes and the Perception of Male and Female Candidates. *American Journal of Political Science*, *37*(1), 119–147.

Jones, J. (2019, June 12). In U.S., Medical Aid Top Reason Why Legal Marijuana Favored. *Gallup*. Retrieved from: https://news.gallup.com/poll/258149/medical-aid-top-reason-why-legal-marijuana-favored.aspx

Jordan-Zachery, J. S. (2007). Am I a Black Woman or a Woman Who Is Black? A Few Thoughts on the Meaning of Intersectionality. *Politics and Gender*, *3*(2), 254–263.

Jordan-Zachery, J. S. (2013). Now you see me, now you don't: My political fight against the invisibility/erasure of Black women in intersectionality research. *Politics, Groups, and Identities*, *1*(1), 101–109.

Jordan-Zachery, J. S. (2018). "I Ain't Your Darn Help": Black Women as the Help in Intersectionality Research in Political Science. In *Black Women in Politics* (pp. 19–30). Routledge.

Kahn, K. F. (1994). Does Gender Make a Difference? An Experimental Examination of Sex Stereotypes and Press Patterns in Statewide Campaigns. *American Journal of Political Science*, *38*(1), 162–195.

Kaplan, T., & Eligon, J. (2012, June 20). Wide Divide Kills Proposal On Marijuana. *New York Times*. Retrieved from: https://advance-lexis-com.proxyga.wrlc.org/api/document?collection=news&id=urn:contentItem:55XM-JJ21-DXY4-X1XV-00000-00&context=1516831

Keyes, K. M., Wall, M., Feng, T., Cerdá, M., & Hasin, D. S. (2017). Race/ethnicity and Marijuana Use in the United States: Diminishing Differences in the Prevalence of Use 2006 to 2015. *Drug Alcohol Depend*, *179*, 379–389.

Koch, D. W., Lee, J., & Lee, K. (2016). Coloring the War on Drugs: Arrest Disparities in Black, Brown, and White. *Race and Social Problems*, *8*(4), 313–325.

Kopicki, A. (2014, May 15). A Measurement of Partisan Unity. *New York Times*. Retrieved from: https://advance-lexis-com.proxyga.wrlc.org/api/document?collection=news&id=urn:contentItem:5C6M-96J1-DXY4-X52X-00000-00&context=1516831

Kovaleski, S., & Apuzzo, M. (2014, February 15). U.S. Issues Marijuana Guidelines for Banks. *New York Times*. Retrieved from: https://advance-lexis-com.proxyga.wrlc.org/api/document?collection=news&id=urn:contentItem:5BHN-2011-DXY4-X27T-00000-00&context=1516831

Lindsay, K. (2013). God, Gays, and Progressive Politics: Reconceptualizing Intersectionality as a Normatively Malleable Analytical Framework. *Perspectives on Politics*, *11*(2), 447–460.

Lovett, I. (2014, September 3). Berkeley Pushes a Boundary on Medical Marijuana. *New York Times*. Retrieved from: https://advance-lexis-com.proxyga.wrlc.org/api/document?collection=news&id=urn:contentItem:5D28-YRG1-DXY4-X2JP-00000-00&context=1516831

Lyman, R., & Sussman, D. (2014, February 27). *Pivotal Point Is Seen on Legalizing Marijuana*. Retrieved from: https://advance-lexis-com.proxyga.wrlc.org/api/document?collection=news&id=urn:contentItem:5BM6-M7X1-DXY4-X2JH-00000-00&context=1516831

MacKinnon, C. A. (2013). Intersectionality as Method: A Note. *Signs*, *38*(4), 1019–1030.

Mansbridge, J. (1999). Should Blacks Represent Blacks and Women Represent Women? A Contingent "Yes." *Journal of Politics*, *61*(3), 628–657.

Mauer, M. (2009). *The Changing Racial Dynamics of the War on Drugs* (p. 24). Sentencing Project.

Minta, M. D. (2012). Gender, Race, Ethnicity, and Political Representation in the United States. *Politics and Gender*, *8*(4), 541–547.

Nash, J. C. (2008). Re-thinking Intersectionality. *Feminist Review*, *89*, 1–15.

Nunn, K. B. (2002). Race, Crime and the Pool of Surplus Criminality: Or Why the "War on Drugs" Was a "War on Blacks." *Journal of Gender, Race, and Justice*, *6*, 381–445.

Phillips, D. (2014, July 24). Bid to Expand Medical Marijuana Business Faces Federal Hurdles. *New York Times*. Retrieved from: https://advance-lexis-com.proxyga.wrlc.org/api/document?collection=news&id=urn:contentItem:5D06-4WT1-DXY4-X0M1-00000-00&context=1516831

Philpot, T., & Walton, H. (2007). One of Our Own: Black Female Candidates and the Voters Who Support Them. *American Journal of Political Science*, 51(1), 49–62.

Politico & Harvard. (2019). Americans' Views on CBD Products and Marijuana for Recreational Use. *Politico*. Retrieved from: https://www.politico.com/f/?id=0000016e-3d52-ddf0-ad6ebfd38a2a0000

Rehavi, M. M., & Starr, S. B. (2014). Racial Disparity in Federal Criminal Sentences. *Journal of Political Economy*, *122*(6), 1320–1354.

Richardson, M. (1987). *Maria W. Stewart, America's First Black Woman Political Writer: Essays and Speeches (Blacks in the Diaspora)*. Indiana University Press.

Sanbonmatsu, K. (2002). Gender Stereotypes and Vote Choice. *American Journal of Political Science*, *46*(1), 20–34.

Schoenfeld, H. (2012). The War on Drugs, the Politics of Crime, and Mass Incarceration in the United States. *Journal of Gender, Race, and Justice*, *15*, 315–355.

Scott, N. A., & Siltanen, J. (2017). Intersectionality and Quantitative Methods: Assessing Regression from a Feminist Perspective. *International Journal of Social Research Methodology*, *20*(4), 373–385.

Simien, E. M. (2007). Doing Intersectionality Research: From Conceptual Issues to Practical Examples. *Politics and Gender*, *3*(02), 264–271.

Simien, E. M., & Clawson, R. A. (2004). The Intersection of Race and Gender: An Examination of Black Feminist Consciousness, Race Consciousness, and Policy Attitudes. *Social Science Quarterly*, *85*(3), 793–810.

Strolovitch, D. Z. (2006). Do Interest Groups Represent the Disadvantaged? Advocacy at the Intersections of Race, Class, and Gender. *Journal of Politics*, *68*(4), 894–910.

Tate, K. (2013). Winds of Change: Black Opinion on Legalizing Marijuana. In *Something's In the Air: Race, Crime, and the Legalization of Marijuana* (pp. 65–78). Routledge.

Uhlaner, C. J. (2012). Potentiality and Representation: The Link between Descriptive Representation and Participation in the United States. *Politics and Gender*, *8*(4), 535–541.

Wadsworth, N. D. (2011). Intersectionality in California's Same-Sex Marriage Battles: A Complex Proposition. *Political Research Quarterly*, *64*(1), 200–216.

APPENDIX

Table 3.2 Traditional Regressions Using ANES Data

	2012	*2016*
Black	0.285**	–0.128
	(0.124)	(0.182)
White	0.543***	0.502***
	(0.0931)	(0.125)
Female	–0.516***	–0.375***
	(0.0737)	(0.0895)
Ideology	–0.542***	0.320***
	(0.0272)	(0.0222)
Age	–0.0192***	–0.0378***
	(0.00229)	(0.00265)
Education	0.0237	0.0254
	(0.0153)	(0.0190)
Constant	2.956***	0.616**
	(0.240)	(0.275)
Observations	3,609	2,608

Standard errors in parentheses
*** p<0.01, ** p<0.05, * p<0.1
Source: *Data from author study*

Chapter 4

The Politics of Marijuana, Immigration, and Latinos

Joe R. Tafoya and Melissa R. Michelson

The Latino politics of marijuana legalization have revolved around drug enforcement arrest rates and incarceration of Latino youth, as well as drug trafficking across the United States–Mexico border. Drug laws have historically been used disproportionately against Latinos (and Black Americans), and the historic link between Mexican immigrants and the flow of marijuana across the United States–Mexico border has been used to criminalize Latino immigrants, including candidate and then president Donald Trump. As a result, debates about cannabis liberalization have generated speculation about how such legal changes might affect attitudes toward immigration. The creation of recreational marijuana markets in several states since 2014 allows for testing of these hypotheses using state-level data. Here, we explore data on attitudes on marijuana legalization and immigration over time, as well as national samples, to compare immigration attitudes of residents from states where marijuana is legalized for recreational use to others where it remains a controlled, illegal drug.

Marijuana was not always illegal in the United States. The first edition (distributed in 1902) of the Sears Roebuck catalog—the Amazon.com of its time—offered bulk cannabis at $1/pound (Campos, 2018; Pruitt, 2019). This period of legal, recreational use was short-lived, however. As anti-immigrant attitudes surged in the early 20th century, coinciding with increasingly popular perceptions of marijuana as something smoked by immigrants, Americans began to extend their nativist, anti-Mexican (and anti-Indian) sentiment to negative attitudes toward marijuana (Waxman, 2019). Dufton (2017, p. 3) notes:

> A 1917 report from the Treasury Department noted its concern that in Texas, only "Mexicans and sometimes Negroes and lower-class whites" smoked

> marijuana for pleasure and warned that "drug-crazed" minorities could harm or assault upper-class white women.

Campos (2018) calls this story of the criminalization of marijuana, including the decision to make it a Schedule-1 narcotic under federal law, the "Mexican hypothesis." While Campos finds fault with the Mexican hypothesis in terms of how accurately it reflects the true history of marijuana's use and criminalization, marijuana and Latinos, especially Mexicans, were linked in the public mind at the time that marijuana was categorized as a dangerous narcotic. In other words, racism against Mexicans, whose "unpredictable and violent behavior" was allegedly caused by marijuana, was used in the 1930s as an excuse for criminalizing marijuana. People believed marijuana was a powerfully addictive drug that gave people superhuman strength and turned them into rapists and murderers. Americans believed that "All Mexicans are crazy, and this stuff is what makes them crazy" (Marion & Hill, 2019: p. 18). When Harry Anslinger, head of the Federal Bureau of Narcotics from 1930 to 1962, testified before Congress in support of criminalizing marijuana, he cited ideas that had come from Mexico about marijuana causing madness and violence (Waxman, 2019).

From the Mexican Cockroach Song (*La Cucaracha*), which has been around for a century, to Cheech and Chong's *Up in Smoke* (1978), the idea that Mexicans are heavy marijuana users is firm in the public imagination, despite data regarding relatively equal rates of use across racial and ethnic groups. In 2014, we wrote about the long history of links between marijuana laws and immigration politics—particularly regarding immigration from Mexico—stemming from stereotypes about Mexican marijuana use and the smuggling of marijuana from across the United States–Mexico border to supply American users (Michelson & Tafoya, 2014). Anti-Mexican sentiment inspired stories of "loco weed" brought across the border by Mexican laborers; domestic, recreational use was blamed on the increase in immigration after the Mexican Revolution of 1910. "The drug became associated with the immigrants, and the fear and prejudice about the Spanish-speaking newcomers became associated with marijuana" (*Frontline*, quoted in Michelson and Tafoya, 2014, p. 117).

In the early 20th century, stories of violent criminal behavior by marijuana-using Mexicans led many state and local legislative bodies to outlaw the drug. This culminated in the 1937 decision to regulate marijuana possession (Gieringer, 2006; Helmer, 1975). In 1937, Congress passed the Marijuana Tax Act, and President Roosevelt signed it. The law required anyone who bought, sold, or grew marijuana to file paperwork with the federal government and buy a stamp from the Department of the Treasury. However, the Treasury did not issue any stamps, which in effect meant that anyone who grew, sold, or possessed marijuana was breaking the law (Marion & Hill, 2019).

The Great Depression of the 1930s triggered fears about economic competition from Mexican immigrants, and inspired research linking marijuana use and violent crime to "racially inferior" communities (Frontline, 2021). Mexican American communities were hit hard by the Depression due to scarcity of jobs and food, but additionally faced growing hostility due to unemployment and competition for the few jobs available (Library of Congress, 2021). Hostility toward Mexicans ramped up and the federal government acted on this sentiment, initiating for the first time large-scale roundups and deportations under a program of repatriation to relocate Mexican immigrants to Mexico. Estimates of Mexicans deported range from 500,000 to 1.8 million and include Mexicans that were American-born U.S. citizens (Little, 2021). Gratton and Merchant (2018) use Census records to show that actual deportations were substantially lower because a great deal of those returning to Mexico consisted of voluntary departures due to government efforts and poor economic conditions in the United States.

In the 1940s, the United States and Mexico implemented the Bracero Program to kick-start the circular migration pattern that provided the United States with steady, cheap labor. The government allowed the agriculture industry to initiate contracts with workers in Mexico and arrange for their transportation, but the program spiraled out of control, leading to unprecedented waves of unauthorized immigration (Anderson, 2003). Waves of deportations increased too and in 1954, the Immigration and Naturalization Service (INS) apprehended 1.1 million Mexican Americans for deportation in "Operation Wetback," the largest mass deportation in American history (Blakemore, 2019).

Years prior, the drug trade from Mexico boomed after World War II coinciding with the mobilization of men to army bases along the border and the development of heroin and marijuana distribution networks (Bucardo et al., 2005). Responding to a rise in drug use among youth, Congress passed the Boggs Act of 1952 and the Narcotics Control Act of 1956 that instituted the first minimum prison sentences for drug-related offenses that included smuggling, selling, or possession of marijuana (Benson, July 2). A sentence for possession required a sentence of two to ten years and/or a fine of up $20,000 (Mills, 2015). The stiff penalties put Mexican immigrants and Mexican Americans in the crosshairs due to their proximity to Mexico and the associations policy makers made about their drug use and involvement in the drug trade. From the beginning, anti-immigrant attitudes influenced anti-marijuana sentiment.

As states began to legalize in the early 2010s, imports shrunk, and some media reported that consumers increasingly turned to domestically produced marijuana (Burnett, 2014). The 2020 National Drug Threat Assessment report notes that "in U.S. markets, Mexican marijuana has largely been supplanted by domestic-produced marijuana." Marijuana seizures by Customs and Border Patrol along the United States–Mexico border have decreased more than 81% since 2013 (NDTA, 2021, p. 47). A lack of robust data makes it difficult to determine just how much marijuana used in the United States originates in Mexico (or other countries) and how much is produced domestically. Regardless of the true degree of marijuana smuggling, debates about securing the United States–Mexico border have consistently cited smuggling as a relevant concern (Michelson & Tafoya, 2014). This historic link between fears of marijuana smuggling and a need for increased border security suggests that as marijuana is decriminalized, concerns about border security and unauthorized immigration might also become weaker, and support for progressive immigration laws stronger.

Of course, there is considerable reason to expect this hypothesized link to fall short. Drug cartels may lose markets as states decriminalize and destigmatize marijuana use, but much of their activity centers on the smuggling of other drugs, as well as on the smuggling of cash and guns (NDTA, 2021). There are also many other sources of attitudes about immigration, including one's sense of social, political, racial, cultural, and economic threat (Cutaia Wilkinson, 2015; Espenshade & Calhoun, 1993; Espenshade & Hempstead, 1996; Burns & Gimpel, 2000; Hainmueller & Hopkins, 2014). Macro-level economic factors such as views of the national economy and anxiety over taxes can also influence immigration attitudes (Citrin et al., 1997). Individuals who reside in predominantly Latino areas are more likely to support restrictive immigration policies (Rocha et al., 2011). Yet, the role of marijuana laws cannot be ignored. As we wrote in 2014, and as noted earlier, marijuana use in the United States has long been associated with importation of the drug from Mexico, and blamed for violent crime by those using the drug recreationally. Criminalization laws banning marijuana use and law-enforcement efforts to prevent marijuana from being smuggled across the United States-Mexican border perpetuate anti-Latino and anti-immigrant stereotypes that Mexicans are drug-crazed criminals. Based on our previous analysis, our hypothesis here is that the decriminalization of marijuana embraced by many state governments in the last decade should also lead to a shift in attitudes about immigration.

HYPOTHETICAL EXPECTATIONS

In this section, we consider evidence that marijuana legality influences views about immigrants. To do so, we employ a measure for how Americans view immigrants in general as a sense of the attitudes Americans have cultivated in the past and more recently. In the past, marijuana criminalization soured immigrant views in public and their lawmaking representatives who enacted anti-Mexican immigrant programs. Nowadays, views on marijuana and immigration are so closely related they might reinforce one another given they share the common thread of law enforcement. In January 2018, White House Press Secretary Sarah Sanders explained that then-president Trump's top priority was enforcement of federal law "regardless of what the topic is, whether it's marijuana or whether it's immigration" (Gurman, 2018).

Immigration politics today contains the reality that 60% of white Americans view Mexican males with stereotypical characteristics as "illegal" (Everding, 2018). Unpacking the public's views about immigration and establishing them as a function of marijuana legality will point to marijuana as the cause and anti-immigration as the effect of racially motivated public policy. Examples from the past establish that marijuana criminalization became a tool to police Mexican immigrant populations. Once ensnared in the criminal justice system, Mexican populations in the United States entered the public mind as a class of crazed, drug-fueled criminals that, when seen as competition for work during periods of high unemployment, became subject to anti-immigration sentiment and government action. We think that this association persists in the public mind today as opponents of marijuana legalization maintain their opposition to immigration.

Given the racialization of immigration politics (Silber Mohamed & Farris, 2020), attitudes about immigration should be linked to marijuana laws. In other words, when states move to decriminalize and even legalize marijuana, this should be reflected in reduced bias against Mexicans and thus increased support for progressive immigration policies. When the stigma of marijuana is reduced for permitted medical purposes, when criminal infractions are reduced, and as legalized recreational use broadens, we expect anti-immigrant attitudes to also diminish. We expect to see that the legalization of marijuana should influence pro-immigrant views because, as we argue, marijuana use, possession, and smuggling is remarkably fused to the presence of immigrants in the United States. We take advantage of the decentralized nature of marijuana laws to explore this hypothesis. We note the status of marijuana laws at the state level to explore whether state attitudes on immigration vary as expected given our hypotheses about how marijuana liberalization affects public opinion.

Our evaluation of publicly available data proceeds by marshaling evidence of a marijuana-immigration link in public opinion. We do so in two phases: first, we evaluate whether attitudes about marijuana are linked over time at the national level. Second, we test whether attitudes toward immigrants differ depending on whether respondents reside in states where

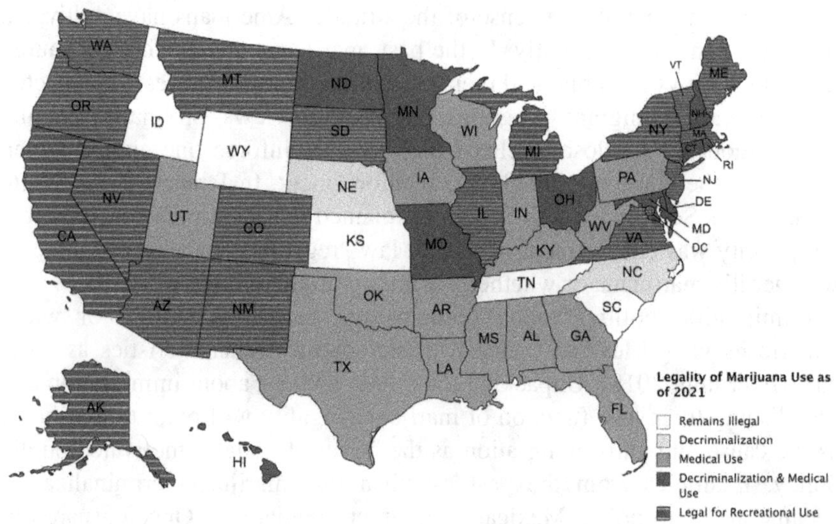

Figure 4.1 Map of State-Level Legal Status of Marijuana. *Source: State classifications are provided by Disa Global Solutions (see Disa, 2021 for a detailed presentation of state laws).*

marijuana remains illegal, if it is medically allowed (but not allowed for recreational use), where it is decriminalized, and whether it is legal for recreational use. Legalization for recreational use refers to the complete removal of criminal punishments for adult possession and ownership, similar to how states treat alcohol and tobacco. Decriminalization refers to the strategy of states declining to prosecute individuals for possession (usually under a set amount that implies use rather than intent to sell). Medical use, as the name implies, allows for the legal use of marijuana by those who have obtained a prescription from a licensed physician. This generates a continuum of policy approaches to marijuana, ranging from compliance with federal law (most conservative) to recreational use (most progressive). In this analysis, we take advantage of the wide variety of state-level treatments of marijuana, as shown in figure 4.1 (see Disa, 2021 for up-to-date state laws on Marijuana use).

We expect to find the following:

H_1: As the public has become more supportive of marijuana legalization, it has also become more likely to think immigrants are beneficial to the United States rather than a burden.

H_2: Support for immigrants will increase among state residents as state marijuana policy moves from most conservative to most progressive.

We test our first hypothesis with data from 1994 to 2019. We test hypothesis two with cross-sectional data from the National Election Pool Poll, a nationally representative survey project providing 20,000 observations per year for the years 2014, 2016, and 2018. In this second phase, we divvy categorize respondents into states of varying marijuana rules and leverage the fact that a growing list of states where marijuana use is liberalized increases our pool of respondents. Specifically, the pool of respondents from legalized, recreational use states expands as state rules change during the 2014–2018 period. We use growing pools of respondents in legalization states to compare views on immigration of residents of states where marijuana remains a controlled, illegal drug.

ATTITUDES TOWARD MARIJUANA AND IMMIGRATION, 1994–2019

A critical part of our story is establishing whether an association exists at the macro level between attitudes toward the legalization of marijuana and attitudes about the impact of immigration. We search for this association nationwide, seeking to prove that an overall association between these two issues exists. In this section, we set the foundation for our later exploration of state-level correlations and between statutory climates related to marijuana and attitudes about immigration.

Our analysis focuses on 1994–2019, when survey data for both issues is available. A unique feature of these data is that Pew often asked both survey questions in the same survey. In a minority of cases, questions did not overlap in the same survey and time interval gaps are present. With this in mind, we constructed a dataset for years and months when data for both measures were available. Our data contain what are known as "toplines" reporting percentages of the public answering each question with support, opposition, or neither (don't know or refused to answer) (see The Audience Agency, 2021 for a description of "topline" reporting of survey findings).

Toplines for the survey measures on marijuana legalization and views about immigrants contain percentages for three possible responses: positive, negative, or neutral positions. The surveys report what the public thinks about legalization and immigrants yearly, sometimes multiple times per year and sometimes skipped years. For skipped years containing no information about public views, we use *interpolation* to generate missing information based on averages of surrounding entries. This process preserves a continuous temporal distribution. In addition, we average multiple entries per year into one entry a year, so that every year between 1994 and 2019 contains aggregate toplines that are rolling averages. We test whether the toplines rise and fall together in the following section.

Survey researchers have measured public attitudes toward marijuana since 1969, when only 12% of Americans supported legalization. In contrast to most public opinion trends, which show very consistent attitudes over time (Page & Shapiro, 1992) this has shifted dramatically over time. Since 2011, a majority of Americans have favored legalization (Dimock et al., 2013), and by April 2021 this percentage had increased to 91% (Green, 2021).

Figure 4.2 contains trend lines of public attitudes on marijuana from 1994 to 2019 (acquired from Pew, 2019a). The dashed trend line is the conservative attitude, signifying the strength of public opposition to marijuana legalization. The solid line is the progressive attitude, signifying support for legalization. The dotted trend line illustrates the relatively small and stable proportion of the public that answered "neither" or "don't know" to each survey. As shown in figure 4.2, a majority of the public has supported legalization since 2011. Support for legalization climbed steadily over time and continued to rise over time, coinciding with statutory change at the state level as an increasing number of states passed more progressive marijuana laws. Dotted vertical lines indicate significant moments in marijuana legalization. In 2012, Washington and Colorado legalized recreational marijuana use. In 2014, Alaska and Washington, DC followed suit. Two years later, 2016 saw the largest increase of states legalizing marijuana for recreational use: California,

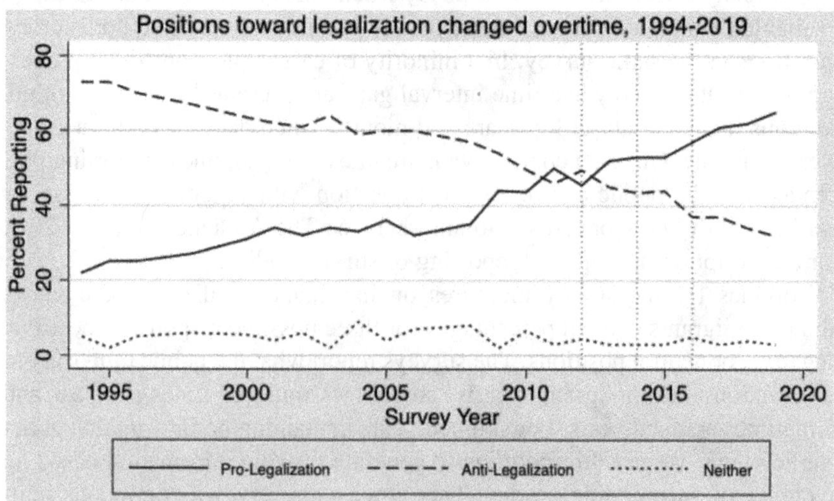

Figure 4.2 Views toward Marijuana Legalization among U.S. Adults (Positions toward Legalization Changed Over Time, 1994–2019). *Source: General Social Survey (GSS), Gallup, Pew Research Center.*

Maine, Massachusetts, Nevada, and Vermont. The growing list of states appears to have bolstered support for marijuana legalization nationwide as it reached majority support in 2011 and continued its steady rise. Additionally, the list of states adjusting rules to liberalize marijuana use from allowing it for medical use to decriminalization grew during this period as well, making changes are far too numerous to list (see Hartman, 2021 for a comprehensive listing of changes to state laws regarding legality of marijuana).

We explore data on marijuana legalization alongside data about attitudes toward immigrants. Since 1994, survey researchers from the Pew Research Center and Gallup have asked the U.S. public whether they believe that immigrants "strengthen our country because of their hard work and talents," or whether immigrants "are a burden on our country because they take our jobs, housing and health care." Even within this truncated time period, we see a rapid shift in public opinion on immigrant views, as shown in figure 4.3. Attitudes have shifted from a majority in opposition to a strong majority in support. The public initially was more likely to report negative attitudes, but here again there has been a relatively large shift in attitudes, from 31% giving positive attitudes (and 63% negative) in 1994, to a reversal in the most recent (2019) survey to 61%–66% reporting favorable attitudes and 24%–36% negative (see Pew, 2017 for 1994–2017; Pew, 2019b for 2017–2019), as shown in figure 4.3.

Figure 4.3 features dashed lines along the *x*-axis similarly demarcate the years 2012, 2014, and 2016 as critical junctures when immigrant attitudes

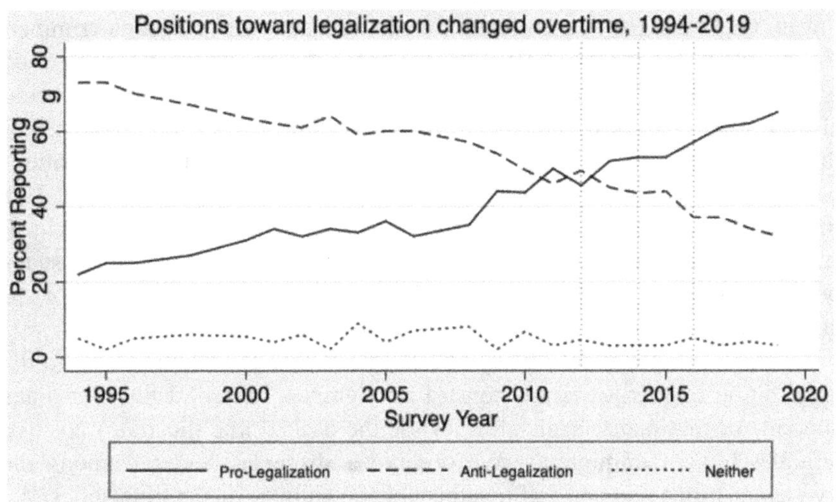

Figure 4.3 Views toward Marijuana Legalization among U.S. Adults (Positions toward Legalization Changed Over Time, 1994–2019). *Source: General Social Survey (GSS), Gallup, Pew Research Center.*

rose rapidly. We speculate that just as support for marijuana rose due to external factors, increasingly liberal attitudes toward immigrants rose according to political events occurring simultaneously. In 2012, President Barack Obama announced the creation of the Deferred Action for Childhood Arrivals (DACA) program as a reprieve from deportation to youths that arrived to this country younger than the age of 16 (Mayorkas, 2012). In 2014, President Obama signed executive actions aimed to address unauthorized immigration at the border, reprioritize deportation to felons instead of families, and require immigrants to pass criminal background checks and pay taxes to stay in the United States temporarily without fear of deportation (USCIS, 2014). In 2016, President Obama's executive order to grant legal status to millions in the country without permission, bypassing Congress, appeared before the Supreme Court. An evenly divided bench due to the death of Antonin Scalia deadlocked 2–2 and the lower court ruling that blocked the program was upheld (Aguilar & Mekelburg, 2016). Lastly, 2016 also saw the candidacy and eventual victory of Donald Trump to the presidency. The Republican campaign advanced an anti-immigrant platform although more than 60% of the American public disagreed due to their support for immigrants.

Overall, it is clear that the public has become far more progressive on these two issues from 1994 to 2019. American adults are both more supportive of the legalization of marijuana and more likely to say that immigrants benefit the United States. This is particularly true for attitudes since 2011, when a majority of Americans have supported progressive positions on these two issues.

Hypothesis 1 advances that attitudes on marijuana and immigrants are linked. Our basis for this association is that a history of marijuana criminalization as a tool to police Latino citizens and Latino immigrants harms public perceptions of immigrants. Conversely, liberalization on marijuana could also be associated with an improvement on views toward immigrants. For the first phase of our analysis, we consider the association in attitudes nationwide; below, we turn to state-level statutory climates about marijuana. This initial test establishes that public opinion on the issues might be intertwined. As a result, attitudes toward immigrants might be improved in specific states where marijuana is legalized. We consider this possibility in the phase of our analysis that follows.

Figure 4.4 displays an overlay of trend lines both for attitudes toward the legalization of marijuana and toward immigrants. The solid line illustrates support for marijuana legalization, while the dashed line illustrates positive attitudes toward immigrants. We observe a strong association among the two as positions rise and fall together for the entirety of the time series. An assessment of this relationship is provided by a Pearson correlation measuring the strength of a linear association between two variables. The Pearson correlation coefficient for this relationship is statistically significant at 0.83,

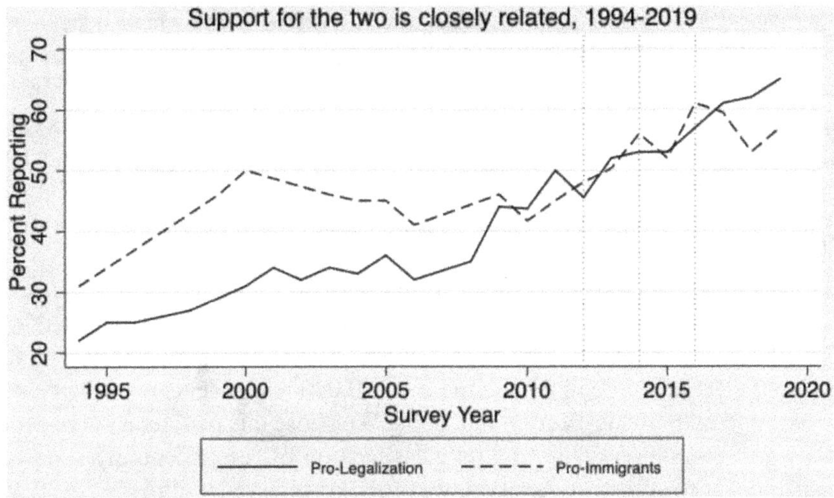

Figure 4.4 Support for Marijuana and Immigrants among U.S Adults (Support for the Two is Closely Related, 1994–2019). *Source: General Social Survey (GSS), Gallup, Pew Research Center.*

indicating a strong association that supports our initial hypothesis. Beginning in 1994 and continuing until about 2008, we observe a considerable gap between attitudes as both legalization and immigrants are opposed by a majority of Americans. The gap disappears as support for both rises above 50% after 2012. In this latter phase, support for legalization and immigrants remain remarkably close. The proximity in support for both immigrants and marijuana legalization persists until about 2016. Diversion of the trend lines here reflects the as nativism and xenophobia that accompanied former president Donald Trump's entry into the national political stage in the summer of 2015 and through his presidency (Anbinder, 2019).

Immigrant Attitudes where Marijuana is Legalized for Recreational Use, 2014–2018

Here, we narrow our search for an association between marijuana legalization and increasingly supportive attitudes toward immigrants. We do so by posing logistic regression tests of cross-sectional data to detect fluctuations in immigrant attitudes reported by respondents residing in states of varying marijuana laws. In other words, our search aims to identify determinants of positive immigrant views, which we hypothesize are associated with residence in states that have moved away from classifying marijuana as an illegal drug. Specifically, individually for survey years 2014, 2016, and 2018, we identify whether respondents to the surveys lived in states where marijuana (A) remained an illegal, controlled substance, (B) was approved for medical use, (C) became decriminalized so that possession amounted to minimal criminal infractions, and (D) has become legal for recreational use. This categorization of respondents by state of residence allows us to compare whether those living in conditions B, C, and D differ from others living in condition A in terms of responses to the dependent variable—support or opposition to immigrants in the United States.

Data come from the National Election Pool Poll sponsored by ABC News, Associated Press, CBS, CNN Fox News, and NBC (Edison Research, 2014; Edison Research, 2016; Edison Research, 2018). The pool consists of a national election exit poll containing over 20,000 respondents of a telephone survey and nationwide election-day polls. We chose this particular survey for its large observation count and its classification of respondents by state of residence. In the preceding section, we relied on reported toplines by the Pew Research Center, but its individual-level, cross-sectional surveys are limited in that they contain roughly 1,500 observations each and classified respondents by geographical region rather than by state.

The large observation count of the National Election Exit Pool Poll is critical because only a handful of states have legalized marijuana. As of 2014, just four states—Alaska, Colorado, Oregon, and Washington—along with Washington DC, legalized marijuana for adult recreational use. Of the over 20,000 observations presented by the poll, 524 (2.6% of the sample) were available to us from these states. The year 2014 also included 8,358 (41.4%) observations from states where marijuana remained completely illegal, 4,941 (24.5%) observations from states where only medical use is allowed, and 6,345 (31.5%) observations from states where marijuana has been decriminalized (Edison Research, 2014).

We further leveraged additional datasets for 2016 and 2018 to observe the growing pool of respondents in states where marijuana is a legalized, recreational drug. By 2016, California, Maine, Massachusetts, Nevada, and Vermont had also legalized recreational adult use of marijuana, increasing the pool of respondents for that statutory context to 4,068 (16.4% of the 2016 sample). The pool of respondents from states where marijuana remained completely illegal was 8,878 (35.8%), where medical use was allowed was 6,386 (25.8%), and where decriminalization was passed was 5,453 (22%) (Edison Research, 2016). By 2018, Michigan joined the ranks of states where recreational use had been legalized and others shifted from illegality to medical use and from medical use to decriminalization (Hartman, 2021; NCLS, 2021). As a result, the proportions of pools of respondents by legal condition shifted. By 2018, the number of respondents living in states where marijuana was completely illegal was 5,591 (29.1%), where medical use was permitted was 4,708 (24.5%), where decriminalization occurred was 4,756 (24.8%), and those where it became legal for recreational use numbered 4,156 (21.6%) (Edison Research, 2018). Ultimately, it is notable that the share of respondents in the samples collected by the National Election Pool Poll where marijuana became legalized went from to 2.6% in 2014, to 16.4% in 2016, and to 21.6% in 2018.

We use increasing sizes of the populations where marijuana is liberalized as a key independent variable to predict state attitudes toward immigration. Our dependent variable indicates whether respondents reported (1) support or (0) opposition to immigrants or immigration based on two different survey questions. The first, used in the 2014 and 2016 surveys, asked, "Should immigrants working in the United States be: (1) offered a chance to apply for legal status or (2) deported to the country they came from." We coded the first response as indicating support for immigrants and the latter as indicating opposition to immigration. The second question, used in 2018, asked respondents, "Are Donald Trump's immigration policies ... (1) too tough, (2) not tough enough, or (3) about right." We coded responses to this question to indicate (0) unsupportive of immigrants (including "not tough enough" and "about right" responses) and (1) supportive of immigrants ("too tough" responses).

We hypothesize that those living in legalization states, all things equal, are significantly more supportive of immigrants than others living in states where marijuana remains illegal. Below we pose logistic regressions models to detect whether the legal context of residence is predictive of immigrant attitudes. The models also take into account individual-level differences such as age, education, income, gender, race/ethnicity, and partisanship to isolate the relationship between state residence and immigrant attitudes as best as possible. Question wording and variable coding for all measures of our multivariate regression models are as follows:

Outcome Measures of respondent opinions to be explained by statistical models for years 2014, 2016, and 2018, possible response options as subpoints:

- 2014: Should most illegal immigrants working in the United States be:
    - (1) Offered a chance to apply for legal status
    - (0) Deported to the country they came from
- 2016: Should most illegal immigrants working in the United States be:
    - (1) Offered a chance to apply for legal status
    - (0) Deported to the country they came from
- 2018: Are Donald Trump's immigration policies:
    - (1) Too tough
    - (0) Not tough enough; about right

Explanatory Measures of respondent characteristics employed to explain Outcome Measures in the statistical model for years 2014, 2016, and 2018, possible response options as subpoints:

- Marijuana State Status:
  - (1) Illegal
  - (2) Medical
  - (3) Decriminalized
  - (4) Legal for Recreational Use
- Age:
  - (1) 18–29
  - (2) 30–44
  - (3) 45–66
  - (4) 65+
- Education:
  - (1) High school or less
  - (2) Some college/AA degree
  - (3) College graduate
  - (4) Post-graduate study
- Income:
  - (1) Under 30K
  - (2) 30K–50K
  - (3) 50K–100K
  - (4) 100K–200K
  - (5) 200K–250K
  - (6) 250K or more
- Gender:
  - (1) Male
  - (2) Female
- Race/Ethnicity
  - (1) White
  - (2) Black
  - (3) Hispanic/Latino
  - (4) Asian
  - (5) Other
- Partisanship:
  - (1) Democrat
  - (2) Republican
  - (3) Independent/Something else

Results are shown in table 4.1 and important associations are illustrated in figures 4.5–4.7. For each column in table 4.1, results from logistic regression

Table 4.1 Predictors of Support for Immigrants According to State Marijuana Status, Logistic Regression Estimates

	2014	*2016*	*2018*
Marijuana: Illegal (Base)	–	–	–
Marijuana: Medical	1.07 (0.09)	1.23* (0.11)	1.17+ (0.11)
Marijuana: Decriminalized	1.07 (0.09)	1.00 (0.09)	1.20* (0.11)
Marijuana: Legal (Recreational)	2.16** (0.52)	1.50*** (0.16)	1.82*** (0.18)
Age	0.95 (0.04)	0.88*** (0.03)	0.75*** (0.03)
Age NA	0.37 (0.26)	0.31** (0.14)	0.16*** (0.07)
Education	1.17*** (0.06)	1.35*** (0.05)	1.31*** (0.04)
Education NA	3.19*** (0.56)	2.13* (0.73)	4.51*** (0.56)
Income	1.00 (0.03)	1.00 (.)	1.00 (.)
Income NA	1.07 (0.19)	1.00 (.)	1.00 (.)
Female	1.22** (0.08)	1.67*** (0.12)	1.44*** (0.10)
Gender NA	1.29 (0.98)	1.26 (0.85)	3.48 (3.03)
Black	2.22*** (0.25)	2.40*** (0.32)	3.51*** (0.41)
Hispanic/Latino	2.82*** (0.45)	1.79*** (0.25)	1.71*** (0.20)
Asian	1.37 (0.38)	0.97 (0.21)	2.08** (0.52)
Other	1.19 (0.22)	1.18 (0.20)	1.02 (0.15)
Party ID	0.71*** (0.03)	0.72*** (0.03)	0.46*** (0.02)
Party NA	0.90 (0.33)	0.59 (0.19)	0.20*** (0.06)
Prob>chi2	0.000***	0.000***	0.000***
Pseudo R2	0.057	0.061	0.149
Observations	3,800	4,585	4,458

Note: Odds Ratios (OR) presented, Standard Errors in parentheses. ORs are measures of association indicating a measure's relationship to the dependent variable—views toward immigrants in 2014, 2016, and 2018. An OR of 1 means a given measure found no higher or lower likelihoods that views toward immigrants changed. An OR above 1 with statistical significance indicates that views toward immigrants improved given increased values of a particular measure. An OR below 1 with statistical significance indicates that views toward immigrants worsened given increased values of a particular measure. *Source:* National Election Pool Poll, National Day Exit Poll, 2014, 2016, 2018. + $p < 0.10$, * $p < 0.05$, ** $p < 0.01$, *** $p < 0.001$, two-tailed tests.

models are presented for 2014, 2016, and 2018. In each of these years, for each of their models, we find that respondents living in states where marijuana is legal are significantly more likely to express support for immigrants. Contextually, our observation of statistical significance in the positive direction for those living in "legalized" states is in comparison to respondents living in states where marijuana remains strictly illegal (the omitted category in the first row).

Detailed results of our analysis are shown in table 4.1. We find consistent evidence that the state-level statutory treatment of marijuana is linked to attitudes about immigration, particularly in the latter two years (2016 and 2018) when there is more variation in the data due to additional states authorizing legalized recreational use. In 2014, 2016, and 2018, respondents from states with legalized recreational use are consistently more supportive of immigrants, compared to states where marijuana remains completely illegal. We

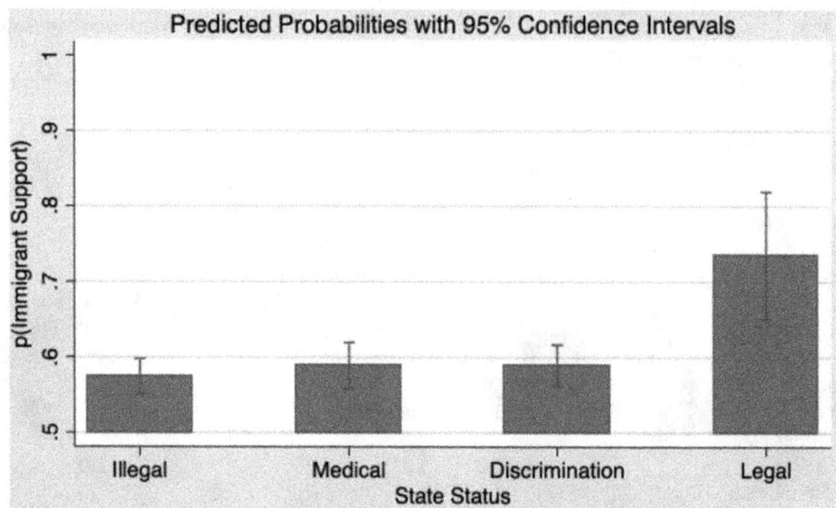

Figure 4.5 Support for Immigrants by State Marijuana Legalization Policy, 2014 (Predicted Probabilities with 95% Confidence Intervals). *Source: National Election Pool, 2014, national exit poll of the United States.*

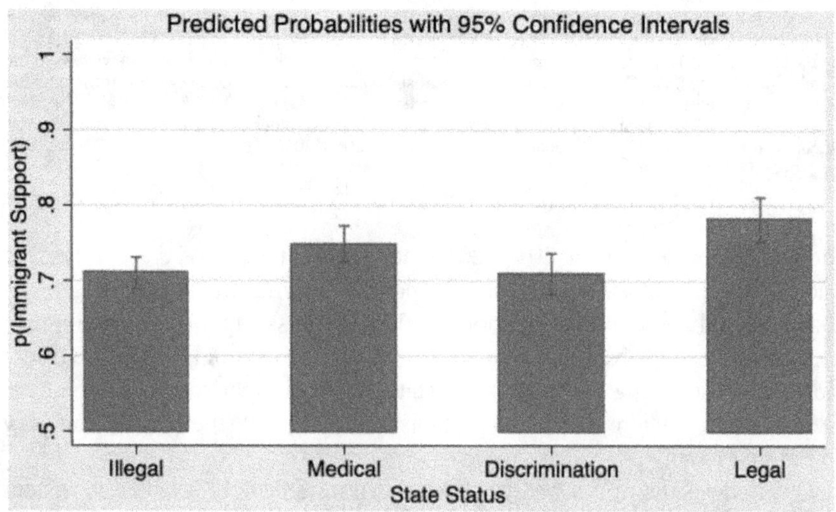

Figure 4.6 Support for Immigrants by State Marijuana Legalization Policy, 2016 (Predicted Probabilities with 95% Confidence Intervals). *Source: National Election Pool, 2016, national exit poll of the United States.*

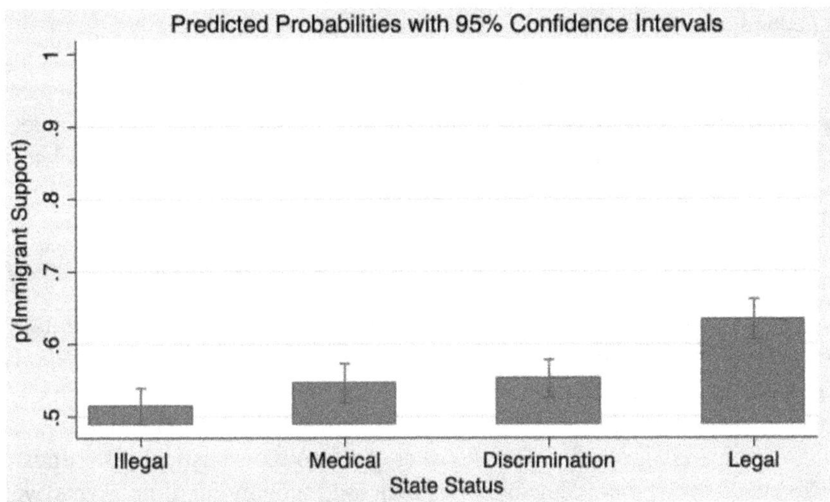

Figure 4.7 Support for Immigrants by State Marijuana Legalization Policy, 2018 (Predicted Probabilities with 95% Confidence Intervals). *Source: National Election Pool, 2018, national exit poll of the United States.*

also tested for differences among those living in states where marijuana is authorized for medical use or is decriminalized. We found that respondents in medical marijuana states in 2016 were more supportive of immigrants than those in states where it remained illegal. A similar result is apparent in 2018, but statistical significance is at the 90% level of confidence.

Other variables are also important predictors of attitudes toward immigration. Consistent with existing scholarship, these include various demographic characteristics as well as partisanship and personal experiences of discrimination. Older individuals are less supportive of immigrants, as are individuals who identify as Republicans. People with more education, who are female, or who identify as a member of a historically marginalized racial or ethnic group (Black, Latino, or Asian American) are more supportive of immigrants.

As shown in figure 4.5, respondents from states where marijuana was legalized for recreational use in 2014 were more than twice as likely to voice support for immigrants, compared to individuals living in states where marijuana remained completely illegal or where it was decriminalized or authorized only for medical use. Recall that in 2014 this included only the states of Alaska, Colorado, and Washington, as well as Washington DC. The difference here is both substantively large and statistically significant.

As shown in figure 4.6, respondents from states where marijuana was legalized for recreational use by 2016 were again more likely to voice support for immigrants, compared to individuals living in states where marijuana remained completely illegal; although the difference is smaller, it is still statistically significant. Support for immigrants was also stronger among individuals living in states where marijuana had been authorized for medical use. We observe no statistically significant difference between respondent attitudes toward immigration in states where marijuana remained completely illegal in 2016 and states where marijuana had been decriminalized. In 2014, places that had legalized recreational use included only Alaska, Colorado, Washington state, and Washington DC. By 2016, they had been joined by California, Maine, Massachusetts, Nevada, and Vermont.

Finally, looking at attitudes in 2018, we again find that respondents in states where marijuana was legal for recreational use were much more likely to voice supportive attitudes of immigrants, compared to states where marijuana remained completely illegal. The difference is both substantively large and statistically significant. For this year, we also see statistically significant differences at the other levels of legalization: support for immigrants was stronger in states with medical and decriminalization policies compared to states where marijuana remained completely illegal, and yet not as strong as in states with legal recreational use. See figure 4.7.

CONCLUSION

In both our national analysis and our state-level analyses, we find consistent evidence that legal contexts toward marijuana and attitudes toward immigrants are linked. As attitudes about marijuana have become more progressive, shifting toward medical use, decriminalization, and legal recreational use, the nation has become more supportive of immigrants and more likely to see them as beneficial to the body public. At the state level, support for immigrants has increased as state laws have moved away from complete bans on marijuana. These findings support our hypothesis that attitudes toward immigrants—who are racialized as Mexican—will move with attitudes toward marijuana due to the historic link between Mexican immigrants and marijuana in the public mind. Even if the "Mexican hypothesis" is not historically accurate, the public consistently stereotypes marijuana as a drug used by Mexicans and as coming to the United States from Mexico.

It is possible that the correlations found in our analyses are not causal, but are spurious and due to a common, underlying factor. For example, it might be argued that attitudes toward marijuana and toward immigration are both based on partisan polarization. However, these correlations persist even when controlling for partisanship, as shown in table 4.1. This increases our confidence that our findings are not spurious remnants of underlying partisan splits. In addition, we note that shifting attitudes toward marijuana are bipartisan—the shift to more progressive policies is supported by both Republicans and Democrats, thus reducing the likelihood that these observed correlations are due to partisanship. It is also possible that the direction of causality is reversed, in that attitudes toward immigrants influence attitudes toward marijuana. We leave explorations of that possibility to future research.

The shift away from strict criminalization of marijuana has downstream effects for immigration attitudes. Less strict laws mean fewer opportunities for racialized enforcement (Michelson & Tafoya, 2014) and fewer media stories about marijuana drug busts at the border. Softening attitudes toward marijuana, and a realization that historical fears about the "loco weed" were racist propaganda, may be leading some Americans to be more skeptical of other negative claims about Mexican and other immigrants. Based on our findings, we predict that attitudes toward immigrants will continue to become more supportive and positive as more states shift toward medical marijuana, decriminalization, and finally to legal recreational use.

REFERENCES

Aguilar, J., & Madlin M. (2016, June 23). U.S. Supreme Court Tie Deals Blow to Obama's Immigration Order. *Texas Tribune*. Retrieved from: https://www.texastribune.org/2016/06/23/supreme-court-rules-obamas-immigration-order/

Anbinder, T. (2019, November 7). Trump Has Spread More Hatred of Immigrants Than Any American in History. *Washington Post*. Retrieved from: https://www.washingtonpost.com/outlook/trump-has-spread-more-hatred-of-immigrants-than-any-american-in-history/2019/11/07/7e253236-ff54-11e9-8bab-0fc209e065a8_story.html

Anderson, S. (2003, November). The Impact of Agricultural Guestworker Programs on Illegal Immigration. *National Foundation for American Policy*. Retrieved from: http://www.nfap.com/researchactivities/studies/Nov_study1.pdf

Benson, T. (2015, July 2). The Real Reason Marijuana Is Illegal in the United States. *Salon*. Retrieved from: https://www.salon.com/2015/07/02/the_real_reason_marijuana_is_illegal_in_the_united_states_partner/

Blakemore, E. (2019, June 18). The Largest Mass Deportation in American History. *History Series*. Retrieved from: https://www.history.com/news/operation-wetback-eisenhower-1954-deportation

Burnett, J. (2014, December 1). Legal Pot in the U.S. May Be Undercutting Mexican Marijuana. *NPR.org*. Retrieved from: https://www.npr.org/sections/parallels/2014/12/01/367802425/legal-pot-in-the-u-s-may-be-undercutting-mexican-marijuana

Burns, P., and James G. G. (2000). Economic Insecurity, Prejudicial Stereotypes, and Public Opinion on Immigration Policy. *Political Science Quarterly*, *115*(2), 201–225.

Campos, I. (2018). Mexicans and the Origins of Marijuana Prohibition in the United States: A Reassessment. *Social History of Alcohol and Drugs*, *32*, 6–37.

Citrin, J., Donald P. G., Christopher M., & Cara W. (1997). Public Opinion Toward Immigration Reform: The Role of Economic Motivations. *Journal of Politics*, *59*(3), 858–881.

Cutaia Wilkinson, B. (2015). *Partners or Rivals? Power and Latino, Black, and White Relations in the 21st Century*. University of Virginia Press.

Dimock, M., Carroll D., & Seth M. (2013, April 4). Majority Now Supports Legalizing Marijuana. *Pew Research Center for the People and Press*. Retrieved from: https://www.pewresearch.org/wp-content/uploads/sites/4/legacy-pdf/4-4-13-Marijuana-Release.pdf

Disa Global Solutions, Inc. (2021, April). Wondering What the Law Is in Your State? *Map of Marijuana Legalization by State*. Retrieved from: https://disa.com/map-of-marijuana-legality-by-state

Dufton, E. (2017). *Grass Roots: The Rise and Fall and Rise of Marijuana in America*. New York: Basic Books.

Edison Research. (2014, November 4). National Election Pool Poll: 2016 National Election Day Exit Poll. *National Election Pool (ABC News, Associated Press, CBS, CNN, Fox News, NBC)*. Retrieved from: https://ropercenter.cornell.edu/ipoll/study/31115091

Edison Research. (2016, November 8). National Election Pool Poll: 2016 National Election Day Exit Poll. *National Election Pool (ABC News, Associated Press, CBS, CNN, Fox News, NBC)*. Retrieved from: https://ropercenter.cornell.edu/ipoll/study/31116396

Edison Research. (2018). National Election Pool Poll: 2016 National Election Day Exit Poll. *National Election Pool (ABC News, Associated Press, CBS, CNN, Fox News, NBC)*. Retrieved from: https://ropercenter.cornell.edu/ipoll/study/31116394

Espenshade, T. J., and Charles A. C. (1993). An Analysis of Public Opinion toward Undocumented Immigration. *Population Research and Policy Review*, *12*(3), 189–224.

Espenshade, T. J., and Katherine H. (1996). Contemporary American Attitudes toward U.S. Immigration. *International Migration Review*, *30*(2), 535–570.

Everding, G. (2018, October 10). White Americans See Many Immigrants as 'illegal' Until Proven Otherwise, Survey Finds. *Washington University in St. Louis: The Source*. Retrieved from: https://source.wustl.edu/2018/10/white-americans-see-many-immigrants-as-illegal-until-proven-otherwise-survey-finds/

Frontline. N.d. (2021). *Marijuana Timeline*. Retrieved from: https://www.pbs.org/wgbh/pages/frontline/shows/dope/etc/cron.html

Gieringer, D. H. (1999). The Forgotten Origins of Cannabis Prohibition in California. *Contemporary Drug Problems*, *26*(2), 237–238.

Gratton, B., & Emily M. (2018). Immigration, Repatriation, and Deportation: The Mexican-Origin Population in the United States, 1920–1950. *International Migration Review*, *47*(4), 944–975.

Green, T. V. (2021, April 16). Americans Overwhelmingly Say Marijuana Should Be Legal for Recreational or Medical Use. *Pew Research Center, Fact Tank: News in the Numbers*. Retrieved from: https://www.pewresearch.org/fact-tank/2021/04

/16/americans-overwhelmingly-say-marijuana-should-be-legal-for-recreational-or-medical-use/

Gurman, S. (2018, January 4). Sessions Terminates U.S. Policy That Let Legal Pot Flourish. *Associated Press*. Retrieved from: https://apnews.com/article/biden-cabinet-cory-gardner-colorado-jeff-sessions-archive-19f6bfec15a74733b40eaf0ff9162bfa

Hainmueller, J., & Daniel H. (2014). Public Attitudes toward Immigration. *Annual Review of Political Science*, 17, 225–249.

Hartman, M. (2021, July 6). Cannabis Overview: Legalization. *NCSL: National Council of State Legislatures*. Retrieved from: https://www.ncsl.org/research/civil-and-criminal-justice/marijuana-overview.aspx#1

Helmer, J. (1975). *Drugs and Minority Oppression*. Seabury Press.

Library of Congress. (2021). Depression and the Struggle for Survival. *Immigration and Relocation in U.S. History*. Retrieved from: https://www.loc.gov/classroom-materials/immigration/mexican/depression-and-the-struggle-for-survival/

Little, B. (2021). The U.S. Deported a Million of Its Own Citizens to Mexico During the Great Depression. *History Studies*. Retrieved from: https://www.history.com/news/great-depression-repatriation-drives-mexico-deportation

Mayorkas, A. (2012, August 15). Deferred Action for Childhood Arrivals: Who Can Be Considered? *The Whitehouse: President Barack Obama*. Retrieved from: https://obamawhitehouse.archives.gov/blog/2012/08/15/deferred-action-childhood-arrivals-who-can-be-considered

Marion, N. E., & Joshua B. H. (2019). *Marijuana 360: Differing Perspectives on Legalization.* Rowman & Littlefield.

Michelson, M. R., & Joe T. (2014). The Latino Politics of Proposition 19: Criminal Justice and Immigration. In *Something's in the Air: Race and the Legalization of Marijuana*, Katherine Tate, James Lance Taylor, and Mark Q. Sawyer, Eds., pp. 115–125. Routledge.

Mills, M. (2015, March 27). Moguls and Mexicans: The American History of Cannabis Legalization. *New Economy*. Retrieved from: https://www.theneweconomy.com/business/a-smear-campaign-a-history-of-the-us-relationship-with-cannabis

NCSL. (2021, July 14). State Medical Marijuana Laws. *NCSL: National Council of State Legislatures*. Retrieved from: https://www.ncsl.org/research/health/state-medical-marijuana-laws.aspx

NDTA. (2021, March). *2020 National Drug Threat Assessment.* U.S. Department of Justice, Drug Enforcement Administration (DEA-DCT-DIR-008-21). Retrieved from: https://www.dea.gov/sites/default/files/2021-02/DIR-008-21%202020%20National%20Drug%20Threat%20Assessment_WEB.pdf

Page, B. I., & Robert Y. S. (1992). *The Rational Public: Fifty Years of Trends in Americans' Policy Preferences*. University of Chicago Press.

Pew Research Center. (2017, October 8). Summer 2017 Political Landscape Survey Final Topline. *Pew Research Center*. Retrieved from: https://www.pewresearch.org/politics/wp-content/uploads/sites/4/2017/10/10-05-2017-Political-landscape-toplines-for-release.pdf

Pew Research Center. (2019a, September 3). 2019 Pew Research Center's American Trends Panel Wave 53: Marijuana Legalization Toplines. *Pew Research Center.* Retrieved from: https://www.pewresearch.org/wp-content/uploads/2019/11/FT_19.11.08_Marijuana_Topline-For-Release.pdf

Pew Research Center. (2019b, September 3). 2019 Pew Research Center's American Trends Panel Wave 53 September Final Topline. *Pew Research Center.* Retrieved from: https://www.pewresearch.org/politics/wp-content/uploads/sites/4/2019/10/10-17-19-impeachment-topline_updated.pdf

Pruitt, S. (2019, March 13). When the Sears Catalog Sold Everything from Houses to Hubcaps. *History.com.* Retrieved from: https://www.history.com/news/sears-catalog-houses-hubcaps

Rocha, R. R., Thomas L., Robert D. W., Benjamin R. K., Polinard, J. L., & James W. (2011). Ethnic Context and Immigration Policy Preferences Among Latinos and Anglos. *Social Science Quarterly*, *92*(1), 1–19.

Silber Mohamed, H., and Emily M. F. (2020). 'Bad *Hombres*'? An Examination of Identities in U.S. Media Coverage of Immigration. *Journal of Ethnic and Migration Studies*, *46*(1), 158–176.

The Audience Agency (2021). *What Is a Topline Report?* Retrieved from: https://support.theaudienceagency.org/support/solutions/articles/43000505445-what-is-a-topline-report-

U.S. Citizenship and Immigration Services (USCIS). (2014, April 15). 2014 Executive Actions on Immigration. *Archive: 2014 Executive Actions on Immigration.* Retrieved from: https://www.uscis.gov/archive/2014-executive-actions-on-immigration

Waxman, O B. (2019, April 20). The Surprising Link Between U.S. Marijuana Law and the History of Immigration. *Time.com.* Retrieved from: https://time.com/5572691/420-marijuana-mexican-immigration/

Chapter 5

Implementing Social Equity

Opportunities and Challenges from Marijuana Legalization in Massachusetts

Jeffrey Moyer

As more and more states have legalized cannabis, both activists and state officials have had to confront questions of equity in the formation of the legal market to grow and sell these products at retail locations. Given the clear disparities in arrest rates and criminal justice system outcomes, as well as the heightened awareness of racial justice brought about by police officer involved deaths and the Black Lives Matter movement, activists for cannabis legalization are increasing demands that legalization should benefit communities that have been targeted during criminalization. My chapter seeks to establish the place the issue of social equity within the context of when the state of Massachusetts sought to make legalization an economic opportunity for those who had been arrested for cannabis offenses before legalization in 2016.

Using primary interviews with activists and state officials involved with legalization, as well as reports and data released by the Cannabis Control Commission of Massachusetts, I narratively describe opportunities and challenges in cannabis legalization in Massachusetts as a means to deliver social equity and increase racial justice. Many of my interview participants identified a number of obstacles that this programmatic effort fell short in, including ensuring that those who might want to start a legal business would be able to navigate the bureaucratic hurdles and obtain financing for their business.

Activists and regulators alike struggle to define and operationalize social equity in the cannabis space. Designing programs that aren't explicitly tied to race is a challenge and often leaves significant numbers of impacted individuals out, while few public officials are willing to entertain designs that explicitly use race for both political and legal reasons. Black communities in particular have systemic disengagement and little material wealth which simply sabotages any effort that doesn't incorporate significant economic transfers.

CONNECTING RACIAL JUSTICE TO CANNABIS LEGALIZATION

Cannabis has a rich history of racialization in American history. Media coverage of the early 20th century led white populations in the American Southwest to associate cannabis directly with their perceptions of Mexican workers and immigrants (Michelson & Tafoya, 2014). Prohibition-era politicians and law-enforcement officials used increased concern about cannabis to crack down on perceived social disorder in jazz clubs and the clubs of major cities. In fact, cannabis sellers in this environment tended to be established whites, while musicians of color avoided it, fearing social and criminal repercussions. Following the repeal of Prohibition in 1933, Federal Bureau of Narcotics head Harry Anslinger began to campaign for heavier restrictions on cannabis and, with the help of a willing press, publicized the details of supposedly cannabis-fueled crimes perpetrated by people of color (Lee, 2012). The policy choice to address perceived social challenges through drug criminalization was taken up in the 1970s by President Richard Nixon, who publicly declared a War on Drugs as part of a strategy to strike back against his political objectors:

> The Nixon campaign in 1968, and the Nixon White House after that, had two enemies: the antiwar left and black people. You understand what I'm saying? We knew we couldn't make it illegal to be either against the war or black, but by getting the public to associate the hippies with marijuana and blacks with heroin, and then criminalizing both heavily, we could disrupt those communities. We could arrest their leaders, raid their homes, break up their meetings, and vilify them night after night on the evening news. Did we know we were lying about the drugs? Of course we did.—*John Ehrlichman as quoted in* (Baum, 2016)

Escalating over the next two decades, the War on Drugs led to a dramatic rise in criminal enforcement that focused disproportionately on communities and people of color (Alexander, *A New Jim Crow*, 2010).

The racial justice implications of cannabis criminalization provide a compelling potential application of social construction of target populations as envisioned by Anne Schneider and Helen Ingram (1993). These authors argued that citizens receive messages through policy design about who is deserving. This received *feedback*, in turn, influences future policy, directed toward these groups. These narratives build off each other in feedback and feed-forward patterns, with previous government policies creating new socially constructed groups targeted with further policy action. These constructions may be flexible at times but they are still quite enduring, as groups that are advantaged and positively constructed enjoy a higher proportion of benefits distributed by the government with few or no burdens, while those with negative constructions and/or little social power will receive few or no benefits and high burdens (Schneider & Ingram, 1993).

Thus, the primary social harm represented by cannabis comes not from its use but from its criminalization; hyper-enforcement in communities of color, in contrast with the comparatively lax scrutiny given to white individuals, serves to destroy community bonds and impair social cohesion in those communities (Iguchi et al., 2002; Iguchi, Bell, Ramchand, & Fain, 2005; Binswanger, Redmond, Steiner, & Hicks, 2012; Williams & Lyons, 2014). People of color are arrested at disproportionately higher rates despite similar usage across racial lines. Through repeated interactions with the justice system, they are subjected to far greater scrutiny and disempowerment, demonstrating not that these individuals are in any way more predisposed to drug use or delinquency, but instead that the criminal justice system, as operated, distributes the burdens of cannabis prohibition disproportionately to people of color (Provine, 2011; Taylor, 2014; Gettman, 2016).

State and federal prosecutions for cannabis possession and trafficking have left in their wake lost generations of potential. A 2013 report released by the ACLU entitled *The War on Marijuana: In Black and White* lays many of the statistics bare, showing over 8 million arrests nationwide for cannabis-related offences between 2001 and 2010 (American Civil Liberties Union, 2013). Cannabis enforcement cost almost $4 billion in 2010 with 889,000 arrests for related crimes, nearly nine-tenths of which were for simple possession. African Americans were 3.7 times as likely to be arrested for cannabis possession, despite nearly identical rates of usage across racial groups. The racial disparity in arrest rates held across every region and type of community (American Civil Liberties Union, 2013). In Michelle Alexander's words,

> Poor people of color are swept into the criminal justice system by the millions for drug crimes that go largely ignored when committed by middle- or upper-class whites. And release from prison or jail marks just the beginning of punishment, not the end. (Alexander, "Think Outside the Bars," 2011)

While some arrests may have led to minor consequences or none at all, that is not the norm in over-policed neighborhoods of color where more individuals than not were saddled with criminal records that rendered them unable to effectively advance their education or careers. This included denial of direct benefits such as higher-education scholarships and loans, welfare, housing, and other transfer payments. Many professions with licensing requirements have so-called "good behavior" requirements; the presence of a criminal record would directly bar access to certain careers and social statuses. In some cases, the mere association with cannabis could hurt an individual's social status, leading to potential losses of economic benefits and employment. Association with cannabis could also impact an individual's perception in venues like family court, splitting up families and breaking social bonds.

Traditional understandings of social construction theory would likely construe those convicted of cannabis offenses as "deviants," meaning they are negatively constructed by society and have little or no power in the policy process (Schneider & Ingram, 1993). Later extensions of the social construction of target population literature explicitly recognize the ability of moral and policy entrepreneurs to challenge their dependent or deviant status and push themselves into another category (Pierce et al., 2014). Just as earlier "moral entrepreneurs" such as Harry Anslinger and Richard Nixon worked to associate perceived social harms linked to cannabis use to people of color (Lee, 2012), leaders of the legalization movement and racial justice activists aim to reverse cultural damage and move policy toward equitable outcomes (Nicholson-Crotty & Meier, 2005). Activism and other external forces can create a policy window where previous constructions lose their force and new policy can be created (Schneider & Sidney, 2005). Those critical of the criminalization of cannabis would ask society to reimagine those who use and sell the product and empower them as contenders by giving them economic power and choice. But it is not enough for activists and scholars to note these effects and ask for change; policy-makers must be willing to exercise the levers of power to change the system and create regenerative policies that aid communities of color.

BUILDING TOWARD LEGALIZATION

Massachusetts wasn't exempt from the over-criminalization of drug regulation. From 1995 to 2008, law-enforcement authorities in Massachusetts arrested over 8,000 individuals per year for cannabis possession and sales offences.

> Guys working at the hotel downtown, they go to Boston English High School. They have to take care of the family, go work a full day until midnight. And they leave and they have a joint in their pocket to help them relax and here comes a [police officer] and snags them off the street, presto, got a record [which] kept them from securing housing [or] employment. And if [they] went to college [they wouldn't be able to study] health education or any of the sciences [if they] had a criminal record. (author interviews with Cannabis Policy Activists, 2020)

Beginning as early as 2000, voters in Massachusetts state elections in various legislative districts voted in favor of petitions to decriminalize cannabis and provide for medical and recreational use. Of the over 80 nonbinding votes (otherwise known as Public Policy Questions) on various forms of liberalization, all passed and often by overwhelming margins. While unnoticed by most voters and political insiders not paying attention to the issue, one of my participants pointed to the common knowledge of these results among liberalization activists: “Massachusetts activists were all cognitive of [the Public Policy Questions]. They were the best kept secret in plain sight. I’m not sure what we could’ve done with them frankly. Beacon Hill ignored them. And most important, politicians ignored them.”

These petitions provide strong evidence for public discontent with the state of drug enforcement in the early 21st century, and any observer of these results would be hard pressed to find the later passage of Question 2 in 2008, Question 3 in 2012, and Question 4 in 2016 surprising or even noteworthy. However, the voters’ judgment in these elections was by no means an automatic exercise. The execution of the escalating political edifice of cannabis liberalization required a great deal of political organizing that has gone unmentioned and underappreciated. Cannabis liberalization required sustained political and cultural organizing that highlighted the disparities in enforcement, the social costs of criminalization, and the identification of an alternative means of regulation and control. These organizers were cognizant of the well-trod if hazy historical path they moved on, and in many cases directly compared their struggle to that of the fight to end Prohibition.

The series of liberalization ballot questions in Massachusetts began in 2008 with Question 2, a proposal to reduce criminal penalties for cannabis-related offenses, which included making possession a civil offense that would prevent citations from appearing on background checks and reducing the priority of enforcement. The initiative enjoyed widespread support, and most opposition came from law-enforcement groups and district attorneys (Campaign for Safe Streets, 2008). The measure ultimately passed with over 65% support across the Commonwealth (Secretary of the Commonwealth of Massachusetts, 2008).

Decriminalization had an immediate impact: data from the Massachusetts ACLU shows that arrests fell by three-quarters in the next year. Meanwhile, usage patterns among the population remained mostly flat, which the report argues is evidence prohibitionist policies are not effective in reducing usage (Gettman, 2016). A follow-up report by the Massachusetts ACLU in 2016 found that racial disparities persisted, however, with African Americans 3.9 times as likely to be arrested for possession and 7.1 times as likely to be arrested for sales (Gettman, 2016), indicating the difficulty of detaching the racial aspect of the drug war despite partial demobilization of the criminal state.

Building on Question 2's popular success, advocates proposed the legalization of the medical use of cannabis in 2012 as Question 3. This proposal generated slightly more opposition, with a similar coalition of law-enforcement groups being joined by some medical groups and newspapers (Young, 2012). Ultimately, voters continued their support of liberalization, with Question 3 winning 63% of the vote and gaining an almost equal share of the vote as decriminalization had four years prior (Secretary of the Commonwealth of Massachusetts, 2012). This vote was part of a nationwide trend that cast a critical eye toward criminalization of cannabis, with voters in Colorado and Washington voting the same year to legalize the recreational use of cannabis.

However, implementation of medical cannabis legalization by the Department of Health was perceived as slow and poorly coordinated. Lamonica, Boeri, and Anderson (2016) investigated implementation from the perspective of crucial stakeholders in the regulatory process, such as doctors, patients, and suppliers. The authors critiqued the Massachusetts Department of Public Health (DPH) for not providing public education materials, and the medical cannabis regulations issued by DPH prevented medical personnel from consulting with dispensaries to assist patients in selecting the proper products for their condition. Lack of communication also prevented patients from accessing financial aid targeted at those in low-income brackets, hampering the overall effectiveness of implementation (Lamonica, Boeri, & Anderson, 2016).

Activists concluded that the only sufficient recourse was full legalization. Emboldened by the success of Questions 2 and 3 and the passage of recreational legalization in Colorado and Washington, cannabis advocates decided to push for full legalization in Massachusetts by proposing what came to be known as Question 4.

WHY A BALLOT MEASURE?

Massachusetts is a relatively recent entrant into the cannabis liberalization debate. Previous legalizing states had a more established history of considering cannabis liberalization measures and were also clustered in the West, where early 20th century progressives had far more political success with initiative laws. Belying the modern reputation of the Commonwealth as progressive, the recent movement toward liberalization mostly speaks to Massachusetts's unique position in New England (Angulov, 2018): it is one of the few states with liberalized ballot access laws, but a stubborn reality of stricter legal prohibitions on controlled substances, including alcohol and cannabis.

Massachusetts constitutional law establishes the ballot initiative process in Articles 48, 74, and 81. This power is broad and allows citizens to submit petitions to pass an initiative, which would become an ordinary law, or a constitutional amendment, which is subject to a higher threshold of legislative action. Voters may also file initiatives to repeal laws passed by the legislature, as well as petitions to ask members of a jurisdiction to instruct their member of the legislature to vote a certain way. The Constitution provides specific restrictions on the ability of initiatives to impact specific areas, such as basic rights or matters specific to local towns, or the power and operations of the judiciary. Furthermore, initiatives are prohibited from appropriating funds in any way, leaving many ballot initiatives subject to the legislature for various aspects of implementation. Most crucially, the Massachusetts Constitution places no limit on the legislature to amend voter-passed initiatives, unlike other states where such changes are prohibited or subject to additional legal threshold.

The literature on ballot initiatives offers a vision of policy diffusion in which the key actors are grassroots policy entrepreneurs and policies can be adopted across states without the support of policy elites—indeed, sometimes even in spite of their opposition (Boehmke, Osborn, & Schilling, 2015). In these cases, grassroots activists typically learn from others through national organizing and activism (Smith, 2004; Boehmke, 2005). When successful, policy elites are forced to implement the policies they had originally opposed. Boehmke (2005) has established that interest groups effectively use ballot initiatives to aid their own legislative lobbying efforts and has looked at the role initiatives play in allowing neglected issues to gain visibility and policy success.[1]

Thus, in response to legislative inaction on cannabis legalization in Massachusetts, activists came to embrace the ballot initiative for its power to give them control of the agenda. Liberalization advocates were first required to press their case to the state legislature, though there was a general expectation that the legislature would push the question to voters. The legislature simply lacked the institutional will to substantively address the issue, despite a recognition that the status quo was untenable, and criminalization should not continue.

As one state legislator stated, "It wasn't something that people were willing to deal with." Another interviewee who had worked for a state legislator involved in the reform bill agreed with this characterization: "It was just more of a, 'I don't want to think about this right now. I feel like this is a hot button issue that I don't want to touch, because people are going to yell at me one way or the other,' so we didn't touch it" (author interviews with Cannabis

Policy Activists, 2020). Another state legislator discussed the tendency of state legislators to listen to their most vocal and conservative constituents when deciding which issues to address. This is consistent with how elected officials assess the beliefs of their constituents, often wrongly (Broockman & Skovron, 2018). As my participant stated, "Every time. Every time there's been [liberalization], for medical and for decrim[inalization] and for this. The people were way ahead of the legislators. We're very risk averse" (author interviews with Cannabis Policy Activists, 2020).

The legislature did not take any official action on the proposed initiative, and per Massachusetts electoral law, supporters were then free to move forward with collecting additional signatures and taking the question to ballot.

DRAFTING QUESTION 4

The drafting committee to get Question 4 to the ballot began meeting in mid-2015 and its membership was a reflection of the larger movement for cannabis liberalization and against drug prohibition. As one of the committee members summarized it:

> In 2016, there was an entire industry already established to raise the issue. There were business owners who would be affected by whatever we did in various industries, not just in cannabis. There were a ton of lawyers who were working on advising their clients, and who were intimately involved with all of the problems and issues related to the implementation of the medical cannabis program who brought a lot of expertise to the room, practical, on the ground helpful stuff. Plus, all of the existing cannabis-related advocacy organizations, the consumer-driven ones, and the medical-driven ones. We got the medical cannabis advocates in who didn't want to do any harm of course to the patients' cause. All the existing organizations that we brought in during the original process. I think our pool of stakeholders just increased between 2012 and 2016 to the point where we were able to put everybody in a room and have them really talk together about the issues. (author interviews with Cannabis Policy Activists, 2020)

The committee was chaired by Dick Evans, who had authored a bill decades prior that would have set up a regulatory regime for cannabis similar to that seen for alcohol. Evans was intimately familiar with the popular support for legalization, having tracked the nonbinding ballot questions closely over the preceding years. Evans and his law partner Mike Cutler, also a committee member, had been fighting on the front lines of liberalization for years, but had seen little success. Members such as Shaleen Title and Kris Krane had early backgrounds in campus organizing and had transitioned to policy groups like the Marijuana Policy Project (MPP) that had been doing work in the liberalization space for several years. Both Title and Krane also had legal educations, which helped them move up quickly and gain influence in these policy groups.

MPP staff spoke of the committee drafting process as important to develop the coalition that would help the initiative gain passage, and that allowing key players to resolve their differences in private and ensure their interests were heard was an important factor in ensuring victory:

> The real benefit was having everybody in the same room, so that all of the activists, everybody who supported reform, could see where the tension was, and see the perspectives from the other side, of stakeholders—it helped them understand the contents of the initiative. It helped everybody understand the constraint we were under, with what we could do under the law, and not do with a single piece of legislation. I think for that reason, it really strengthened the coalition that was behind the initiative when it was introduced. (author interviews with Cannabis Policy Activists, 2020)

The Question 4 drafting committee faced legal limits to the methods by which they could mandate state action. Primary among their challenges was the single-subject rule, which prevented drafters from incorporating a broader subset of issues in the initiative. This rule is written into 43 state constitutions and is intended to prevent legislation and initiatives that cover multiple issues and thus might confuse or manipulate those reading the law (Cooter & Gilbert, 2010). The main purposes of this restriction are to prevent the merging of differing proposals to take advantage of majority support, to prevent the use of a more popular proposal to ensure passage of a less popular one, and to otherwise ensure transparency in the political process surrounding ballot measures.[2] Ballot initiatives by nature, then, have to go through more layers of review and are nearly always subject to legal challenges on issues of wording, structure, and content. As a result, the scope of legalization was always constrained.

Racial justice advocates that served on the drafting committee viewed their work as primarily to ensure passage of a legalization bill and to prevent their initiative from falling to legal challenge prior to or after the vote.[3] There was a sense that the longer criminalization continued, the more damage would occur. Yet they were successful in getting some provisions into the initiative, such as a legal prohibition that previous cannabis convictions could not be used as a disqualifier for licensing, as well as mandate the selection of commissioners and advisory board members with experience in social justice. They also sought to limit fees and other barriers to entry for potential applicants. Other provisions that supporters of greater equity desired, such as expungement and licensing priorities, did not find consensus among drafters or senior staff at the MPP, who sought to keep the ballot issue focused on the issue of legalization and avoid challenges on the single-issue question.

The drafting committee was ultimately successful: the measure was officially certified on July 6, 2016, and after resolution of some court challenges over language,[4] the public campaign commenced.

Campaigning for Question 4

Legalization for recreational use attracted far more controversy and organized opposition than previous initiatives on cannabis. Both the pro- and anti-Question 4 ballot campaigns attracted nearly $10 million in donations combined, nearly four times the amount raised for both the 2008 and 2012 ballot campaigns, indicating a great deal more interest from the general population and interest groups than the previous campaigns (National Institute on Money in State Politics, 2018).

While equity served as a discussion point, the campaign focused on a more general message. The talking points for legalization advocates always returned to the "failure of prohibition," which let speakers mention the disparate enforcement of cannabis criminalization, but in the context of the broader failure. As one campaign official stated:

> I always talked about the harms of prohibition. But our overall message was the failure of prohibition. Part of that message was the problem that prohibition had caused certain communities [to be] disproportionately impact[ed]. That was not our lead message [but] it was always a component of our messaging. (author interviews with Cannabis Policy Activists, 2020)

This did not dampen enthusiasm for the initiative, as those who had fought for more racial justice measures in the initiative viewed the primary goal of the legal changes mandated by the campaign as the end of criminalization. A video published by the Yes on 4 campaign in early October 2016 demonstrates this, with drafting committee member and campaign advocate Shanel Lindsay emotionally recounting her personal experience with being detained by law enforcement in the period after decriminalization had passed. She framed her story as a refutation of claims made by legalization opponents that individuals were no longer being arrested for cannabis, a key point of dispute between the two sides.

Despite the resistance of elected officials in the legislature, the development of the ballot initiative forced some institutional action on the issue. The Special Senate Committee on Marijuana convened in early 2016 was chaired by Senator Jason Lewis and eight other members of the State Senate. This committee conducted hearings, took information from a number of sources inside and outside Massachusetts, and took a well-publicized trip to Colorado funded in part by the Milbank Memorial Fund.

The participants on this trip included Senator Lewis himself, members of the special panel, staffers, and state government officials. The trip spanned four days in mid-January 2016, and included meetings with Colorado's Andrew Freedman (former director of Marijuana Coordination for CO Governor Hickenlooper), Rick Garza (director of the Washington State Liquor Control Board), public health officials, Colorado state legislators, representatives from the Colorado Department of Agriculture and the City of Denver, law enforcement including the Rocky Mountain High Intensity Drug Trafficking Area Task Force, and experts on banking and finance. Participants also toured a grow facility and retail stores. Notably, the trip included no meetings with racial justice advocates or license owners of color who could speak to the concerns of their communities.

Despite exposure to evidence that the social benefits of legalization regimes outweigh the harms, legislators continued to oppose legalization. The committee issued a report in March 2016, and while it did not take an official position on legalization, the authors warned of "serious concerns" about moving forward (General Court of Massachusetts, 2016). Specific concerns in this report included the lack of a standard test for determining impairment, increased public health costs not offset by revenues from taxes on recreational sales, and continued uncertainty on the federal level (General Court of Massachusetts, 2016). According to one respondent, Senator Lewis entered the committee process as a legalization advocate but was convinced by his experiences traveling that the form of legalization seen in the drafted Question 4 would be dangerous.

Senator Lewis came out in opposition and represented the No side in public debates throughout the state. Six of his colleagues on the panel joined the campaign in opposition, with 98 out of 160 members of the State House and 22 out of 40 members of the state Senate in total officially endorsing the No side. Statewide leaders such as Governor Charlie Baker and Attorney General Maura Healey, as well as Boston Mayor Marty Walsh loudly endorsed the No side. Members of the legislature cited specific flaws in the initiative that influenced the decision to publicly oppose it, though some like Senator Lewis stated that they might otherwise support legalization if the legislature should take it up.

Passage

On November 7, 2016, nearly 1.77 million voters in Massachusetts voted on ballot Question 4 or the "Regulation and Taxation of Marijuana Act." The results of this election continued the theme started in 2008, with voters supporting Question 4 by a reduced yet still decisive 53% of the vote (Secretary of the Commonwealth of Massachusetts, 2016).

Legislative resistance to legalization continued after the election, with legislators opting to delay the enactment of Question 4 by six months and expressing interest in rewriting parts of the law themselves. The resulting law, House Bill 3818 (HB3818), which was passed in July 2017, allowed them to put their own stamp on legalization and make significant changes to the regulatory and tax structure envisioned by Question 4.

Still, in the legislative process, racial justice benefited from the continued activism of drafting committee members and other organizers, as well as the voice of the African American legislative caucus in the State House. As one activist put it, "For communities of color, this was the first time in essentially 400 years that we have been as close to equal partners to the economic planning process as we ever have been" (author interviews with Cannabis Policy Activists, 2020). From this perspective, communities of color needed to take advantage of this rhetorical space offered by racial justice advocates to carve out a space for themselves and ensure that impacted communities and individuals could get an early share of the licenses and business. The persistence with which these voices pressed leadership helped to underscore to legislators how important these issues were and helped ensure the addition of stronger equity measures to the final bill. One activist describes this process:

> I have to give [state legislator] a lot of credit because he had the balls enough to fight. We would feed him, "We need this in there. This is how you should respond to that." And yeah, he would regurgitate. And that worked. And [legislative leadership] didn't expect to have as many of us [and] underestimated our knowledge with how we did business with the press. The speaker and majority leader usually [operate] behind closed doors, but the press kept it going. (author interviews with Cannabis Policy Activists, 2020)

In the end, the legislature adopted several measures into its bill. Establishing the Cannabis Control Commission, appointing authorities were tasked with adding a commissioner "whom shall have a background in legal, policy or social justice issues related to a regulated industry," and the bill specified several members of the Advisory Board and a subcommittee of the same to focus on issues of social equity. The bill included a general mandate for the Commission to

> prioritize review and licensing decisions for applicants [that] demonstrate experience in or business practices that promote economic empowerment in communities disproportionately impacted by high rates of arrest and incarceration for

> offenses under chapter 94C. —as found in House Bill 3818 of the 190th Session of the General Court.

The bill also tasked the Commission with conducting research on the issues that limited ownership and business formation in impacted communities and to file reports on the status of social equity with the legislature yearly.

While initiative drafting committee members and racial justice advocates appreciated the legislature's willingness to give specific instructions to the Cannabis Control Commission on expungement, and to empower one commissioner to advocate for those interests, there was a strong desire for legislators and state officials to do more. One activist shared their view as follows:

> Looking back at it now, there are so many things that could have been much more improved. But it was better than every other state. Like it allowed for homegrown, six plants per person, 12 per household, gifting, [and] keeping all of your homegrown. Aside from that portion about social equity being such a crucial part and so embedded within the mission and mission statement of the Cannabis Control Commission, that's what I found as the best piece to the Massachusetts law. (author interviews with Cannabis Policy Activists, 2020)

While the Legislature was able to better bring principles of social justice to the forefront during the amendment process, other states have been able to more comprehensively address equity as part of their legalization proposals.

EMBEDDING SOCIAL EQUITY IN LEGALIZATION

Despite many of the challenges in getting equity addressed in the statute book, senior Commission staff were committed to addressing equity in some way. The lack of comprehensive prior examples provided little in the way of guidance, but allowed the Commission to experiment with a variety approaches.

When seeking to address its mandate to address social equity, the Commission first sought to learn more about the issue. In Spring 2018, the Commission distributed a survey online that invited respondents to detail their thoughts about how the agency should approach the social equity question. As a result of this process, the Commission adopted the following language on their website that defines their mission of social equity:

> The Commission is committed to implementing a variety of programs to actively engage people from communities of disproportionate impact and ensure

> their inclusion in the legal cannabis industry. Many programs were developed in response to evidence which demonstrates that certain geographic areas and demographic populations, particularly Blacks and Latinos, have been disproportionately impacted by high rates of arrest and incarceration for cannabis and other drug crimes as a result of state and federal drug policy. Criminalization has had long-term negative effects, not only on the individuals arrested and incarcerated, but on their families and communities. We now have the opportunity to redress the historic harm done to those specific individuals and communities. (Cannabis Control Commission website, 2020)

ECONOMIC EMPOWERMENT PROGRAM

The first program the agency created to assist impacted communities was the Economic Empowerment Program, through which the Commission would certify licensee applicants as having met at least three of six possible criteria:

- Majority of ownership belongs to people who have lived in areas of disproportionate impact[5] for five of the last ten years.
- Majority of ownership has held one or more previous positions where the primary population served were disproportionately impacted, or where primary responsibilities included economic education, resource provision or empowerment to disproportionately impacted individuals or communities.
- At least 51% of current employees/subcontractors reside in areas of disproportionate impact and will increase to 75% by first day of business.
- At least 51% of employees or subcontractors have drug-related CORI, but are otherwise legally employable in a cannabis-related enterprise.
- A majority of the ownership is made up of individuals from black, African American, Hispanic or Latino descent.
- Owners can demonstrate significant past experience in or business practices that promote economic empowerment in areas of disproportionate impact (Cannabis Control Commission, 2018b).

Economic empowerment (EE) applicants were to be given first consideration, alongside registered medical dispensaries (RMDs), when the Commission considered final applications. However, given the logistical, financial, and technical head start many RMDs had, there was little opportunity for EE applicants to meaningfully benefit from this. The application period for the EE program opened in April 2018 and preceded the general license application period by less than a month. Meanwhile, the Commission didn't finalize certifications for the program until early June, after licensing had begun. By the time the regulations were finalized in August 2019, none of the EE licensees had received final approval.

While issues at the state level contributed to the delay, particularly in the way applications were processed and in what order they were placed in the queue, obstacles applicants faced in gaining local approval were a major factor. The discretion offered by state lawmakers to Massachusetts towns and cities resulted in extreme delays as local officials took months to establish their licensing procedures and then go through all the steps outlined under the law, such as public comments and zoning approval. One licensee explained:

> Because the federal illegality and the so-called gray area, and local control, it actually encourages corruption and puts a lot more power into the hands of smaller local politicians who are not well versed on these issues. . . . They can come down heavy-handed on their own side of these issues in these municipalities. (author interviews with Cannabis Policy Activists, 2020)

Delays had a huge negative impact on EE applicants with pending licenses, as they had to continue to pay rent and other expenses on businesses that would take years to be approved and open. During the public comment session for these regulations, many licensees appeared before commissioners detailing the difficulties they were facing with the delays, with at least one directly stating that they would be giving up their plans to establish a business. Commissioners were well aware of many of the challenges these applicants were working through but were not able to address them through the challenges of limited authority, budget, and political capital. There was little consensus on how to address it through regulation or legislation. Commissioner Shaleen Title advocated for the Commission to regulate and govern local approvals more closely, but the other Commissioners did not feel that they had the authority to do so. There was more consensus that the legislature should address the issue, but those legislators and aides I was able to speak to made clear that there was little immediate appetite to develop a solution. This unfortunate political reality will likely serve to drive additional applicants from the legal market as their limited funding dries up.

The final regulations adopted by the Commission in August 2019 made some limited progress to streamline the process, such as allowing the Commission to give preliminary approval to some applicants to allow them to acquire the financing needed to run their business, but this did not address the substance of the delays at the local level. While recreational sales were permitted beginning in July 2018, the first stores did not open for months afterward. This slow pace of roll-out would continue, with many jurisdictions, including those in the greater Boston area (Adams, 2017).

Social Equity Program

The Commission also created the Social Equity Program (SEP),

> A free, statewide, technical assistance, and training program that provides education, skill-based training, and tools for success in the cannabis industry. The SEP focuses on those most impacted by the War on Drugs, marijuana prohibition, disproportionate arrests and incarceration, and provides education and entry across four areas: entrepreneurship, entry- and managerial-level workforce development, and ancillary business support. (Cannabis Control Commission, 2021)

The SEP was seen as a way for the Commission to help bridge the business startup and skill development stage for those who lacked these tools. Agency staff and Commissioners took it upon themselves to personally assist many of those in this program. After several delays, the Commission began searching in early 2019 for trained vendors to provide the specific type of skills that SEP participants had requested, though staff developed an initial set of trainings at agency headquarters to give a head start to the first classes.

Positive Impact Plans

Another key part of the Commission's strategy to ensure social equity in the cannabis market was developed through the requirement that each licensee applicant submit a Positive Impact Plan (PIP) as part of their application to be considered by the Commission. As recommended by the Commission, this impact plan should contain a proposal for how the licensee's operations could reduce barriers to entry in the recreational market, provide professional and technical services to those facing barriers, and promote socially responsible practices in the industry.

Along with a report from the Commission on the contents of PIPs it had received and the results of initial surveys and data collection conducted over the first year of regulated operations, my analysis suggests that PIPs can form the basis of a sustainable equity program for the Cannabis Control Commission. This equity program does not require any legislative appropriation and gives cannabis companies in the market the power to direct assets to communities where they feel that the need is greatest. Many of the plans suggest great promise and potential. Cannabis establishments may be able to play a particularly important role in hiring diverse workforces, creating mentorship and training programs for future business owners in the industry, and providing talent pipelines and access to resources and equipment for smaller operators.

At the same time, the PIP program by its very nature also has flaws that might limit its overall capacity and reach. First, the Commission has only begun considering how to hold licensed companies responsible for the promises they make in the PIPs. While Commissioners are fully willing to reject licensees who do not live up to these promises, the Commission may be limited in how much independent auditing they are able to do to evaluate effectiveness. Second, the research demonstrates that in the neoliberal model of philanthropy, the individual actors with financial privilege to give often operate at deficits of information and expertise in deciding how to appropriate their giving resources and may not be effective in achieving widespread or systemic change (Katz, 2005; Dean, 2015). The PIP program model embraces both the advantages and flaws of this resource delivery model. By using licensees to independently direct their efforts and resources, the Commission is unlikely to be able to reach all the communities and a representative approximation of those impacted by criminalization. Even if all licensees live up to their promises, the number of individuals receiving mentorship and other career resources might be small and these initiatives might fail to provide substantive help to those who need it. While well-intentioned, many of the individuals designing these plans are not experts in the difficult work of reaching individuals in need of business development skills, and it is possible that many of the efforts of these licensees will be underutilized or not accessed by those who need them.

FINANCING AND OWNERSHIP IN CANNABIS

Perhaps the largest and still most thorny practical issue for those from impacted communities to participate in the legalized market is getting the necessary financing to obtain a space, pay employees, and pay other costs associated with the requirements established by state and local officials. Even the most basic cannabis establishments require hundreds of thousands of dollars in initial investments before any revenue comes in. This was a difficult hurdle for the initial investors in the cannabis market, who often turned to so-called "angel" investors that were willing to take a greater risk for more return. Many players in the worlds of financing and venture capital operate on personal networking and connections. These spaces can be highly difficult if not impossible for non-experienced participants to succeed in. One participant in the Question 4 campaign framed it as such:

> Getting the right mix of people into the industry is difficult and that's a problem that everybody is facing. A lot of kinds of people who are aversely impacted, they don't have the capital to open up a conservation facility. So how can we

> get these folks who may not be able to get private banking to attract private wealth to finance them? Because right now these people have to have a network of investments to build up private [financing] to move forward with this. (author interviews with Cannabis Policy Activists, 2020)

While many of those who had participated in the illicit market were able to build skills and experiences that would help them in transitioning to the legal space, the value of these connections and the kind of personal involvement needed to work with local officials, residents, and state officials to ensure success was an entirely different element that these applicants wholly lacked.

While licensees could hire consulting firms that would help guide them through the process, these firms cost a great deal themselves. One such consultant I talked with stated that he charged clients over $100,000 and required that they have at least a minimum of a million in financing:

> But if you pay even a cheap lobbyist, it's going to cost you 60,000 a year and you need a real lawyer to do just the business structure. Then, you need a local lawyer to do the city hall stuff. That's going to cost you probably at least as much as me, so now you're just saying, you're likely to see a tripling of already 250,000 for your first year before you bring in a penny. (author interviews with Cannabis Policy Activists, 2020)

While he also said that he was willing to consult with EE applicants on a pro bono basis, such clients were, in fact, rare.

This funding shortage has resulted in the Commission undertaking additional efforts to help businesses gain access to financing. My interviews with Commission staff revealed an effort to encourage small- and medium-sized banks to lend to EE applicants, and commissioners celebrated some successes in convincing these institutions to offer financing. These smaller local and middle-size financial institutions are often the first to give financing to small businesses and provide capital to underserved communities, especially through federal programs designed explicitly for this purpose. With a double obstacle of continued federal illegality and the threat of possible prosecution, this financing is basically unavailable, and it is likely that the Commission will have to continue providing such lobbying for the industry. It is difficult to imagine a government regulator playing such a role for a more established industry, but with their limited ability to drive social equity under the law and a frustration at the pace of progress, this sort of advocacy is likely a necessary component of their mandate to ensure equal participation in the industry.

Another thorny issue for both cannabis regulators and racial justice activists to tackle is determining the comparative value of driving equal participation in the market through employment or ownership of businesses.

While registered cannabis agents, often employees of firms, are relatively equitable, as compared to the general Massachusetts population, similar gains are not present in ownership. Even within ownership, there are significant barriers in how to understand this, as the complicated ownership systems present in many cannabis businesses demonstrates. This quote from an activist is telling:

> You know, it's the same thing that happened in the 1960s during the Great Society Programs of the sixties. Where the white establishment figured out how to use co-op black faces to continue to be in control. (author interviews with Cannabis Policy Activists, 2020)

Media reporting and anecdotal evidence from other states shows that wealthy investors have recruited qualifying individuals to apply for licenses while maintaining effective control of the businesses and making a mockery of the provisions intended to help impacted populations (Healy, 2019). Regulators like the Cannabis Control Commission will likely need additional expertise to unravel the complicated structures, and some operators may still remain opaque to them.

There is disagreement in determining how valuable it is that these impacted communities have actual ownership of businesses. For some activists, this is key to ensure that communities of color have the opportunity to build wealth and financial security, while others are willing to accept a financial settlement as recognition and an acknowledgment that this concession might be the most concrete benefit they are able to get.

This also points to the larger question of who actually benefits from legalization. While refocusing the criminal justice system is an obvious win for advocates, opponents of legalization and those in communities of color are united in a belief that the primary financial winners of this policy change are a select group of wealthy, white male investors who have a combination of savvy and liquid capital to get in early and take advantage of a complicated and inconsistent regulatory environment due to their capacity to sustain the high initial costs in order to monopolize the emerging market. In the capitalist-dominated world of venture capital and investing, these advantages would be praised with the implication that the "winners" of the market were thus more deserving.

However, the political alliances crafted behind legalization measures included activists who were deeply skeptical of this model of economic success, and with a changing narrative around racial justice and the topic of reparations, the critiques of a wealthy, white male-dominated cannabis industry have gained ever more steam. Some in these groups were happy to ally with legalization skeptics and slow down legalization if their communities did not see any measurable economic benefits. They also did not want to be forced to divide among each other, as this licensee discussed:

> We have higher standards of hiring and ownership. It's not a game. We're out here throwing elbows trying to get these things established against the tide. That's what's happened. I don't think that's working. It needs to be more open, it needs to be more objective, it needs to be more free to not immediately put people up against each other before they're even making money. We want to compete. We don't want to kill each other and slice each other's throats. We want to compete like the dispensaries are able to. (author interviews with Cannabis Policy Activists, 2020)

One local official I interviewed put the situation in Massachusetts in stark terms: even as declined arrest rates did benefit all communities, the primary beneficiaries of legalization were middle-class whites who could now buy their cannabis without feeling like they were supporting the drug trade.

DIFFUSING SOCIAL EQUITY

In the years since cannabis legalization passed in Massachusetts, the nature of the discussion among those in communities of color both nationally and in states such as Illinois, New York, and New Jersey, has fundamentally changed. The institutions of mass incarceration are still thriving, and critics have called for the rechanneling of legalization proceeds away from any potential benefit to law enforcement. The money, they argue, should instead be used to repair and strengthen the social fabric of communities of color damaged by mass incarceration (a concern echoed by current calls to "defund" the police). A legislative staffer I interviewed identified this argument:

> It's a constant battle, because the same structural inequality that caused the disparity in enforcement also factors into all these other things that affect you from getting on to business. Without access to banking, people who are starting these companies are normally relying on friends and family, who have millions and millions of dollars. Like, if you grew up poor in a community that was decimated by the War on Drugs enforcement, you probably don't have a bunch of friends and family with millions of dollars who can just spot you. (author interviews with Cannabis Policy Activists, 2020)

The legalization bill that passed in Illinois was cited by several of my sources as directly inspiring these concerns. There are multiple pieces of this bill that the racial justice supporters I've interviewed in Massachusetts have expressed a desire for. Perhaps the biggest element has been expungements. Illinois has flipped the traditional logistics of expungements, putting the burden on state police to affirmatively search their databases for cannabis arrests and eliminate them. In contrast, in Massachusetts and other jurisdictions, those who had been convicted of cannabis crimes had to apply for expungement on their own, finding little assistance with that long, complex process. Illinois also sought to ensure that the revenue from legalization would benefit disproportionately impacted communities, with 25% being devoted to "restore, reinvest and renew" these areas. Social Equity Applicants (SEAs) who had resided in them could also benefit from waived fees and priority on the licensing front, while license buy-back restrictions limited the incentives for wealthy investors to target early adopters. SEAs were additionally eligible for statewide loan and grant programs that would help give them an edge over these wealthy investors.

A fundamental challenge for racial justice in Massachusetts was that despite decisions throughout the process to focus conversations on the issue and develop policy solutions, it suffered from a reluctant engagement from those most equipped to provide resources to address the problems, namely legislators and the governor. These policy actors, who had never fully embraced legalization, viewed their work as complete on the passage of the legislative reform package and disengaged from cannabis almost completely except to express their objection to certain proposals of the Commission. Unless legislative leaders prioritize the issue, it seems difficult to imagine Massachusetts embracing the bolder proposals seen in Illinois, where legislators responded to a mandate from the governor to create an equitable legalization system from the ground up rather than being compelled to do so by voters.

The progress of legalization in early states and the challenges Massachusetts has encountered in fostering a diverse marketplace have shown communities of color and the activists that represent them that the economic beneficiaries of legalization are often wealthy and white. As a result, many activists and legislators in states that have considered legalization since 2016 have not been willing to press forward with legalization without explicit guarantees that they would be given a place in the new industry. The racial justice movement challenges policy-makers adopting legalization to demonstrate that those impacted by criminalization derive some benefit from it. Recent campaigns for legalization in New York and New Jersey have demonstrated that racial justice advocates are willing to hold up bills if their concerns are not adopted, and the success of legalization in Illinois required the inclusion of social equity measures such as expungement and addressing distribution of tax revenues. There is also a clear impact on the level of trust in institutions by people of color. Many already had a low regard for the government that dispossessed their communities, and these same people are now seeing white individuals of wealth and status making large sums of money doing something that only several years ago would have gotten them a stiff jail sentence and permanent record. At least some activists are seeing the models of legalization and determining that a flawed legalization is worse than none at all.

NOTES

1. The structure of the ballot initiative is enough on its own to give interest groups a boost, with those states with initiatives seeing a 17% increase in interest group population and up to a 29% increase in citizen issue-focused groups (Boehmke, 2002).

2. There is no such rule in the federal Constitution, and as a result Congress is criticized for passing long bills that address many different policy areas as well as omnibus budget riders that have significant policy impact. There is significant political science and legal research into the element of voter confusion and apathy for long ballots with many initiatives, with many scholars critiquing initiatives for providing confusing choices to voter that don't let them effectively express their policy preferences (Gafke & Leuthold, 1979; Farley, Gaertner, & Moses, 2013; Burnett & Kogan, 2015). Courts in many jurisdictions have been less enthusiastic about enforcing these restrictions on a sovereign branch of government and have more often been willing to strike initiatives down before they are given to voters (Cooter & Gilbert, 2010).

3. The fear of jeopardizing the initiative by pushing issues like expungement was not merely theoretical. The Massachusetts Supreme Judicial Court threw out a proposed constitutional amendment to create a "millionaire's tax" that would have appeared on the 2018 ballot because it specified where the revenue for from those taxes should go.

4. Question 4's language was challenged on the grounds that it could allow for super-concentrated edibles, as well as suggestions that the ballot title was misleading. The Supreme Judicial Court ordered revisions to the drafted language of the ballot measure to clarify these issues.

5. The Cannabis Control Commission commissioned two reports by well-cited cannabis researcher Jon Gettman to help identify those areas in Massachusetts that would be defined as having been disproportionately impacted by criminalization (Gettman, 2017, 2018). Gettman specifically cited the factors that went into the identification criteria of the California cities and constructed a six-variable index that included the numbers of arrests for sales and possession of cannabis, the total number of arrests, the total population size, number of families under the poverty rate, and the unemployment rate. The Commission used this index to identify 29 communities of impact, with the cities of Boston, Springfield, and Worchester being further divided to obtain specific census tracts that had been impacted (Cannabis Control Commission, 2018).

Most notably, this index excludes a racial variable, which has left a number of racially diverse localities off of the list of impacted communities, such as Lawrence, which has a 43% white population, while including localities like the tiny town of

Monson with under 10,000 residents and a white population exceeding 97% of residents (Gettman, 2017).

REFERENCES

Adams, D. (2017, December). *Cannabis Panel Backs Pot Bars, Home Delivery, and Stoned Yoga*. Retrieved from Boston Globe: https://www.bostonglobe.com/business/2017/12/13/cannabis-cafes-marijuana-delivery-and-stoned-yoga-get-preliminary-from-state/NZS5P2oIO7lbTLm2CYka9K/story.html

Alexander, M. (2010). *A New Jim Crow*. New York: New Press.

Alexander, M. (2011). Think Outside the Bars. *Yes Magazine*. Retrieved from: http://yesmagazine.org/issue/beyond-prisons/2011/06/08/think-outside-the-bars

American Civil Liberties Union. (2013). *The War on Marijuana in Black and White*. New York: American Civil Liberties Union.

Angulov, N. (2018). *From Criminalizing to Decriminalizing Marijuana: The Politics of Social Control*. New York: Lexington.

Baum, D. (2016, April). Legalize It All. *Harpers Magazine*. Retrieved from: http://harpers.org/archive/2016/04/legalize-it-all/

Binswanger, I., Redmond, N., Steiner, J., & Hicks, L. (2012). Health Disparities and the Criminal Justice System: An Agenda for Further Research Action. *Journal of Urban Health*, *89*(1), 98–107.

Boehmke, F. (2002). The Effect of Direct Democracy on the Size and Diversity of State Interest Group Populations. *Journal of Politics*, *63*(3), 827–844.

Boehmke, F. (2005). *The Indirect Effect of Direct Legislation*. Columbus: Ohio State University Press.

Boehmke, F., Osborn, T., & Schilling, E. (2015). Pivotal Politics and Initiative Use in the American States. *Political Research Quarterly*, *68*(4), 665–677.

Broockman, D., & Skovron, C. (2018). Bias in Perceptions of Public Opinion among Political Elites. *American Political Science Review*, *112*(3), 542–563.

Burnett, C., & Kogan, V. (2015). When Does Ballot Language Influence Voter Choices? Evidence from a Survey Experiment. *Political Communication*, *32*(1) 109–126.

Campaign for Safe Streets. (2008, September 20). *Our Supporters*. Retrieved from Vote No on Question 2 (archived): https://web.archive.org/web/20080920130241/http://noquestion2.org:80/?page_id=8

Cannabis Control Commission. (2018). *Guidance: Summary of Equity Provisions*. Boston, MA: Cannabis Control Commission.

Cannabis Control Commission. (2018, May 22). *Cannabis Control Commission Approves 204 Potential Licensing Applicants to Receive Priority Review* [Press release]. Retrieved from: https://mass-cannabis-control.com/5619-2/

Cannabis Control Commission. (2021). *Equity Programs*. Commonwealth of Massachussets, Cannabis Control Comission. Retrieved from: https://mass-cannabis-control.com/equityprograms/

Cooter, R., & Gilbert, M. (2010). A Theory of Direct Democracy and the Single Subject Rule. *Columbia Law Review*, *110*(3), 687–730.

Dean, J. (2015). Volunteering, the Market, and Neoliberalism. *People, Place, and Policy*, *9*(2), 139–148.

Farley, A., Gaertner, M., & Moses, M. (2013). Democracy under Fire: Voter Confusion and Influences in Colorado's Anti-Affirmative Action Initiative. *Harvard Educational Review*, *83*(3), 432–462.

Gafke, R., & Leuthold, D. (1979). The Effect on Voters of Misleading, Confusing, and Difficult Ballot Titles. *Public Opinion Quarterly*, *43*(3), 394–401.

General Court of Massachusetts. (2016). *Report of the Special Senate Committee on Marijuana*. Boston, MA: General Court of Massachusetts.

Gettman, J. (2016). *The War on Marijuana in Black and White: A Massachusetts Update*. Boston, MA: ACLU.

Gettman, J. (2017). *The Impact of Drug and Marijuana Arrests on Local Communities in Massachusetts*. Boston, MA: Cannabis Control Commission.

Gettman, J. (2018). *The Impact of Drug and Marijuana Arrests within the Largest Cities in Massachusetts*. Boston, MA: Cannabis Control Commission.

Healy, B. (2019, March 19). "You Can't Own More Than 3 Pot Shops, But These Companies Test the Limits—and Brag about It." *Boston Globe*. Retrieved from: http://bostonglobe.com/news/special-reports/2019/03/21/seahunter/okkkbxkh38kt-kh9hdiifxl/story.html

Iguchi, M., Bell, J., Ramchand, R., & Fain, T. (2005). How Criminal System Racial Disparities May Translate Into Health Dispartities. *Journal of Healthcare to the Poor and Underserved*, *16*(4), 48–56.

Iguchi, M., London, J., Forge, N. G., Hickman, L., Fain, T., & Riehman, K. (2002). Elements of Well-being Affected by Criminalizing the Drug User. *Public Health Reports*, *117*(1), S146–150.

Katz, S. (2005). What Does It Mean to Say That Philanthropy Is "Effective"? The Philanthropists' New Clothes. Proceedings of the American Philosophical Society, 123–131.

Lamonica, A., Boeri, M., & Anderson, T. (2016). Gaps in Medical Marijuana Policy Implementation: Real-Time Perspectives from Marijuana Dispensary Entrepreneurs, Health Care Professionals and Medical Marijuana Patients. *Drugs: Education, Prevention, and Policy*, *23*(5), 1–13.

Lee, M. A. (2012*). Smoke Signals*. New York: Simon & Schuster.

Michelson, M., & Tafoya, J. (2014). The Latino Politics of Proposition 19: Criminal Justice and Immigration. In K. Tate, J. L. Taylor, & M. Sawyer (eds.), *Something's in The Air: Race, Crime, and the Legalization of Marijuana* (pp. 115–125). New York: Routledge.

National Institute on Money in State Politics. (2018). *Search*. Retrieved from FollowTheMoney.org: https://www.followthemoney.org/

Nicholson-Crotty, S., & Meier, K. (2005). From Perception to Public Policy: Translating Social Constructions into Policy Designs. In A. Schneider, & H. Ingram (eds.), *Deserving and Entitled: Social Constructions and Public Policy*. Albany, NY: SUNY Press.

Pierce, J., Siddicki, S., Jones, M., Schumaker, K., Pattison, A., & Peterson, H. (2014). Social Construction and Policy Design: A Review of Past Applications. *Policy Studies Journal*, *42*(1), 1–29.

Provine, D. M. (2011). Race and Inequality in the War on Drugs. *Annual Review of Law and Social Science*, *7*, 41–60.

Schneider, A., & Ingram, H. (1993). Social Construction of Target Populations: Implications for Politics and Policy. *American Political Science Review*, *87*(2), 334–347.

Schneider, A., & Sidney, M. (2005). What Is Next for Policy Design and Social Construction Theory? *Policy Studies Journal*, *37*(1), 103–120.

Secretary of the Commonwealth of Massachusetts. (2008). *Q2/Initiative Petition/2008*. Retrieved from PD43+ Election Statistics: http://electionstats.state.ma.us/ballot_questions/view/2181/

Secretary of the Commonwealth of Massachusetts. (2012). *Q3/Initiative Petition/2012*. Retrieved from PD43+ Election Statistics: http://electionstats.state.ma.us/ballot_questions/view/2258/

Secretary of the Commonwealth of Massachusetts. (2016). *Q4/Initiative Petition/2016*. Retrieved from PD43+: http://electionstats.state.ma.us/ballot_questions/view/2742/

Smith, D. (2004). Peeling away the Populist Rhetoric: Towards a Taxonomy of Anti-Tax Ballot Initiatives. *Public Finance and Budgeting*, *24*(4), 88–110.

Taylor, J. L. (2014). Building Minority Community Power Through Legalization. In K. Tate, J. L. Taylor, & M. Sawyer (eds.), *Something's in the Air: Race, Crime, and the Legalization of Marijuana* (pp. 92–114). New York: Routledge.

Williams, C., & Lyons, T. (2014). Public-Health Considerations in the Legalization Debate. In K. Tate, J. L. Taylor, & M. Sawyer (eds.), *Something's in the Air: Race, Crime, and the Legalization of Marijuana* (pp. 31–39). New York: Routledge.

Young, S. (2012, June 12). *Mass Medical Marijuana Opponents Mobilize Efforts*. Retrieved from Boston.com: http://archive.boston.com/news/local/massachusetts/articles/2012/06/03/mass_medical_marijuana_opponents_mobilize_efforts/

Chapter 6

The Regulation of Medical Cannabis

Bureaucracies and Policy Implementation Challenges

Céline Mavrot

INTRODUCTION: OPENING THE BUREAUCRATIC BLACK BOX OF CANNABIS POLICIES

Since the beginning of the worldwide wave of legalizing medical or recreational cannabis that was initiated by U.S. states (starting in 2012), Uruguay (2013), and Canada (2018), numerous studies have been carried out to shed light on this turning point in contemporary drug policies. Crucial questions regarding the effects of the legalization on consumption levels and patterns (Smart & Liccardo Pacula, 2019), the public health impact (Hall & Lynskey, 2016), the effects on social justice (Adinoff & Reiman, 2019), and the economic consequences (Shanahan & Ritter, 2014) have received priority interest from both the authorities and scientific researchers. This chapter examines the roles of governments and the bureaucratic agencies responsible for the implementation of cannabis policies—a still under-studied yet crucial dimension of these endeavors. The focus is on public agencies as a key factor in shaping the content of these policies across time. More specifically, the chapter examines the dilemmas faced by the public servants in charge of the implementation of the medical cannabis policy and how they addressed them based on their professional ethos. It is based on the results of a policy evaluation of the Federal Act on Narcotics and Psychotropic Substances in Switzerland (Mavrot et al., 2018).

As research tradition on public administration has long shown, the study of bureaucratic behavior in public policy implementation is crucial because civil servants are key players of the policy process, able to steer policy implementation in various directions—sometimes far away from the original political intent. Public administration research has therefore been extensively discussing the dilemma between discretion and accountability with regard to the constitutional role of public service (Rhodes, 2014). Street-level bureaucracy literature has particularly insisted on the leeway bureaucrats and their implementation partners enjoy in redefining a policy during its everyday implementation. However, the necessary leeway granted to public servants is not arbitrary, as "discretion is filled by rules professionals impose upon themselves" (Hupe & Hill, 2007: 282). These observations call for a strong focus on the policy implementation nexus, which is far from just being a residual step subordinated to higher-level political decisions (Hupe & Hill, 2015). Moreover, not only do bureaucrats have the latitude to move a policy away from initial expectations, but it might also happen—more often than expected—that politicians show a great deal of indifference as to the actual implementation of a policy, thus leaving its success or failure in the hands of the bureaucrats (Mavrot & Hadorn, 2021). In that regard, the policy implementation phase entails a whole array of players who carry their own values, norms of action, and agendas, which might differ from the ones prevailing during the public deliberations or legislative debates. In addition, important responsibilities are also placed on administrations, which are expected to remain true to the policy objectives of these sensitive regulations, such as fulfilling patients' rights in the case of medical cannabis, while having to constantly adapt to rapidly changing and unexpected realities.

Given these considerations, this chapter proposes to open the bureaucratic black box of cannabis legalization from a policy implementation perspective. Based on a case study on the regulation of the use of cannabis for medical purposes in Switzerland, it analyzes the role of the public agency responsible for the policy enforcement over a seven-year period. The Swiss Federal Office of Public Health, which is the Swiss national public health department, has the exclusive enforcement competence regarding medical cannabis. In the rest of the chapter, it is referred to as the public health agency. It identifies six particular challenges bureaucrats face during policy implementation regarding various legal, ethical, medical, and political dimensions and forms some lessons for the future of cannabis regulation. Although based on the Swiss case, the results can be of a more general interest because of the similarities of the challenges faced around the world regarding cannabis policies—which are quickly evolving from criminalization to legalization in a global prohibitionist context.

Theoretical Framework, Data, and Methods

Bureaucratic Discretion and the Implementation of Cannabis Policies

This evaluation was a formal study commissioned to an interdisciplinary research team of the University of Bern by the Swiss Federal Office of Public

Health. The study aimed to assess various aspects of the enforcement of the Narcotics Act, especially the policy that followed the regulation of medical cannabis in the country in 2011. Unlike in the United States, the medical cannabis policy in Switzerland is defined by the federal government at the national level. The study was based on the policy cycle evaluation model, which aims at analyzing the different steps of a public policy, including its conceptualization by various social, political, and administrative actors, the delivery system, the implementation process and the policy outcomes (Bussmann et al., 1997: 69–70). The rationale of this model is to consider a public policy as a whole, while assessing each component with precise evaluation criteria (*op. cit.*). The main evaluation criteria defined here were the legal conformity, the adequacy, and the relevance of the implementation praxis in relation to the policy's goals regarding the medical coverage of patients in need of cannabis for therapeutic reasons (Mavrot et al., 2018: 4). The fact that the study was a commissioned policy evaluation granted the research team excellent access to confidential data and information.

The patients treated with cannabis are the main policy targets. Policy stakeholders are understood as players involved in the policy or having an interest in it. They can be policy-makers, policy implementers, or other policy beneficiaries (Mehrizi et al., 2009: 431). In this study, the focus is on the agencies and professional groups participating in the policy's enforcement—for instance, the federal public health agency or referring physicians—as well as other third parties taking a direct part in the policy, such as cannabis growers, producers, and providers. Moreover, cannabis legalization usually requires complex policy mixes spread among various public agencies and administrative divisions. Hence, the coherence of the implementation of policy packages is also crucial (Kern et al., 2019), and cross-sectoral policy coordination efforts are a key factor in policy success (Trein et al., 2020). Policy success can be defined a minima as the effective implementation of the policy and the achievement of its objectives without generating adverse side effects. These coordination efforts were therefore also part of the study. Finally, cannabis policies can be considered as morality policies, implying specific policy dynamics linked to the nature of this disputed topic (Engeli et al., 2013). The effects of the moral nature of the cannabis issue on policy formulation and policy implementation must be taken into account, and can be approached through the political debates, the media controversies, and implementation struggles.

Hence, this policy evaluation takes a close look into the bureaucratic structures and processes involved in cannabis regulation policies. Insightful observations on cannabis legalization can be made through a focus on policy implementation from within the state. In a particularly useful study, Wesley and Salomons (2019) review what they call the "government machinery" in various Canadian provincial and territorial governments. The authors detail what kind of committees were introduced within public agencies in the wake of legalization, in particular to tackle the challenge of cross-departmental coordination (*op. cit.*, 590–591). They propose to classify cannabis legalization policy models in a typology including market-based (i.e., based on the delegation of some aspects of the policy to private corporations), network-based (i.e., based on horizontality and on cooperation flows between a multitude of cross-sector players), and hierarchical approaches (i.e., based on structured organizational frameworks and on vertical accountability). This typology helps sorting through the different models of cannabis legalization according to their dominant pattern, and to be aware of their respective strengths and weaknesses (e.g., responsiveness vs. accountability, diffusion of responsibilities vs. inflexibility). Kilmer (2019: 666) notes that regardless of the adopted model, however, the "power to regulate" remains in the hand of the government. Within this context, however, whether the regulatory authority is attributed to public health agencies or other bodies such as liquor control commissions will greatly influence the orientation of the policy (*op. cit.*). Indeed, legalization automatically implies governmental arbitrations between various players. The use of the government's regulatory capacity is notably crucial for protecting public health from corporate interests when it comes to the choice of the economic model underpinning cannabis legalization (Shover & Humphreys, 2019). At the dawn of a new era regarding legalization, some have underlined the importance to "place regulatory control in the hands of a public-health minded agency that views its job as protecting consumers from being abused by industry" (Caulkins, 2019: 283). The discussion here is about whether the commercialization of a product like cannabis should be put in the hand of for-profit corporations, or if public organizations might take better care of the consumers in case of state-based markets (e.g., avoiding aggressive marketing, integrating cannabis policies into a more general harm-reduction policy framework, being in touch with health organizations). In some models, special task forces have been set up to help develop public health-oriented regulations building on decades of tobacco and alcohol prevention experience (Ghosh et al., 2016), for instance regarding advertising restrictions, packaging and product access for youth.

Moreover, cannabis legalization requires a fundamental rethinking of the related regulatory regimes, because new agencies are called to perform "governance tasks that were previously undertaken by the criminal justice system" (Aaronson & Rothschild-Elyassi, 2021: 2, citing Beckett & Murakawa, 2012: 231). Stohr et al. (2020), for instance, investigated cannabis legalization from the perspective of the police as key implementation players whose practices will have to be adapted on the ground. If the authorities fail to carry out a profound reform of the prohibitionist system, which is still deeply entrenched in the state, cannabis policies will be at risk of remaining within the scope of "carceral paradigms of policing" (Aaronson & Rothschild-Elyassi, 2021: 11). This is even more the case when those policies are historically anchored in decades of a repressive approach to drug consumption, such as in the United States where Reagan's "war on drug" took over from Nixon's "war on crime" approach, strongly directed against African American and Latino minorities (Anguelov, 2018: 51). This targeted repressive approach combines with a focus on youth arrests, creating long-term adverse effects within age groups. As Bender notes, "marijuana use by youth of color has been the focal point of the War on Drugs from its inception"; most arrests for cannabis possession are found among the groups of young African Americans and Latinos despite the fact that white youths consumption rate lies at the same level (2016: 691).

Whether a society is really prepared or put in motion the promise of social reparation through a genuine turn in the cannabis policy path will also have to be reflected in the administrative structures set up to materialize the legalization (Moyers, 2020: 1). Finally, some specific governance issues arise in countries where the legalization is undertaken at an intra-national level, especially regarding the question of policy coherence between states as well as inter-state interactions (or interprovincial in the case of Canada) in a context where different regulatory regimes coexist (Bear, 2017). This chapter adds to the reflections on legalization enforcement by analyzing the policy delivery system established for medical cannabis in Switzerland. As medical cannabis is exclusively regulated at the national level in the Swiss federal system, and as the states are not involved in the policy implementation, the case does not specifically allow to make observations on federal dynamics in matters of cannabis. However, it provides an example of a suboptimal policy concept that provoked implementation crises and required considerable adjustment over the years. It can therefore be of interest with regard to any national of subnational process of cannabis regulation, both for policy designing and policy implementation.

Evaluation of the Swiss Medical Cannabis Policy

The study is based on five methodological modules that allowed qualitative triangulation of different sets of data, in the sense of "corroborating evidence from different . . . types of data . . . or methods of data collection" (Creswell, 2005: 252, cited in Carter & Baghurst, 2014: 456). To contextualize the policy reform, the study first included a qualitative analysis of parliamentary debates on the topic at the federal government level from 2004 to 2018 (i.e., from the beginning of the medical cannabis regulation debate to the time of the study). This context analysis was completed with an analysis of media reports on the topic from 2000 to 2017 (i.e., from the first press articles about a possible future reform to the last complete year before the analysis) in the two main national languages (German and French). Second, the study included a quantitative analysis of the authorizations for medical use of cannabis granted by the responsible agency—the federal public health agency—between 2012 and 2017 (from the beginning of law enforcement to the time of the study), to analyze trends in the authorization-granting praxis. The 8,400 authorization requests received by the public health agency were coded according to the International Classification of Diseases (ICD-10) of the World Health Organization to determine for which medical indications (conditions and symptoms) authorizations were granted.

Third, the study also included an online survey of all referring physicians who had submitted authorization requests for their patients to the public health agency for a cannabis-based treatment during the 18 months prior to our study (N = 353). This survey assessed the physicians' practice related to the medical use of cannabis and their opinions regarding the policy delivery system (special authorization and double-gatekeeper systems, relationship with the public health agency, effectiveness of the process, evolution of the context). The fourth module consisted of an organizational study of the administrative processes of the public health agency through a document analysis and 21 semi-structured qualitative interviews with all players involved in the policy. These interviews comprised jurists, physicians from the public health agency responsible for the authorizations (formerly or currently in office) and their administrative hierarchy, a member of the public health agency's external advisory board for medical cannabis (medical experts), the Swiss Agency responsible for the surveillance of therapeutic products (Swissmedic), the representative of the medical authorities at the state level (president of the cantonal physicians), cannabis producers, and cannabis providers (heads of the drugstores certified for medical cannabis delivery). Fifth, the study comprised a legal opinion on the legality of the law-enforcement practice and potential needs for adaptation. The whole analysis in this chapter is based on data retrieved from this study (Mavrot et al., 2018).

Case Study

The Swiss case is familiar to drug policy specialists because of its groundbreaking model of harm-reduction policy. The so-called "four-model" pillar is a policy mix relying on prevention, repression, harm reduction, and therapy as the key elements of the approach to drugs. Especially interesting is the harm-reduction component of the mix, which was developed in the early 90s after Switzerland had become a major European epicenter of drug consumption. Its images of impressive open-air consumption scenes in the city of Zurich were circulated around the world. The strong political and public prominence of the issue in the midst of the devastating AIDS epidemic forced the local and national governments to react. Actively pushed by experts from public agencies and professionals in the field, an audacious harm-reduction model including supervised injection rooms and medically prescribed heroin programs was set up (Kübler, 2001), inaugurating a new era for the drug policy of this otherwise highly conservative country. Since then, the federal public health agency and its administrative experts have played a central role in the definition and implementation of drug policies in Switzerland.

Interestingly, the liberalization of cannabis policies occurred much later, starting with the regulation of cannabis use for medical purposes. The recreational use of cannabis is still banned at the moment, although some cities have recently been temporarily authorized by the federal government to organize pilot testing the effects of different legalization models on a small scale.[1] Cannabis, however, remains a strongly controversial topic in Switzerland. One of the reasons it did not enjoy the same flexibility as opioid consumption is related to the fact that cannabis never generated a visible and a dramatic public problem as heroin. In 2011, however, after years of heated parliamentary debates, the paragraph 5, article 8, of the Federal Act on Narcotics and Psychotropic Substances, allowing the restricted use of cannabis for medical purposes, entered into force. This new statutory provision states that the federal public health agency can issue exceptional authorizations for the cultivation, importation, manufacturing, and use of (i) opium; (ii) diacetylmorphine (i.e., synthetic heroin); (iii) lysergide (LSD-25); and (iv) cannabis for research, drug development, or limited medicinal purposes.[2] This national legislation is applicable in all 26 Swiss states (cantons). Law enforcement began in 2012; the use of cannabis for medicinal purposes was banned prior to this legislative change. Under the new regulatory regime, cannabis for medical purposes can be obtained under a set of specific criteria: the use of cannabis must be supported by the referring physician, who has to submit an authorization request to the federal public health agency; it must concern medical indications that are scientifically recognized; all other existing therapies must have been tried before moving to the cannabis option; and the authorization is granted on a temporary basis and must be regularly renewed.

The Swiss regulatory model for medical cannabis has two crucial characteristics. First, it was defined by the legislature as a juridical regime of exceptional authorizations. This means that a request meeting all the criteria does not automatically require the public health agency to grant the authorization. The regime of exceptional authorizations foresees that the public health agency enjoys discretionary power in its decisions to accept or to decline patients' requests. The system is purposefully made to keep the use of cannabis for medical reasons occasional and to avoid cannabis becoming a regular therapeutic option. It is therefore a case of medical cannabis regulation and not of full legalization. Second, double-gatekeeper system is utilized in which both referring physicians and experts from the public health agency must agree on the use of the product for a specific patient. In Wesley and Salomons' typology (2019), this places the Swiss medical cannabis system among the hierarchy-based models. However, after policy evaluation and following recurrent criticisms related to the cumbersome nature of the process, the system is currently being revised and will evolve toward a single gatekeeper process, with referring physicians being directly allowed to prescribe cannabis like it is commonly the case in the American and Canadian models.[3] In the timespan studied by the evaluation, medical cannabis was used mostly for medical conditions related to diseases of the nervous system (40.3% of the authorizations) and diseases of the musculoskeletal systems (27.8%). The symptoms mostly considered for medical cannabis authorizations were chronic pain (51.1%) and spasticity (i.e., spasms, for instance in Parkinson's conditions) (33.8%) (Mavrot et al., 2018: 15–16).

The enforcement of the new medical cannabis policy has been assigned to two groups of bureaucrats within the public health agency that have different professional backgrounds: physicians and jurists. Both are civil servants employed by the government and belong to the federal administration. Contrary to the physicians working in the public health agency, all referring physicians, including those who submit medical cannabis requests for their patients, are private market actors. The public health agency's physicians review the authorization requests and decide whether to grant them, while a group of agency jurists is responsible for ensuring that the enforcement of the policy remains within the juridical framework. Although the physicians are specialists on the medical cannabis policy, the jurists also work on other policies. None of these bureaucrats was involved in the topic of cannabis prior to the medical cannabis legislation. Before this regulation, cannabis was fully banned (although possessing small amount for personal consumption was decriminalized in 2012) and mostly fell within the scope of police, security, and justice agencies at the state level. A strong conflict quickly arose between the physicians and the jurists of the public health agency regarding the degree of severity to adopt for authorizations. In the years following the regulation of medical cannabis, a sharp increase in authorization requests occurred, jumping from 291 in 2012 to 2,309 in 2017 (Mavrot et al., 2018: 14). The figures cover only the time span from January 1 to September 15 for the year 2017 (the data available at the time of the evaluation). While the public health agency's physicians thought this evolution should have no impact on their authorization-granting practice, the jurists felt it endangered the nature of the system, which was based on the principle of exceptional authorizations. According to the referring physicians (i.e., the ones requesting authorizations for their patients), this sharp rise in the number of requests occurred because of the increased notoriety of cannabis as a therapeutic product. The media analysis performed as part of the policy evaluation also showed increased social acceptance of cannabis in the public discourse across the study period, especially in the wake of the 2016 authorization of low-THC/high-CBD cannabis products in Switzerland (Anderfuhren-Biget et al., 2020: 330) and the boom in related businesses.

In addition, almost all authorization requests were accepted by the physicians of the public health agency. According to them, this fact showed that the referring physicians did a good job of selecting the patients for whom to grant a request, while the jurists accused the agency's physicians of being too loose. The rationale behind the attitude of the public health agency's physicians was double: they trusted the judgment of the referring physicians submitting requests on the one hand, and they prioritized patients' rights to access a therapeutic product on the other. A point of contention was the criterion that authorizations should be granted only for patients who have tried all other available therapeutic options (i.e., authorized medications). For the jurists, this criterion should have been closely verified by the public health agency before granting any authorization. However, the agency's physicians were against close monitoring of this aspect for several reasons. They thought this would be unnecessary micromanagement since the referring physicians could be trusted and were best placed to know their patient's therapeutic best interests. They were also overwhelmed with the drastic increase in authorization requests they had to manage with the same human resources as at the beginning of law enforcement and deemed it impossible to check this aspect within the deadline attributed to them for reviewing each request. These points led to a serious clash of professional ethos between the public health agency's physicians and jurists. The physicians underlined the patients' rights to be treated and the autonomy of medical knowledge, while the jurists invoked respect for the legal order and the lack of legitimacy of bureaucrats to overlook the will of democratically elected politicians who originally defined the system of exceptional authorizations. In addition, whereas the quantitative analysis showed that the authorization practice indeed remained fairly consistent across time as far as cannabis was concerned, there was flexibility regarding the granting of exceptional authorizations for the use of LSD for medical experiments in university hospitals, which began in 2014 (Mavrot et al., 2018: 18).

Interestingly, the policy evaluation results showed that the main cause of the mismatches between the legal provisions and the reality was that the members of the legislative commission in charge of drafting the law worked under the assumption that a cannabis-based legal medication having undergone all necessary trials would be put on the market in the following years by pharmaceutical companies. However, this turned out not to be the case because of the pharmaceutical industry's limited financial interest in developing a drug based on cannabis (Mavrot et al., 2018: 59). Hence, the double-gatekeeper system of exceptional authorizations was initially conceptualized as a temporary solution until better options were developed. However, this system was ultimately maintained because of the lack of alternatives and turned out not to be viable in the medium term. Not only was the bureaucratic system in charge of the policy's implementation maintained, but it also was never fundamentally updated to face the challenges that came up with the time, especially the sharp increase in authorization requests that was not in line with an exception system anymore. This can be explained by the fact that although the dispute between the agency's jurists and physicians was strong within the office, they also feared publicizing their conflict and thereby attracting unwarranted political attention to a topic they knew was highly sensitive. The physicians feared that some politicians would take the opportunity to attack medical cannabis regulation and attempt to take it a step backward, and the jurists feared that the legality of the agency's behavior would be questioned.

Crucial to this deadlocked situation was that while the physicians had the power to make the authorization decisions, the jurists felt they were the ones who would be legally responsible for them. This decoupling of implementation and legal capacity increased the tensions between the two parties. Another disagreement was highly representative of the legal ambiguities around the regulation of medical cannabis. The referring physicians and the physicians from the public health agency themselves wished that the federal agency had published more information on various aspects of the therapeutic use of cannabis, including a continually updated list of indications for which the use of the product had been scientifically recognized. The public health agency's jurists were skeptical about the idea, arguing that the federal government shouldn't advertise the use of a still banned product (except in cases of special authorizations). The continuous adaptation of an indication list to current medical evidence was also contentious. The legal division of the agency instead insisted on limiting the indications to those that were explicitly mentioned during the political debates that led to the regulation, especially within the legislative commission in charge of the law's formulation of the law. For their part, the referring physicians would have welcomed the publication of official information on the use of medical cannabis as its indications, posology, and effects are less well-known than those of manufactured medications that would be on the market for a long time (Mavrot et al., 2018: 24). The medical division of the public health agency had the same opinion because they wanted to grant authorizations for new medical indications if scientifically relevant.

The institutional design of the policy and the administrative processes between the physicians and jurists of the public health agency were not optimally conceptualized, which worsened the conflicts. The two groups of bureaucrats answered to distinct parallel hierarchies within the public health agency's organizational chart. The physicians responded to public health managers, while the jurists were subordinated to managers with legal backgrounds. The first common hierarchical level was high up in the organization, where only the most sensitive dissentions were escalated. This resulted in two distinct hierarchical lines with a lack of common mutual transparency. The jurists wanted to be virtually able to have a look into each special authorization case, while the physicians wanted to involve them only in the most complex and questionable cases. From an organizational perspective, no procedure was established regarding the workflows between them. The division of tasks was neither precisely defined nor formalized. Moreover, no conflict resolution procedure was put in place, which resulted in ad hoc conflict management among the two parallel line of hierarchies.

Finally, beyond the intra-agency organization and processes, several issues also came up regarding external players involved in the policy's delivery. The agency responsible for the surveillance of therapeutic products—Swissmedic—must ensure national compliance with international treaties. The process of determining whether the new legislation and its implementation were still in line with international drug treaties was complex and required a lot of coordination with the public health agency. Other key players were the drugstores specialized in the preparation and delivery of medical cannabis. In the Swiss case, they buy cannabis oil from cannabis producers and prepare the final product for the patients according to the indications of the medical prescription (based on a magisterial formula). Over the years, the public health agency's legal division pushed to strengthen several inspection and documentation requirements of these drugstores to ensure the proper law enforcement regarding the cannabis' traceability. Among other changes, the duration of the drugstores' licenses to prepare and deliver cannabis products was shortened from two years to six months. The review of renewal requests for these licenses was performed extremely thoroughly by the public health agency, which led to dangers of product shortages in the field, according to the drugstores. Hence, the question of inspections raises important issues related to their frequency and degree of severity, which led to further disagreement between the involved players. Cannabis producers—that is, the companies buying cannabis flowers from the growers and extracting and formulating its oil—were also in an argument with the public health agency at the time of the study. The producers wanted to be granted authorization to produce cannabis for exportation because a neighboring country, Germany, had recently legalized cannabis for medical purposes. However, the agency's interpretation of the law was that only production for domestic use was allowed. As a consequence, the producers threatened the public health agency with court litigation on this point.

Results and Discussion

Based on this case study, six major challenges of the cannabis policy implementation are identified from the perspectives of the implementing public agencies. In the following, each of these challenges is presented and discussed.

Law Obsolescence, Legal Uncertainty, and Legislative Incoherence

One major challenge policy implementers faced in the case of cannabis regulations is the obsolescence of the law. Although not specific to cannabis policies, an increasing mismatch between quickly evolving realities on the ground and rules decided at a given point in time is a major problem for cannabis policies. This is exacerbated by decisions on cannabis usually being taken in contexts of political polarization and uncertainty. The case of medical cannabis in Switzerland provides an example of the kind of problems that may result from law obsolescence. When the law was decided, policy-makers expected that the special authorizations system would be a temporary solution before the development of legal and manufactured cannabis-based drugs. The development of such drugs by pharmaceutical companies ultimately did not occur as expected because the return-on-investment for such products was deemed too low. Public agencies in charge of issuing the special authorizations consequently faced an unsustainable situation, with a dramatic increase in authorization requests from patients meeting the attribution criteria, but within a legal framework foreseeing an exceptional use of cannabis. This led to vivid conflicts among implementation players disagreeing on how to react to this contradiction.

Legislative incoherence can be an issue at the domestic level (e.g., between narcotics laws and laws on therapeutic products). In addition, a risk of law incoherence—or at least of legal uncertainty—exists across governance levels. This is the case in the United States, with the uncertain reaction of the federal government after the introduction of the first state-level cannabis legalization (Mallinson & Hannah, 2020: 347). In fact, the incoherence affects several governance levels, to the point that "the inconsistency in marijuana laws between the federal government and many states, among the states, and between the states and Native American tribes raises serious and often unprecedented federalism issues" (Chemerinsky, 2017: 859). Moreover, the question of the compatibility of national cannabis legalization policies with international drug treaties has also been raised in various countries. It seems that the initial tendency "turning a blind eye to the conflicts with international treaties" is still pretty much part of the policy path (Room, 2013: 346). While national legislation is quickly evolving in various countries around the globe, international treaties remain in line with the prohibitionist paradigm to this day (see for instance the United Nations Single Convention on Narcotic Drugs of 1961). Finally, differences in legislation across jurisdictions are also a challenge regarding many aspects such as the fear of out-of-state cannabis tourism (Santaella-Tenorio et al., 2020). There can be a legislative patchwork even within a state, where local governments may issue more restrictive legal provisions in their jurisdictions like for instance experienced in Colorado (Ghosh, 2016: 25). All these tendencies will have to be closely monitored to ensure as much legal certainty as possible for the future developments of cannabis legislation. In fact, these legislative uncertainties and incoherencies have not been resolved yet almost a decade after the first regulations—for instance, for medicinal and recreational cannabis in numerous U.S. states and for medicinal cannabis in Switzerland.

Evolving Medical and Empirical Evidence

Closely related to the problem of law obsolescence is the question of the evolving medical and empirical evidence. In a matter such as cannabis policy, which has high public health stakes (e.g., public health consequences of the criminalization of consumption, access to a therapeutic option in the case of medical cannabis) and social stakes (e.g., social justice, stigmatization), the periodic adaptation of the policies to up-to-date evidence would be crucial. However, the dynamics and temporality of policy-making are not always compatible with continuous and rapid policy adjustments. Implementing agencies can consequently be trapped in outdated models with regard to a changing reality. Medical cannabis regulatory regimes raise specific challenges in this regard. The scientifically recognized list of medical indications for a therapeutic use of cannabis—for instance, spasticity and pain in neurodegenerative diseases—might evolve according to new trials and scientific results. Policy-makers can be torn between the willingness to define a catalogue of indications for which medical cannabis is authorized—to maintain control over the use of this product—and the necessarily changing medical evidence. Such contradictions are difficult to resolve as long as medical practice is constrained by laws. This situation is representative of the paradox in which cannabis regulations are caught, at the crossroads of morality and medical considerations.

Beyond the medical aspects, many kinds of evidence are also highly relevant to cannabis regulations. Numerous studies analyzing the first effects of the various cannabis regulatory models are being conducted. Valuable lessons will undoubtedly be drawn about the comparative advantages and drawbacks of each policy mix; for instance, regarding their consequences on youth consumption (Hammond et al., 2020), racial inequalities (Tran et al., 2020), or the criminal justice system (Fischer et al., 2021). Behind these key issues, some specialized subsets of questions will also require close inquiry, such as the effects of various advertising or pricing regulations on levels of consumption (Stockwell et al., 2020) or the possibility to incentivize consumers toward reduced-risk consumption modes (Fischer & Bullen, 2020). Both intended and unintended consequences arise from the new cannabis policies and each must be examined. The possibility of inter-state policy variations in federal systems such as the United States provides interesting prospects for experimentation and innovation (Pierson, 1995), which may be used at the advantage of policy learning in novel and uncertain regulatory areas such as cannabis legalization (Mallinson & Hannah, 2020). Comparative research designs taking advantage of inter-state differences in federal contexts can be used for this purpose (Vatter & Rüefli, 2003). Therefore, policy-making processes will have to allow room for policy-learning processes (Dolowitz & Marsh, 2000) that help regulatory models to adapt to upcoming evidence. In that regard, the Canadian approach that foresees a legislative review of cannabis legalization every three years to check upon the achievement of its goals might constitute a good model.[4] Regular and early legislative reviews are especially crucial that it has been shown that commercial interests and corporate players tend to quickly grow within the system and become powerful parties steering the agenda away from public health (Jesseman, 2019, cited in Zwicky et al., 2021: 65).

Litigation Threat: Physicians' Liability and Economic Freedom

On the legal side, cannabis regulations also raise a series of issues that have to be disentangled regarding litigation risks. At this level, professionals and agencies in charge of policy implementation are likely to be torn between contradicting requirements. First, in the case of medical cannabis, patients' rights to be treated are a core issue that needs to be seriously considered. When it comes to alleviating pain for patients for whom therapeutic alternatives have failed, referring physicians are likely to consider the cannabis option because of its pharmacological properties, regardless of the product's sometimes-ambiguous legal status. However, physicians also express important medical concerns when it comes to prescribing these products because their use and effects might be less predictable than that of drugs that have received marketing authorizations and have undergone extensive medical trials. Such uncertainty places great responsibility on physicians with the use of non-standardized and non-manufactured products such as cannabis. Depending on the legal arrangement in place for the use of medical cannabis (i.e., whether a procedure exempts physicians from any liability), referring physicians could be vulnerable to litigation in cases of medical complications. This may in turn decrease the physicians' willingness to open the door to that therapeutic option. Second, public agencies in charge of the policy are at risk of lawsuits from the various economic interests invested in the cannabis market. The question that arose in the Swiss case was the authorization of the concerned companies to expand toward international business. This legal uncertainty is also an issue in the United States at the domestic level, with the uncertainties regarding the future of inter-state commerce.

Professional Conflicts and Clashes of Professional Ethos

Cannabis legalization implies arbitration between a wide array of competing political, economic, and social interests. With the legislative U-turn they involve, those policies also alter deeply rooted professional routines and practices within governmental structures. Although adapting to new political orders is an intrinsic part of administrative duties, such changes carry the risk of causing professional conflicts among bureaucrats in charge of the policy. The case study of medical cannabis showed how far such professional conflicts could go toward provoking disputes within implementation agencies but also toward creating problems on the ground. Because of the historical categorization of the product as an illegal psychotropic, medical cannabis policies lie at the crossroads of medical and juridical expertise. This double nature is likely to be reflected in the policy delivery system, bringing together bureaucrats with different professional ethos and dramatically diverging priorities. In the case at hand, jurists prioritized the letter of the law and the strict respect of the political will as originally formulated, to guarantee the constitutional order and the separation of state powers. On their part, the physicians acted primarily according to patients' rights and claimed a certain degree of medical autonomy. In the short run, such disputes run the risk of leading to implementation incoherence and delays. From a wider perspective, they can have consequences of more importance, including prolonged administrative dysfunctions and enhanced risks of politicization.

Although the professionals analyzed here were physicians and jurists, the same type of conflicts can occur with different professional groups such as social workers or law-enforcement agents. This issue also bears repercussions regarding implementation partners and policy targets. Various groups of professionals having a conflicting understanding of the legislation are likely to disagree on key dimensions of the policy. The degree of strictness in law enforcement is likely to be a matter of disagreement as in the Swiss case and as underlined in the U.S. context (Kilmer, 2019: 667). The degree to which controls and inspections have to be deployed—for instance regarding cannabis production, selling arrangements in retail outlets or consumption in the streets—and which consequences will occur therefrom is a salient dimension of policy enforcement. The freedom granted to field actors is also a point for discussion: in the states where cannabis is authorized only for medical use, are the referring physicians completely entrusted with the right to decide for their patients, or does a review process exist like in the case study? The answer to these questions requires anticipating the potentially conflictual patterns of policy implementation among policy stakeholders.

Organizational Challenges: Intra- and Inter-Agency Processes

The experience with changes in cannabis regulations also bears some lessons from an organizational perspective. Expecting that the implementation of new regulatory arrangements can occur within the previously existing policy delivery systems is a mistake. The division of tasks and responsibilities that were relevant within the previous legislative paradigm—for instance, the preponderant role of the criminal justice system—has been fundamentally altered and must be reflected in the decisional and enforcement structures. A decoupling of implementation capacities and responsibilities (Mavrot & Hadorn, 2021) such as the one observed in the case study must be avoided. To avoid such mismatches, not only the new responsibilities have to be clearly defined, but corresponding and effective hierarchical lines must be put in place. Similarly, in a context of legalization, public authorities have to establish cooperation with new range of players such as cannabis growers, producers and retailers, and pharmaceutical companies or physicians in the case of medical cannabis, which might require the involvement of agencies that were not previously involved in the prohibitionist legislative framework. This finally raises the question of inter-agency cooperation. With legalization, consequent shifts are likely to occur regarding the location of the policy among agencies due to the emergence of new stakeholders (e.g., offices in charge of the licensing system and the economic aspects of the enforcement). Public authorities have to conceptualize these critical aspects ahead of the enactment of new legislation. In the United States, the picture is completed by the social equity and racial justice objectives of cannabis legalization, which includes additional crucial policy stakeholders. These policy objectives imply radical changes in law-enforcement practice or the attribution of exploitation licenses to members of the communities that have primarily suffered from the effects of unequal implementation of prohibitionist policies. The equity and justice objectives of cannabis policies will therefore require the establishment of adequate structures and procedures within the state to enable their fulfillment. It is otherwise likely that the implementation of fundamentally new policies within old enforcement structures is bound to fail.

Risks of Politicization: Policy Implementation under Pressure

Finally, as morality policies, cannabis regulations are particularly salient in the public debate and at constant risk of politicization. This has an effect on the enforcement practice, especially for public agencies. In the Swiss medical cannabis case, this pressure had a perverse effect. Fearing unnecessary public attention, the involved agencies carried on implementing legislation that had become misadjusted to reality. Key implementation problems such as production shortfalls threatening to deprive patients of treatment or the quick increase in requests in a system of exceptional authorizations remained long undeclared. Public agents dealt with those problems on a case-by-case basis and were reluctant to escalate them to the political level because of negative experience with political overreaction concerning the issue. Consequently, the original mismatch remained and the gaps between field needs and the law continued to widen. This dynamic also made it consistently more difficult to denounce the original problem without revealing what had been done by the administration to deal with it during the past implementation phases—for instance, stretching the law. Such effects should be anticipated, and effective problem-resolution procedures should be put in place. The early creation of stakeholder panels commissioned with the task of supervising policy implementation and helping to solve ongoing problems could be a useful approach. The experience also shows the difficulty of keeping the debates between medical and recreational cannabis separate in countries and states that have only legalized consumption for medical purposes. The frequent confusion between these two topics puts cannabis policies further at risk of political polarization during the debates.

CONCLUSION

While bearing the promise of a shift toward a less repressive state presence, legalization does not necessarily mean a decreased importance of governments in cannabis policies, the role of which deserves close analytical attention. Depending on the chosen regulatory and economic model, the roles of public agencies vary greatly between states and countries that have chosen to move toward some form of cannabis legalization—be it for medical or recreational purposes. Reflecting upon the evolution of the implementation of a cannabis policy over a ten-year period may hold some useful lessons in a context where numerous countries in the world are taking an ambitious turn toward legalization policies. Despite being a less spectacular aspect of the recent cannabis legalization wave, the question of policy implementation by public agencies is worthy of analytical interest. Opening the black box of bureaucratic action in that regard can shed light on some major success or failure factors for cannabis policies during these first post-prohibitionist steps. Governments oversee various coordination, enforcement, and reviewing activities that are central to these reforms. Thus, their capacity to adapt their structures and processes to tackle this emerging issue is crucial, from an intra- and inter-agency perspective as well as regarding their interactions with external policy stakeholders. Whether we want it or not, governments play a central role in these policy pathways, if only by their centralizing and redistributive capacity regarding the choice of an economic model, the attribution of retail licenses, and the taxation of cannabis products. They also play a key role in setting regulatory limitation to preserve consumers' health. Finally, governments are central to the repressive historical legacy of cannabis policies that led to a strong reproduction of social and racial inequalities (Owusu-Bempah & Luscombe, 2021). From a historical institutionalist perspective, given the tendency toward path dependency in policy implementation processes (Bali, 2020), bureaucratic behavior in this new era must therefore be closely scrutinized to determine whether if it matches the new promises of legalization. In that regard, a comprehensive research agenda that more systematically links studies focused on the public health and social effects of cannabis policies and close analyses of policy enforcement processes would offer promising perspectives.

NOTES

1. https://www.admin.ch/gov/fr/accueil/documentation/communiques.msg-id-82917.html
2. https://www.fedlex.admin.ch/eli/cc/1952/241_241_245/de. The medical use of synthetic heroin was already allowed under other legislative provisions.
3. https://www.bag.admin.ch/bag/de/home/medizin-und-forschung/heilmittel/med-anwend-cannabis.html
4. https://highgreennews.com/article/cannabis-industry-needs-step-canada-prepares-review-effects-legalization

REFERENCES

Aaronson, E., & Rothschild-Elyassi, G. (2021). The symbiotic tensions of the regulatory–carceral state: The case of cannabis legalization. *Regulation and Governance*, early online.

Adinoff, B., & Reiman, A. (2019). Implementing social justice in the transition from illicit to legal cannabis. *American Journal of Drug and Alcohol Abuse*, *45*(6), 673–688.

Anderfuhren-Biget, S., Zobel, F., Heeb, C., & Savary, J-F. (2020). Swiss cannabis policies. In T. Decorte, S. Lenton & C. Wilkins (Eds.), *Legalizing Cannabis: Experiences, Lessons and Scenarios* (pp. 323–336). London/New York: Routledge.

Anguelov, N., & McCarthy, M. P. (2018). *From Criminalizing to Decriminalizing Marijuana. The Politics of Social Control*. Lanham, MD: Lexington Books.

Bali A. S. (2020). Navigating Complexity in Policy Implementation. In H. Sullivan, H. Dickinson & H. Henderson (Eds.), *The Palgrave Handbook of the Public Servant* (early online). Cham: Palgrave Macmillan.

Bear, D. (2017). From Toques to Tokes: Two challenges facing nationwide legalization of cannabis in Canada. *International Journal of Drug Policy*, *42*, 97–101.

Bender, S. (2016). The Colors of Cannabis: Race and Marijuana. *U.C. Davis Law Review*, *50*, 689–706.

Bussmann, W., Klöti, U., & Knoepfel, P. (Eds.). (1997). *Einführung in die Politikevaluation*. Basel/Frankfurt am Main: Helbing & Lichtenhahn.

Carter, D., & Baghurst, T. (2014). The influence of servant leadership on restaurant employee engagement. *Journal of Bussiness Ethics*, *124*, 453–464.

Caulkins, J. (2019). Legalising drugs prudently: The importance of incentives and values. *Journal of Illicit Economies and Development*, *1*(3), 279–287.

Chemerinsky, E. (2017). Introduction: Marijuana laws and federalism. *Boston College Law Review*, *58*(3), 857–862.

Creswell, J. (2005). *Education Research: Planning, Conducting, and Evaluating Quantitative and Qualitative Research* (2nd ed.). Upper Saddle River, NJ: Pearson.

Dolowitz, D. P., & Marsh, D. (2000). Learning from abroad: The role of policy transfer in contemporary policy-making. *Governance*, *13*(1), 5–23.

Engeli, I., Green-Pedersen C., & Larsen L. T. (2013). The puzzle of permissiveness: understanding policy processes concerning morality issues. *Journal of European Public Policy*, *20*(3), 335–352.

Fischer, B., & Bullen, C. (2020). Emerging prospects for non-medical cannabis legalisation in New Zealand: An initial view and contextualization. *International Journal of Drug Policy*, *76*, 102632.

Fischer, B., Daldegan-Bueno, D., & Reuter, P. (2021). Toward a "post-legalization" criminology for cannabis: A brief review and suggested agenda for research priorities. *Contemporary Drug Problems*, *48*(1), 58–74.

Ghosh, T., Van Dyke, M., Maffey, A., Whitley, E., Gillim-Ross, L., & Wolk, L. (2016). The public health framework of legalized marijuana in Colorado. *American Journal of Public Health*, *106*(1), 21–27.

Hall, W., & Lynskey, M. (2016). Evaluating the public health impacts of legalizing recreational cannabis use in the United States. *Addiction*, *111*(10), 1764–1773.

Hammond, D., Goodman, S., Wadsworth, E., Rynard V., Boudreau, C., & Hall, W. (2020). Evaluating the impacts of cannabis legalization: The International Cannabis Policy Study. *International Journal of Drug Policy*, *77*, 102–698.

Hupe, P. L., & Hill, M. J. (2007). Street-level bureaucracy and public accountability. *Public Administration*, *85*(2), 279–299.

Hupe, P. L., & Hill, M. J. (2015). "And the rest is implementation": Comparing approaches to what happens in policy processes beyond Great Expectations. *Public Policy and Administration*, *31*(2), 103–121.

Jesseman, R. (2019). *What Have We Learned from One Year of Cannabis Legalization?* Policy Options. Retrieved from: https://policyoptions.irpp.org/magazines/december-2019/what-have-we-learned-from-one-year-of-cannabis-legalization/

Kern, F., Rogge, K. S., & Howlett, M. (2019). Policy mixes for sustainability transitions: New approaches and insights through bridging innovation and policy studies. *Research Policy*, *48*(10), 103832.

Kilmer, B. (2019). How will cannabis legalization affect health, safety, and social equity outcomes? It largely depends on the 14 Ps. *American Journal of Drug and Alcohol Abuse*, *45*(6), 664–672.

Kübler, D. (2001). Understanding policy change with the advocacy coalition framework: an application to Swiss drug policy. *Journal of European Public Policy*, *8*(4), 623–641.

Mallinson, D. J., & Hannah, A. L. (2020). Policy and political learning: The development of medical marijuana policies in the states. *Publius: The Journal of Federalism*, *50*(3), 344–369.

Mavrot, C., & Hadorn, S. (2021). When politicians do not care for the policy: Street-level compliance in cross-agency contexts. *Public Policy and Administration*, early online.

Mavrot, C., Hadorn, S., Sprecher, F., & Sager, F. (2018). *Evaluation spezifischer Vollzugsaufgaben des BAG im Rahmen des Betäubungsmittelgesetzes (BetmG).* Center for Public Management and Institute for Public Law, University of Bern. Retrieved from: https://boris.unibe.ch/130600/

Mehrizi M. H. R., Ghasemzadeh, F., & Molas-Gallart, J. (2009). Stakeholder mapping as an assessment framework for policy implementation. *Evaluation*, *15*(4), 427–444.

Moyer, J. (2020). *Innovation through Popular Diffusion: Seeking Social Equity Through Cannabis Legalization in Massachusetts* [Doctoral dissertation, University of Massachusetts Boston]. ProQuest Dissertations Publishing.

Owusu-Bempah, A., & Luscombe, A. (2021). Race, cannabis and the Canadian war on drugs: An examination of cannabis arrest data by race in five cities. *International Journal of Drug Policy*, *91*, 102937.

Pierson, P. (1995). Fragmented welfare states: Federal institutions and the development of social policy. *Governance*, *8*(4), 449–478.

Rhodes R. A. W. (2014). Public administration. In R. A. W. Rhodes & P. T. Hart (Eds.), *The Oxford Handbook of Political Leadership* (pp. 101–116). Oxford: Oxford University Press.

Room, R. (2014), Legalising a market for cannabis. *Addiction*, *109*(3), 345–351.

Santaella-Tenorio, J., Wheeler-Martin, K., DiMaggio, C.J., et al. (2020). Association of recreational cannabis laws in colorado and washington state with changes in traffic fatalities, 2005–2017. *JAMA Internal Medicine*, 180(8), 1061–1068.

Shanahan, M., & Ritter, A. (2014). Cost-benefit analysis of two policy options for cannabis: Status quo and legalisation. *PLOS ONE*, *9*(4), e95569.

Shover, C. L., & Humphreys, K. (2019). Six policy lessons relevant to cannabis legalization. *American Journal of Drug and Alcohol Abuse*, *45*(6), 698–706.

Smart, R., & Pacula R. L. (2019). Early evidence of the impact of cannabis legalization on cannabis use, cannabis use disorder, and the use of other substances: Findings from state policy evaluations. *American Journal of Drug and Alcohol Abuse*, *45*(6), 644–663.

Stockwell, T., Giesbrecht, N., Sherk, A., Thomas, G., Vallance, K., & Wettlaufer, A. (2020). Lessons learned from the alcohol regulation perspective. In T. Decorte, S. Lenton & C. Wilkins (Eds.), *Legalizing Cannabis: Experiences, Lessons and Scenarios* (pp. 211–232). London/New York: Routledge.

Stohr, M., Makin, D., Stanton, D., Hemmens, C., Willits, D., Lovrich, N. et al. (2020). An evolution rather than a revolution: Cannabis legalization implementation from the perspective of the police in Washington state. *Justice Evaluation Journal*, *3*(2), 267–293.

Tran N. K., Goldstein, N. D., Purtle, J., Massey, P. M., Lankenau, S. E., Suder, J. S., & Tabb, L. P. (2020). The heterogeneous effect of marijuana decriminalization policy on arrest rates in Philadelphia, Pennsylvania, 2009–2018. *Drug and Alcohol Dependence*, *212*, 108058.

Trein, P., Biesbroek, R., Bolognesi, T., Cejudo, G. M., Duffy, R., Hustedt, T., & Meyer, I. (2021). Policy coordination and integration: A research agenda. *Public Administration Review*, early online.

Vatter, A., & Rüefli, C. (2003). Do political factors matter for health care expenditure? A comparative study of Swiss cantons. *Journal of Public Policy*, *23*(3), 301–323.

Wesley, J. J., & Salomons, G. (2019). Cannabis legalization and the machinery of government. *Canadian Public Administration*, *62*(4), 573–592.

Zwicky, R., Brunner, P., Caroni, F., & Kübler, D. (2021). A research agenda for the regulation of non-medical cannabis use in Switzerland. *Zürcher Politik- und Evaluationsstudien*, *20*. Zurich, Department of Political Science.

Chapter 7

Consumer Well-Being and Cannabis Spending Habits

Evidence from Massachusetts

Steven White, Catharine M. Curran-Kelly, Paul Bacdayan, and Marion McNabb

INTRODUCTION

The legal U.S. cannabis market is projected to be between $22–26.4 billion in 2021 and employs over 400,000 workers (Marijuana Business Daily, 2021). In the United States today, legalized medical cannabis is the norm and legal recreational cannabis is a growing trend (Ludlum, Ford, & Barger-Johnson, 2019). All but five U.S. states (table 7.1) have some form of legal cannabis consumption of varying degrees.

From a business perspective, the study of the cannabis market is both interesting and historic. What started as a cottage industry is morphing into big business with national implications. The largest limiting factor to industry growth is current U.S. federal cannabis policy. Until the U.S. federal government establishes a unified national policy, state operators are left to navigate a myriad of legal, policy, regulatory, banking, and tax systems that limit growth and operations. Cannabis business operators are forced to find creative, or expensive, solutions to access to banking, in some instances paying monthly service fees to banks or credit unions to have access to banking services. Additional challenges related to banking include the payment of taxes to municipalities when one doesn't have access to adequate financial options. Some cannabis business operators pay in cash, as a result. Finally, cannabis businesses are not able to file for federal bankruptcy nor are they able to write-off business expenses when filing taxes. From an operation perspective, states have different regulations regarding vertical integration in the industry as well as the ability of national cannabis operators to purchase

Table 7.1 2021 U.S. State and Territory Cannabis Status

Cannabis Status	*Illegal (5)*	*Highly Restrictive Medical—CBD/Low THC (9)*	*Medical (20)*	*Recreational (20)*
States	Alabama	Kansas	Arkansas	Alaska
	Idaho	Kentucky	Connecticut*	Arizona
	Indiana	Georgia	Delaware*	California
	Nebraska	Mississippi	Florida	Colorado
	Wyoming	North Carolina*	Hawaii*	Illinois
			Iowa	Maine
		South Carolina	Louisiana	Massachusetts
		Tennessee	Maryland*	Michigan
		Texas	Minnesota*	Montana
		Wisconsin	Missouri	Nevada
			New Hampshire*	New Jersey
			North Dakota*	New Mexico
			Ohio*	New York
			Oklahoma	Oregon
			Pennsylvania	South Dakota
			Rhode Island*	Vermont
			Utah	Virginia
			West Virginia	Washington
Territories			Puerto Rico	Washington, DC
			U.S. Virgin Islands	Guam

*Cannabis Possession Decriminalized
Source: *Based on author calculations.*

local operations, the latter of which is designed to protect small independent cannabis business operators.

Palali and van Ours (2017) posit "that as the share of cannabis users in the population increases, support for cannabis legalization will also increase" (p. 1769). The United States has reached the tipping point and that cannabis is destined to become legal in some form in all 50 states. It is time for U.S. federal cannabis policy to catch up.

Synopsis of Current U.S. Policy

The U.S. Government criminalized cannabis with the Marijuana Tax Act of 1937 (Musto, 1972). Modern federal law codified cannabis as illegal in the Controlled Substances Act of 1970 (Sacco, 2014). Because of these acts, cannabis is classified as a Schedule 1 controlled substance in the same category as heroin (Clark, 2018).

From early colonization through 1936, cannabis was legal in the United States and considered to be a poor man's pain reliever (Ludlum et al., 2019). In fact, during the colonial period U.S. colonist farmers were required by law to grow hemp and could use it to pay taxes (Will III, 2004). According to Will III (2004), the last legal U.S. hemp crop was harvested in 1958. California, with its passing of the Compassionate Use Act of 1996, was the first state to approve use of cannabis as a medical product (Bridgeman & Abazia, 2017).

According to Kees, Fitzgerald, Dorsey, and Hill (2020), cannabis legalization policy in the United States lacks a clear framework. Currently, the cannabis policy debate predominantly focuses on the negative impacts of consumption (c.f. Arseneault, Cannon, Witten, & Murray, 2004; Brook, Balka, & Whiteman, 1999; Ellickson, Collins, & Bell, 1999; French, Roebuck, & Alexandre, 2001; Palali & van Ours, 2017). Fischer et al. (2017) operate from the perspective that the use of cannabis possesses substantial health risks and offer ten "concrete recommendations" on how to mitigate the potential negative health impacts of cannabis use. The authors grade their evidence for each of the ten recommendations in various degrees from limited to substantial. Of the ten recommendations, six are identified as having substantial evidence against consumption (early use, high THC products, inhalation, frequent use, driving, higher risk for adverse effects). The authors end with a call for the development of "public health tools to further population-oriented prevention goals" (Fischer et al., 2017, p. e7). van Ours and Williams (2015) contend that there are no serious harmful effects of moderate cannabis use except in cases of heavy users possessing existing mental health issues.

Policy issues are not limited to public health perspectives. Increasingly, employers in both medical and recreational cannabis states are confronted with the reality that their employees may be using a substance banned by the federal government. Truxillo, Cadiz, Bauer, and Erdogan (2012) point out important discrepancies in employment policy based on use of medical cannabis. They recommend different policies based on the safety sensitivity associated with the job: The higher the safety sensitivity, the stricter the policy. Until cannabis policy is harmonized across states by the federal government, employers are unsure of their rights and responsibilities concerning employee use of cannabis outside of working hours. Bridgeman and Abazia (2017) concur, indicating that until a national cannabis policy is enacted, the use of cannabis in treating medical conditions remains limited to states in which the use of cannabis is approved, with federal facilities (Department of Veterans Affairs) in those states as the exception.

Regardless of the lack of a unified national cannabis policy, cannabis businesses operate in a majority of U.S. states and territories. Similar to California, most of the state legalization initiatives are based on potential medical benefits of cannabis for addressing a myriad of conditions. Bridgeman and Abazia

(2017) provide a comparative summary of approved medical conditions by state. Given the lack of federally sponsored studies regarding the efficacy of cannabis in treating ailments, self-reported consumer benefits provide the foundation for the approval of medicinal and recreational cannabis on which state approvals are based. In a sense, cannabis is viewed as homeopathic medicine and the self-reported benefits of consumption proved justification for its use as a medical treatment. Thus, how well cannabis addresses the symptoms identified by its users is the proximate reason for state justification for legalization. These self-reported consumer benefits address outcomes associated with an improved quality of life: that is, cannabis consumption contributes the overall self-perceived well-being of the consumer.

Consumer Well-Being/Quality of Life

Arndt (1981) developed a conceptualization of quality of life based on both objective and subjective approaches. In short, the consumers act in a way that promotes satisfaction. Consumer well-being uses quality-of-life research as its foundation (Sirgy, 2001; Sirgy & Lee, 2003). Consumer well-being is defined as "bringing self-gratification and fulfillment through consumption avenues" (Manchandra, 2017, p. 2).

Well-being is a complex, multidimensional construct based on different theoretical foundations: hedonic well-being (orientation to pleasure), eudaimonic well-being (flourishing), and prudential well-being (subjective well-being) (Delle Fave, Brdar, Freire, Vella-Brodrick, & Wissing, 2011; Ganglmair-Wooliscroft & Wooliscroft, 2019). Pancer and Handleman (2012) provide a thorough historical treatise of the development of consumer well-being and propose the existence of a new approach, "transformative consumer research" focusing on the benefits of consumer welfare and quality of life.

Closely related to quality of life and consumer well-being is the concept of ethical consumerism. Bennett (2018) defines ethical consumerism as a "theory to describe, explain, and evaluate the ways in which producers and consumers use the market to support social and environmental values" p. 295. Ganglmair-Wooliscroft and Wooliscroft (2019) tie the two research streams together by focusing on the commonality of quality-of-life research. Consumers are posited to act in a way that supports their subjective well-being through the purchase of products or services deemed by the consumer as ethical. Subjective well-being, quality of life, and ethical consumerism represent major advances in understanding consumer well-being (Pancer & Handleman, 2012; Sirgy, 2008).

Focusing on consumer self-reported quality of life provides the foundation for this research. Specifically, Sirgy, Lee, and Kressman's (2006) need satisfaction model offers the largest overlap with self-reported benefits from consuming medical cannabis. Consumers have unmet perceived needs and use cannabis to enhance their sense of well-being. Legitimately, one can question the actual efficacy of cannabis as a treatment, but until federal policy provides a venue for examining the impacts, both positive and negative, of using cannabis as a treatment, consumer reported outcomes remain the only basis on which efficacy can be judged. Finally, the use of cannabis as medicine is not a new concept. Throughout history, civilizations have identified and used homeopathic medicines as treatments for medical conditions.

The History of Cannabis as Medicine

Ludlum et al. (2019) confirm that cannabis has been used by humans for more than five millennia. Pisanti and Bifulco (2019) document the use of cannabis as an herbal medicine in China and Japan over 4,000 years ago. In Traditional Chinese Medicine (TCM) cannabis is useful in treating rheumatic pain, constipation, and malaria among other things (Pisanti & Bifulco, 2019). In Japanese Traditional Medicine, cannabis is considered to be a mild laxative and useful for asthma, and in India, the use of cannabis in religious and ritual practices began in 1000 BCE (Pisanti & Bifulco, 2019). In Ayurvedic medicine, cannabis is used as relief from cough, asthma, headache, mania, and insomnia (Knorzer, 2000). Furthermore, cannabis was used by both the Scythians and Egyptian (Pisanti & Bifulco, 2019).

There are no known recorded fatal overdoses attributed to cannabis use in history (Ludlum et al., 2019). Boehnke, Gangopadhyay, Clauw, and Haffjee (2019b) document the most widely cited medical conditions for those who obtain medical cannabis cards in the United States: Chronic pain is the most cited medical condition. The authors further document evidence of efficacy of cannabis for addressing conditions. They cross-referenced state-reported data with the 2017 National Academies of Sciences, Engineering, and Medicine report to classify self-reported efficacy by state-approved medical condition. According to Boehnke et al. (2019b), cannabis shows limited efficacy in addressing anxiety, PTSD, HIV/AIDS, Tourette syndrome, and traumatic brain injury. Substantial evidence of efficacy exists for multiple sclerosis and chronic pain. Finally, conclusive efficacy exists for addressing chemotherapy-induced nausea and vomiting. In addition to chronic pain, cannabis is reported to provide benefits for those afflicted with depression and insomnia (Bhattacharyya, Atakan, Martin-Santos, Crippa, & McGuire, 2012; Chagas et al., 2014; Hill et al., 2009; Kees et al., 2020; Russo, 2008). Furthermore, cannabis has been shown to reduce the number of prescriptions for opioids (Bradford, Bradford, Abraham, & Adams, 2018; Kees et al., 2020).

Solomon and Solomon (2019) criticize Boehnke et al.'s (2019b) research indicating the positive effect of cannabis on chronic pain for focusing on neuropathic pain and not musculoskeletal pain. Their biggest concern is that extant studies do not control for cannabis potency, dose, and application. Boehnke, Clauw, and Haffjee (2019a) in their rebuttal agree and indicate that the aforementioned limitations point to the need for more research. However, for 85.5% of conditions listed for certification of use of medical cannabis, consumers indicate that cannabis provides either substantial or conclusive evidence of efficacy (Boehnke et al., 2019b).

METHODOLOGY

In summer of 2018 the authors launched one of the first national research panels of U.S. cannabis consumers, consisting of 1,050 respondents recruited via Qualtrics from U.S. medical and recreational cannabis states. Of the national sample, 54 respondents resided in Massachusetts. In addition, Massachusetts medical cannabis patients were able to participate in the study by scanning a QR code displayed in multiple medical cannabis dispensaries in the state. Scanning the QR code took respondents to the same version of the national Qualtrics questionnaire but using the SurveyMonkey platform. This convenience sample resulted in 966 responses. Therefore, respondents consist of national panelists from Massachusetts plus a convenience sample of medical patients.

The survey consists of 67 questions including four for screening respondents affirming consent to participate, cannabis use, legal age for consumption, and location. Data was collected between May and August 2018. Since the goal of the research is exploratory, and with the absence of a census of cannabis users, the use of the panel plus convenience sample is appropriate. Only summary statistics are reported.

The goal of the project is to determine consumer reported benefits of cannabis use on their quality of life. Consumer well-being provides the framework for interpreting the results. Additional data collected includes purchase preferences (forms of cannabis), cannabis advertising, importance of recommendations of dispensary personnel, and favorite strains of cannabis. Only the data regarding self-reported consumer benefits from cannabis consumption are included in this chapter.

RESULTS

A total of 1,020 Massachusetts cannabis users (54 via Qualtrics and 966 via dispensaries) responded to the survey. On average, each respondent spends $80 per week on cannabis with 77% of their total purchases coming from legal, regulated sources (defined as state-approved cannabis businesses). This translates to each consumer spending $4,160 annually on cannabis with $3.203.20 spent at the dispensaries and $956.80 spent via illegal transactions. Extended to all participants, respondents generated $3,267,264 in annual sales via legal market and $975,936 annually in illicit sales. Bennett (2018) specifically addressing the Oregon cannabis market defines it as a semi-legal market because it consists of both legal and illegal distribution. This study confirms Bennett's premise and finds that the illicit market continues to exist in Massachusetts.

Respondents were asked to indicate under what circumstances they use cannabis by checking all of the options that applied. Those using cannabis for medicinal purposes, either with a medical card (top response) or self-medicating (third largest response), dominated the responses. Recreational consumers accounted for the second largest category of respondents overall.

When asked to select the primary condition for which they consume cannabis, the top five responses are for chronic pain (consistent with previous research), depression, anxiety, other, and insomnia. Fibromyalgia was the most noted "other" condition as identified by write-in responses. Interestingly, the condition for which cannabis was identified as having the highest efficacy by Boehnke et al. (2019b), to treat nausea and vomiting, was selected by 13 respondents. But are consumers substituting cannabis for their prescriptions of opioids, narcotics, antidepressants, anxiolytics, or muscle relaxants? The answer to this question is presented in the ensuing discussion (figure 7.6).

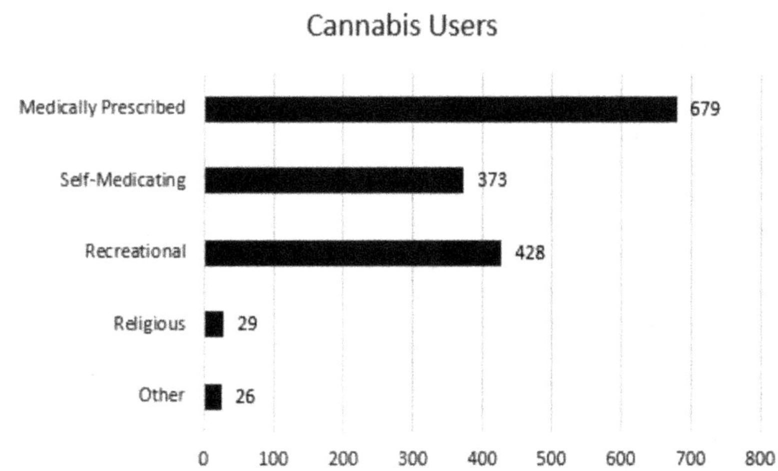

Figure 7.1 Cannabis Users. *Source: White, D. S., Curran, C. M., Bacdayan, P., & McNabb, M. (2018).*

Primary Condition

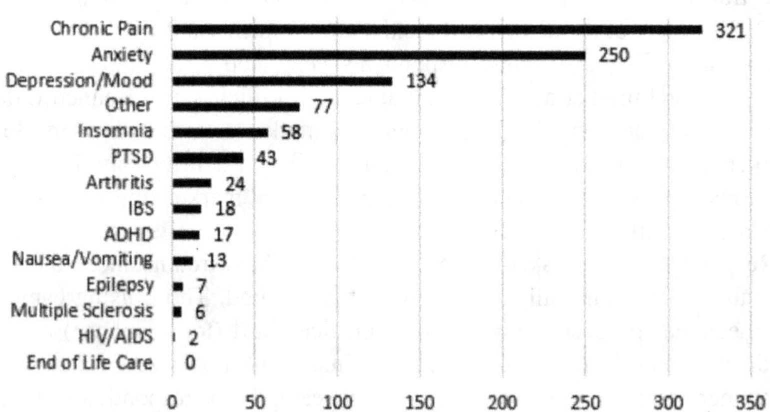

Figure 7.2 Primary Condition. *Source: White, D. S., Curran, C. M., Bacdayan, P., & McNabb, M. (2018).*

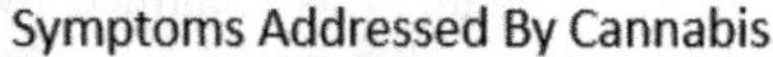

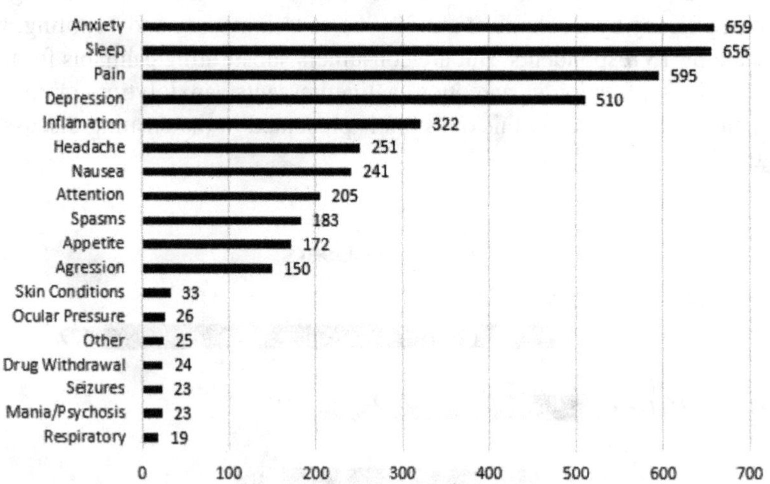

Figure 7.3 Symptoms Addressed by Cannabis. *Source: White, D. S., Curran, C. M., Bacdayan, P., and McNabb, M. (2018).*

When queried to identify which symptoms related to the primary condition for which cannabis is used, respondents identified anxiety, sleep, pain, depression, and inflammation as the top five (figure 7.3). Figure 7.4 presents the self-reported perceived impact that cannabis use has on the daily life of consumers. Consistent with the premise of consumer well-being, respondents

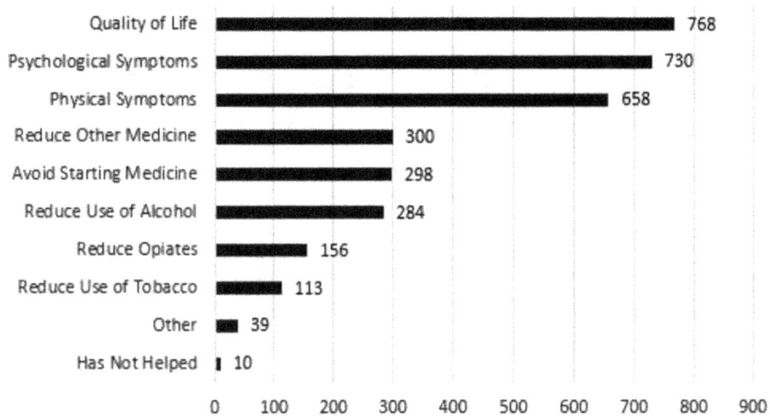

Figure 7.4 How Has Cannabis Helped Your Daily Life? *Source: White, D. S., Curran, C. M., Bacdayan, P., and McNabb, M. (2018).*

affirm that cannabis has provided a positive impact on overall quality of life. Other self-reported benefits include cannabis helping with psychological symptoms, physical symptoms, use of medicine including opioids, alcohol, and tobacco. That cannabis is used to reduce reliance on alcohol and tobacco is one of the more interesting self-reported benefits.

Asked specifically how cannabis use has impacted quality of life, respondents overwhelmingly report positive impact (figure 7.5) with 66.8% of respondents selecting Highly Positively Impacted. Those reporting a positive impact account for 14.74% of respondents. The category Moderately Positive Impact is selected by 12.16% of respondents. Overall, 96.186% of respondents reported some self-perceived positive benefit from cannabis consumption for the treatment of conditions. Only 3.8% of respondents report a negative (31 respondents) or no impact (6 respondents) on quality of life.

When asked to identify what type of prescriptions the cannabis users are trying to reduce, respondents who are trying to reduce the use of medicine identify reducing the use of antidepressants, NSAIDs, narcotics/opioids, muscle relaxants, and anxiolytics as the top five. The inclusion of opioids as one of the top responses in figure 7.6 is consistent with previous research. So to answer the question that was posed earlier, the answer is yes: cannabis consumers are substituting cannabis for reliance on the use of prescription drugs.

Respondent demographics are presented in figures 7.7 through 7.14. The majority of respondents are between the ages of 30–39, female, have a household income of over $150,000 per year, have earned a bachelor's degree, are married, employed full-time, are heterosexual, and white. This may be an

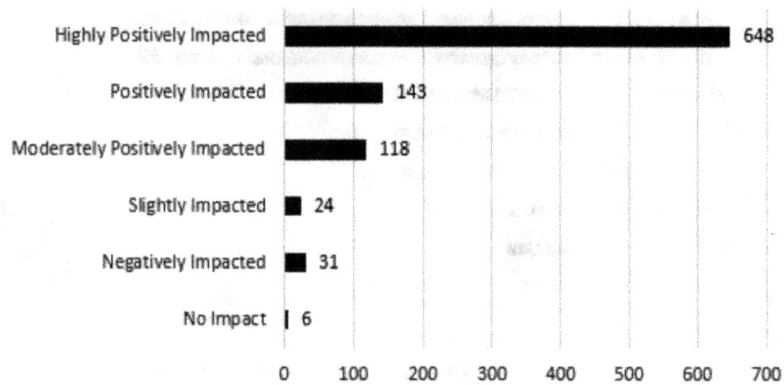

Figure 7.5 To What Extent Has Cannabis Use Impacted Your Quality of Life? *Source: White, D. S., Curran, C. M., Bacdayan, P., and McNabb, M. (2018).*

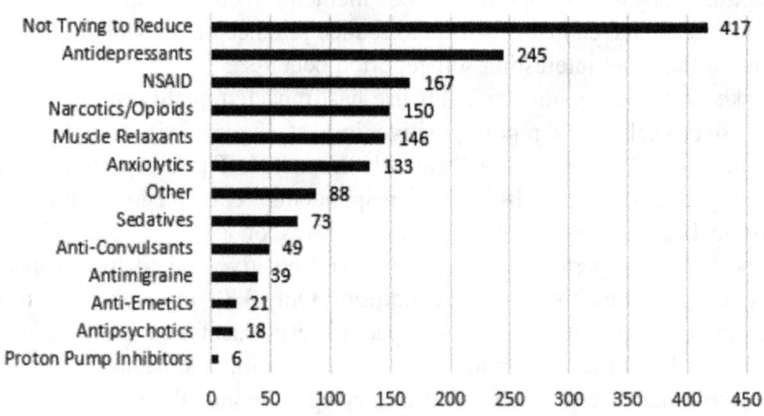

Figure 7.6 Actively Trying to Reduce Prescription Medicine Using Cannabis. *Source: White, D. S., Curran, C. M., Bacdayan, P., and McNabb, M. (2018).*

atypical cannabis consumer profile given the general demographics of the population of Massachusetts.

As indicated earlier, respondents were asked to provide the amount spent per week on cannabis and the percent of purchases from legal regulated sources. Interesting contrasts are highlighted in table 7.2. Respondents who indicate that they use cannabis for reasons other than medical, recreational,

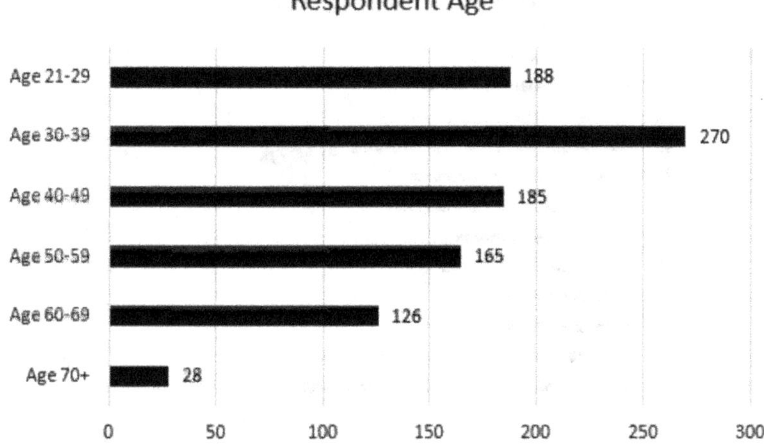

Figure 7.7 Respondent Age. *Source: White, D. S., Curran, C. M., Bacdayan, P., and McNabb, M. (2018).*

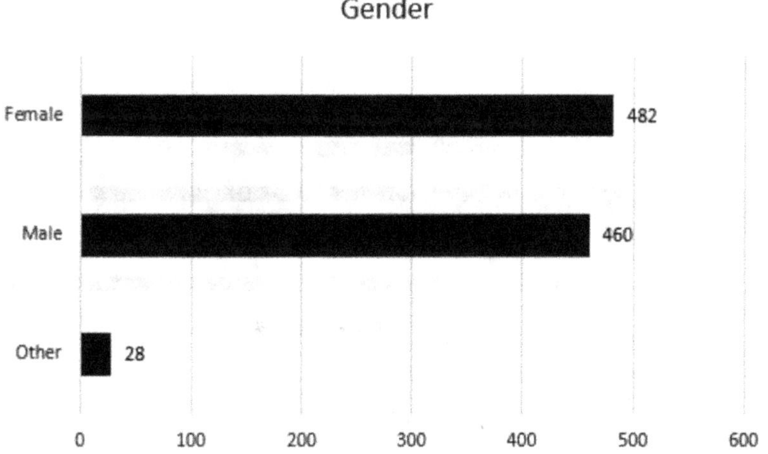

Figure 7.8 Gender. *Source: White, D. S., Curran, C. M., Bacdayan, P., and McNabb, M. (2018).*

or religious spend $117.54 per week on cannabis, or $6,112 per year. Those respondents who indicate no impact on quality of life from cannabis use purchase the least amount of cannabis from legal, regulated sources (42%). Average spending per week ranges from $27.14 (Epilepsy) to $117.54 (Other Reason for Use). Average legal purchase percent ranges from 42% (No Impact on Quality of Life) to 100% (Epilepsy).

Contrary to previous research indicating that males consume significantly more cannabis than do females (Fergusson, Boden, & Horwood, 2008;

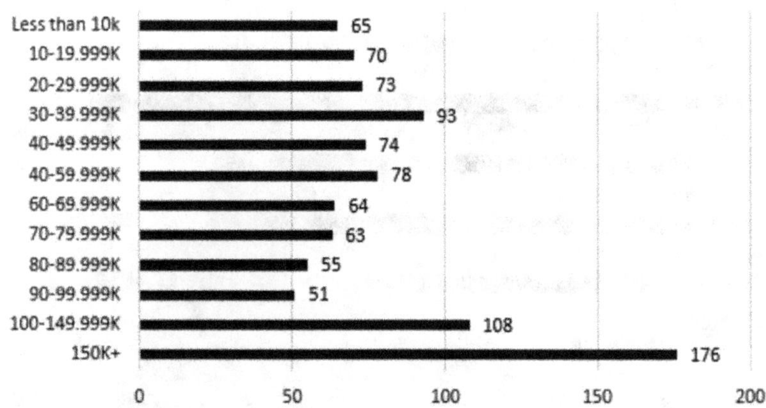

Figure 7.9 Household Income (U.S. Dollars). *Source: White, D. S., Curran, C. M., Bacdayan, P., and McNabb, M. (2018).*

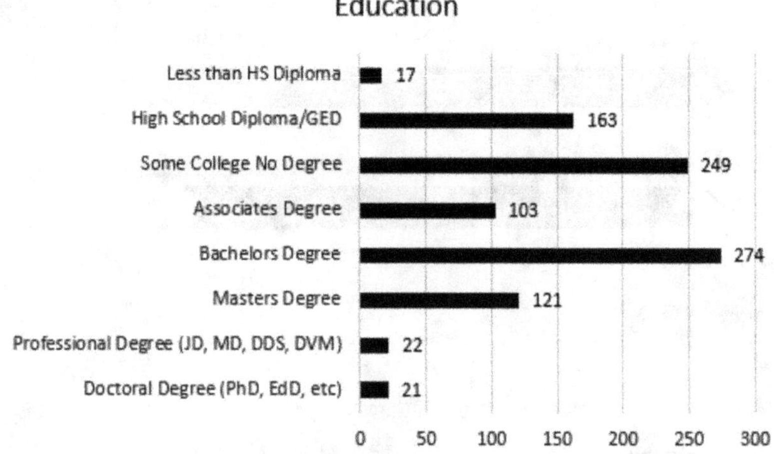

Figure 7.10 Education. *Source: White, D. S., Curran, C. M., Bacdayan, P., and McNabb, M. (2018).*

Tartaglia, Miglietta, & Gattino, 2017), the majority of respondents for this survey are females although males do spend more per week on average. One possible reason for this is that research by Smith (2008) contends that females are more favorably predisposed to participating in surveys than are males. Regardless, males spend an average of $84.95 per week on cannabis while females spend $76.44 per week on average. Both utilize legal cannabis

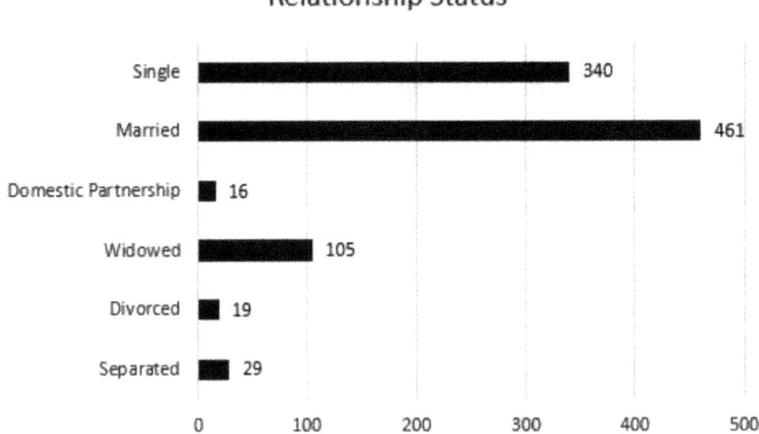

Figure 7.11 Relationship Status. *Source: White, D. S., Curran, C. M., Bacdayan, P., and McNabb, M. (2018).*

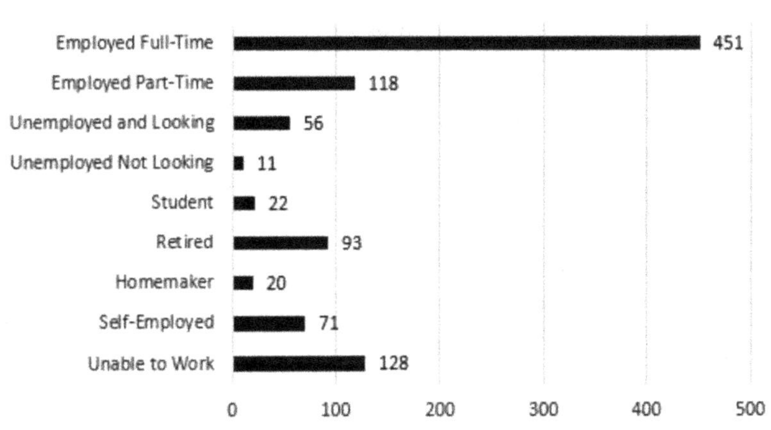

Figure 7.12 Employment Status. *Source: White, D. S., Curran, C. M., Bacdayan, P., and McNabb, M. (2018).*

sources in similar proportions with approximately 24% of total purchases coming from outside of state-approved retailers.

Overall, the results indicate support for using self-reported well-being and quality of life for analysis of cannabis consumers. A majority of respondents (96.186% as presented in figure 7.5) indicate that cannabis has highly positively impacted their quality of life. In addition, the results support the use of cannabis to address chronic pain, among other conditions, and to reduce

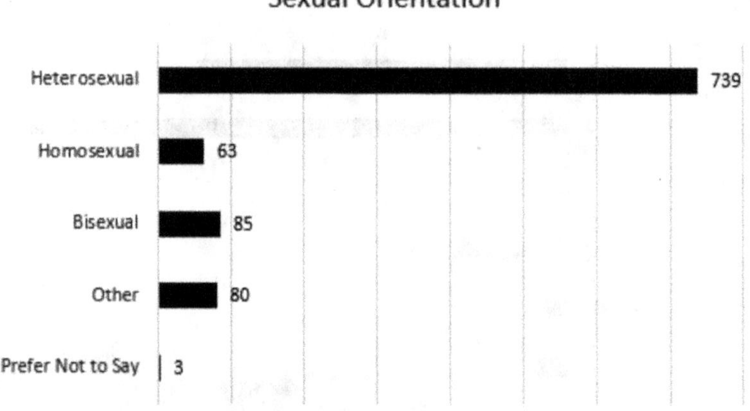

Figure 7.13 Sexual Orientation. *Source: White, D. S., Curran, C. M., Bacdayan, P., and McNabb, M. (2018).*

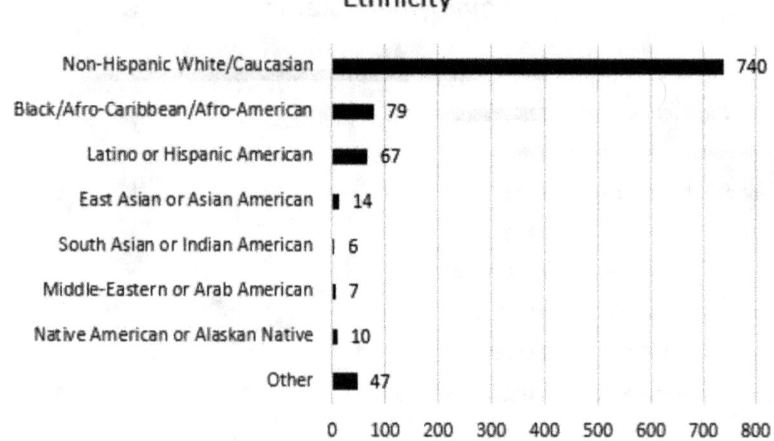

Figure 7.14 Ethnicity. *Source: White, D. S., Curran, C. M., Bacdayan, P., and McNabb, M. (2018).*

reliance on other medications. As highlighted by Solomon and Solomon (2019), dose and application should be investigated through formal research processes.

Policy Needs

With all but five states having some type of medical or recreational cannabis use, the absence of federal policy on legal cannabis use remains an outlier

Table 7.2 Average Spending and Legal Purchases by Response

	n	*Average $ Per Week*	*Average Percent Legal Purchase*
Medical Prescribed	678	85.75	87.67
Self-Medicated	369	79.44	71.7
Recreational	425	73.76	66.24
Religious	29	111.97	80.45
Other Reason for Use	26	117.54	75.31
Chronic Pain	318	86.67	80.29
Anxiety	249	86.82	76.17
Depression/Mood	133	70.41	73.58
Other Conditions	76	75.55	62.5
Insomnia	58	53.52	77.72
PTSD	43	81.4	78.19
Arthritis	24	75	87.62
IBS	18	82.5	67.06
ADHD	17	73.24	77.59
Nausea/Vomiting	13	91.15	77.54
Epilepsy	7	27.14	100
Multiple Sclerosis	6	98.33	67.17
HIV/AIDS	2	75	50
Reducing Narcotics	150	107.2	77.19
Reducing Anxiolytics	132	100.05	78.17
Reducing NSAIDS	166	82	77.96
Reducing Sedatives	73	98	82.21
Reducing Muscle Relaxants	142	101.53	78.35
Reducing Anti-Emetics	21	106.33	84.76
Reducing Anti-Convulsants	49	105.16	79.73
Reducing Antimigraine	39	123.08	73.36
Reducing Antipsychotics	18	68.33	76.94
Reducing Proton Pump Inhibitors	4	63.75	77.5
Reducing Other Medicines	88	101.98	78.27
Highly Positively Impacted	648	88.98	81.26
Positively Impacted	142	65.56	73.08
Moderately Positively Impacted	117	54.05	72.23
Slightly Impacted	23	49.61	32.87
Negatively Impacted	28	99.11	43.67
No Impact on Quality of Life	6	55	42
Not Reducing Medicines	401	70.46	72.9
Female	477	76.44	76.57
Male	459	84.95	76.04
Other Gender	28	74.39	82.89
Heterosexual	735	82.42	76.77
Other Sexual Orientation	229	74.06	75.63

Source: White, D.S., Curran, C.M., Bacdayan, P. and McNabb, M. (2018).

(Ludlum et al., 2019). Current U.S. cannabis policy has shortcomings from a public health perspective (Barry & Glantz, 2018). Current policy is based on a "private-for-profit" model instead of public health. Opponents of legal cannabis claim that any form of use is illegal due to the federal Controlled Substance Act (Ermasova, 2020). Until the lack of an industry-friendly U.S. federal policy is addressed, the cannabis industry cannot move forward on a national scale.

Kees et al. (2020) lays out the framework for the development of a national cannabis policy. Three important policy considerations for guiding a national policy include: reducing consumption among risky communities, optimizing regulation of cannabis marketing activities, and proactively educating consumers. These national policies exist for both alcohol and tobacco and may serve as a starting point for the development of a national policy for cannabis. To guide the development of a federal cannabis policy, Clark (2018) calls for the use of a normative regulatory framework and normative public policy to be built around the potential public health impacts of legalized cannabis. A normative regulatory framework is one that provides for choice (Pistor & Cafaggi, 2013) and acts as a model for examining trade-offs. In this context, it means that both the framework and policy developed should provide a broad range of alternative courses of action based on potential public health impacts.

In addition, from a business perspective, clarity is needed for owners of cannabis enterprises. Taylor, Bunker, Johnson, and Rodriguez (2016) document the difficulty that cannabis businesses face in walking the line between a federally illegal business activity and one sanctioned by the states. The pressure on cannabis operators is immense. Cannabis businesses cannot file for bankruptcy. The application of Section 280E to legal cannabis businesses prevents them from deducting business expenses from gross income albeit these businesses can deduct cost of goods sold using inventory costing methods. Banking and financial institutions are penalized for accepting cannabis businesses as clients. The tax burden placed on cannabis businesses is extreme. The disparate state policies, as conceived and enacted, continue to provide more benefit to illegal operators in the cannabis industry than to legal operators.

SUMMARY/CONCLUSION

In terms of medical and recreational cannabis use in the United States, it is clearly too late to attempt to return to prohibition. As the industry nationalizes, cohesive federal policies are needed. More research should be conducted on the impact of the different components of cannabis on medical conditions, on safe use, and on acceptable business practices. Items for research consideration include efficacy, safe dosing, and potential negative consequences. Once legal cannabis federal policies are established, the United States will be able to compete in the growing global cannabis market.

REFERENCES

Arndt, J. (1981). Marketing and the quality of life. *Journal of Economic Psychology, 1*(4), 283–301.

Arseneault, L., Cannon, M., Witton, J., & Murray, R. M. (2004). Causal association between cannabis and psychosis: Examination of the evidence. *British Journal of Psychiatry, 184*(2), 110–17.

Barry, R. A., & Glantz, S. A. (2018). Marijuana regulatory frameworks in four U.S. states: An analysis against a public health standard. *American Journal of Public Health, 108*(7), 914–23.

Bennett, E. (2018). Extending ethical consumerism theory to semi-legal sectors: Insights from recreational cannabis. *Agriculture and Human Values, 35*(2), 295–317.

Bhattacharyya, S., Atakan, Z., Martin-Santos, R., Crippa, J. A., & McGuire, P. K. (2012). Neural mechanisms for the cannabinoid modulation of cognition and affect in man: A critical review of neuroimaging studies. *Current Pharmaceutical Design, 18*(32), 5045–54.

Boehnke, K. F., Clauw, D. J., & Haffajee, R. L. (2019a). Editorial: Medical cannabis and chronic pain: The authors reply. *Health Affairs, 38*(4), 694.

Boehnke, K. F., Gangopadhyay, S., Clauw, D. J., & Haffajee, R. L. (2019b). Qualifying conditions of medical cannabis license holders in the United States. *Health Affairs, 38*(2), 295–302.

Bradford, A. C., Bradford, W. D., Abraham, A., & Adams, G. B. (2018). Association between U.S. state medical cannabis laws and opioid prescribing in the Medicare Part D population. *JAMA Internal Medicine, 178*(5), 667–72.

Bridgeman, M. B., & Abazia, D. T. (2017). Medical cannabis: History, pharmacology, and implications for the acute care setting. *Pharmacy and Therapeutics, 42*(3), 180–88.

Brook, J. S., Balka , E. B., & Whiteman, M. (1999). The risks for late adolescence of early adolescent marijuana use. *American Journal of Public Health, 89*(10), 1549–54.

Chagas, M. H. N, Eckeli, A. L., Zuardi, A. W., Pena-Pereira, M. A., Sobreira-Neto, Sobreira, E. T., Camilo, M. R., Bergamaschi, M. M., Schenck, C. H., Hallak, J. E. C., Tumas, V., & Crippa, J. A. S. (2014). Cannabidiol can improve complex sleep-related behaviours associated with rapid eye movement sleep behaviour disorder in Parkinson's Disease patients: A case series. *Journal of Clinical Pharmacy and Therapeutics, 39*(5), 564–66.

Clark, H. W. (2018). Editorial: Marijuana initiatives versus legislation and public health, *American Journal of Public Health, 8*(7), 854–56.

Delle Fave, A., Brdar, I., Freire, T., Vella-Brodrick, D., & Wissing, M. P. (2011). The eudaimonic and hedonic components of happiness: Qualitative and quantitative findings. *Social Indicators Research*, *100*(2), 185–207.

Ellickson, P. L., Collins, R. L., & Bell, R. M. (1999). Adolescent use of illicit drugs other than marijuana: How important is social bonding and for which ethnic groups? *Substance Use and Misuse*, *34*(3), 317–46.

Ermasova, N. (2020). Fiscal and health effects of U.S. marijuana legislation at the state level. *Journal of Social, Political, and Economic Studies*, *45*(1–2), 151–77.

Fergusson, D. M., Boden, J. M., & Horwood, L. J. (2008). The developmental antecedents of illicit drug use: Evidence from a 25-year longitudinal study. *Drug and Alcohol Dependence*, *96*(1), 165–77.

Fischer, B., Russell, C., Sabioni, P., van den Brink, W., Le Foll, B., Hall, W., Rehm, J., & Room, R. (2017). Lower-risk cannabis use guidelines: A comprehensive update of evidence and recommendations. *American Journal of Public Health*, *107*(8), e1–e12.

French, M. T., Roebuck, M. C., & Alexandre, P. K. (2001). Illicit drug use, employment, and labor force participation. *Southern Economic Journal*, *68*(2), 349–68.

Ganglmair-Wooliscroft, A., & Wooliscroft, B. (2019). Well-being and everyday ethical consumption. *Journal of Happiness Studies*, *20*(1), 141–63.

Grossman, J.C., Goldstein, R., & Eisenman, R. (1974). Undergraduate marijuana and drug use as related to openness to experience. *Psychiatric Quarterly*, *48*(1), 86–92.

Hill, M. N., Hillard, C. J., Bambico, F. R., Patel, S., Gorzalka, B. B., & Gobbi, G. (2009). The therapeutic potential of the endocannabinoid system for the development of a novel class of antidepressants. *Trends in Pharmacological Sciences*, *30*(9), 484–493.

Kees, J., Fitzgerald, P., Dorsey, J. D., & Hill, R. P. (2020). Evidence-based cannabis policy: A framework to guide marketing and public policy research. *Journal of Public Policy and Marketing*, *39*(1), 76–92.

Knorzer, K-H. (2000). 3000 years of agriculture in a valley of the high Himalayas. *Vegetation History and Archaeobotany*, *9*(4), 219–22.

Ludlum, M., Ford, D., & Barger-Johnson, J. (2019). The year in pot: 2018. *Southern Journal of Business and Ethics*, *11*, 96–109.

Manchanda, R. (2017). Consumer well-being: Contemporary conceptualization, *Indian Journal of Economics and Development*, *5*(1), 1–4.

Marijuana Business Daily (2021). Marijuana business factbook projects nearly $45 billion market by 2025. Retrieved from: https://mjbizdaily.com/new-marijuana-business-factbook-projects-nearly-45-billion-us-market-by-2025/

Musto, D. F. (1972). The marihuana tax act of 1937. *Archives of General Psychiatry*, *26*(2), 101–8.

National Academies of Sciences, Engineering, and Medicine (2017). *The Health Effects of Cannabis and Cannabinoids: The Current State of Evidence and Recommendations for Research*. Washington, DC: National Academies Press.

Palali, A., & van Ours, J. C. (2017). Cannabis use and support for cannabis legalization. *Empirical Economics*, *53*, 1747–70.

Pancer, E., & Handelman, J. (2012). The evolution of consumer well-being. *Journal of Historical Research in Marketing*, *4*(1), 177–89.

Pisanti, S., & Bifulco, M. (2019). Medical cannabis: A plurimillennial history of an evergreen. *Journal of Cellular Physiology*, *234*(6), 8342–51.

Pistor, K., & Cafaggi, F. (2013). Regulatory Capabilities: A Normative Framework for Assessing the Distributional Effects of Regulation. Columbia Law School Public Law & Legal Theory working paper no. 13-354. Retrieved from: https://scholarship.law.columbia.edu/faculty_scholarship/2281

Russo, E. B. (2008). Cannabinoids in the management of difficult to treat pain. *Journal of Therapeutics and Clinical Risk Management*, *4*(1), 245–59.

Sacco, L. N. (2014). Drug enforcement in the United States: History, policy, and trends. *Congressional Research Service, 7-5700, October 2*, Retrieved from: https://fas.org/sgp/crs/misc/R43749.pdf

Sirgy, M. J. (2001). *Handbook of Quality-of-Life Research: An Ethical Marketing Perspective*. Social Indicators Research Series, Volume 8, Dordrecht, Netherlands: Kluwer Academic Publishers.

Sirgy, M. J. (2008). Ethics and public policy implications of research on consumer well-being. *Journal of Public Policy and Marketing*, *27*(2), 207–12.

Sirgy, M. J., & Lee, D-J. (2003). Developing a measure of consumer well being in relation to personal transportation. *Yonsei Business Review*, *40*(Spring), 73–101.

Sirgy, M. J., Lee, D-J., & Kressman, F. (2006). A need-based measure of consumer well being (CWB) in relation to personal transportation: A nomological validation. *Social Indicators Research*, *79*(2), 337–67.

Smith, W. G. (2008). Does gender influence online survey participation? A record-linkage analysis of university faculty online survey response behavior. Retrieved from: https://files.eric.ed.gov/fulltext/ED501717.pdf

Solomon, G. D., & Solomon, C. S. (2019). Editorial: Medical cannabis and chronic pain. *Health Affairs*, *38*(4), 694.

Tartaglia, S., Miglietta, A., & Gattino, S. (2017). Life satisfaction and cannabis use: A study on young adults. *Journal of Happiness Studies*, *18*(3), 709–18.

Taylor, K., Bunker, R. B., Johnson, L. R., & Rodriguez, R. (2016). An analysis of the accounting and financial effects of inconsistent state and federal laws in the recreational marijuana industry. *Journal of Legal, Ethical and Regulatory Issues*, *19*(2), 11–25.

Truxillo, D. M., Cadiz, D. M., Bauer, T. N., & Erdogan, B. (2012). Reactions to employer policies regarding prescription drugs and medical marijuana: The role of safety sensitivity. *Journal of Business and Psychology*, *28*(2), 145–58.

van Ours, J. C., & Williams, J. (2015). Cannabis use and its effects on health, education and labor market success. *Journal of Economic Surveys*, *29*(5), 993–1010.

White, D. S., Curran, C. M., Bacdayan, P., & McNabb, M. (2018). *Consumer Study of Cannabis in Legal Recreational and Medical States*. Unpublished raw data.

Will III, O. H. (2004). The forgotten history of hemp cultivation in America. *Farm Collector*, Retrieved from: https://www.farmcollector.com/farm-life/strategic-fibers/

Chapter 8

Exaggerated Panic or Valid Concerns? Post-Legalization Youth Drug Use

Renee Scherlen and José Antonio Cisneros-Tirado

INTRODUCTION

"What about the children?!?" This is a common refrain encountered in the history of marijuana legalization (Dufton, 2017). While many are familiar with the use of scare tactics to shape public debate, the emphasis on dangers to youth may not be as clear. However, the threat posed to children by legalization has been central in the discussion surrounding cannabis legislation. This chapter evaluates the concerns expressed about the impact of legalization of recreational use of marijuana on youth drug use. What does the evidence suggest regarding the claim that following marijuana legalization "adolescent cannabis use may increase substantially" (Dineen Wagner, 2019, 4).

In 2015, the Pew Research Center conducted a series of studies on public opinion regarding marijuana legalization (Pew Research Center, 2015). The organization found that 43% of opponents of legalization view marijuana as a dangerous drug that inflicts damage on people and society. A further 8% of those surveyed mentioned that marijuana was particularly harmful to young people. Research on news coverage of the marijuana legalization debate reveals the critical role that health concerns play in reporting. Analysis of reporting shows that arguments against legalization focused on adverse public health consequences, such as detriments to youth health and well-being (E. E. McGinty et al., 2016).

Medical research on the harms of marijuana has paid particular attention to youth drug use (Hadland & Harris, 2014; Dougherty et al., 2013; Skalski et al., 2018). Identification and discussion of short- and long-term negative health effects on minors have been explored by the National Institute for Drug Abuse, the Food and Drug Administration, and the Drug Enforcement Administration (Larkin, 2018). Most of the public health issues connected to recreational marijuana use relates to "its effects on youth health and educational attainment, cannabis use disorder, and marijuana-impaired driving" (E. E. McGinty et al., 2016). The American Academy of Pediatrics "opposes legalization of marijuana because of the potential harms to children and adolescents" while at the same time is "supports studying the effects of recent laws legalizing the use of marijuana to better understand the impact . . . (on) adolescent marijuana use" (Committee on Substance Abuse, Committee on Adolescence Pediatrics, 2015). This chapter seeks to do this.

Can we determine whether or not the fears associated with marijuana legalization were overstated or well-founded? Federalism in the United States provides us with a quasi-experimental situation. Some states have legalized marijuana while others have not. Many macro-level factors are the same for states regardless of their legalization status; this minimizes some of the external threats to validity. Because of federalism, it is possible to compare youth drug use pre- and post-legalization with youth drug use from the same time period in non-legalized states as well as the national average.

How can youth drug use in the United States be determined? Researchers, policy-makers, and politicians have relied upon The National Survey on Drug Use and Health (NSDUH) since 1971 (under various names). The National Survey is sponsored by the Substance Abuse and Mental Health Services Administration (SAMHSA), an agency in the U.S. Department of Health and Human Services (HHS). The survey itself has been conducted by RTI International, a nonprofit research organization based in Research Triangle Park, North Carolina since 1988. For our purposes, a recently published report comparing drug use data from 2008–2009 to 2018–2019 is especially useful. There is information for every state for years (2008–2009) prior to legalization anywhere as well as data post-legalization for some states (2018–2019).

In-depth analysis of pre- and post-legalization data indicates that marijuana legalization has not increased youth drug use. Below is the evidence and analysis that leads to this conclusion. Since youth drug use has been and continues to be a key concern for the public and policy-makers, these findings should be comforting for both supporters and opponents of marijuana legalization.

FRAMING THE DEBATE OVER LEGALIZATION

How do people decide whether or not to support marijuana legalization? Prospect theory, which models decision-making under conditions of uncertainty, can provide insight into this process (Edwards, 1996). Of particular relevance is the emphasis that prospect theory places on how context and framing influence decision-making. Kahneman and Tversky (1979) developed the theory as an alternative economic model for which Kahneman was awarded 2002 Nobel Prize in Economics (Tversky was deceased by that time). Subsequently, the insights have been applied beyond economics into politics and international relations (Jervis, 2004).

In the context of marijuana legalization arguments, the most critical components of prospect theory are framing, domain, risk aversion, and loss aversion. Tversky and Kahneman argue that decision-making differs depending upon how the problem is framed. The framing of an issue creates the context in which the decision is viewed and affects the preferred choice depending upon the "domain" that emerges from the framing. Kahneman and Tversky suggest that there are two possible domains: loss and gain. A loss domain is one in which the person sees the issue as a problem or a policy as unsuccessful. In contrast, in a gain domain, people do not consider the issue as problematic or a policy as a complete failure. The importance of a domain relates to its impact on risk acceptance. All decisions made under conditions of uncertainty involve a degree of risk. In terms of policy choice, retaining the status quo can be considered less risky than adopting a new policy. Prospect theory research reveals that a person's degree of risk aversion/acceptance differs depending upon the domain in which they find themselves. Under conditions of loss, people are more risk accepting. In contrast, under conditions of gain, the same people are more risk-averse (Kahneman & Tversky, 1979; Tversky & Kahneman, 1992).

Application of prospect theory to the debates over the legalization of marijuana offers insights into the utility and persuasiveness of differing arguments. As noted above, if people perceive themselves to be in a condition of loss, they are more open to risk and change. If an existing public policy can be successfully portrayed as a failure, this places the decision-making into the loss domain. Since the loss domain is associated with risk acceptance and increases the possibility that people will be open to changing the status quo. In contrast, a policy that is framed as successful (even mildly so) places the discussion into a gain domain; this is associated with risk aversion and thereby decreases the likelihood of openness to policy change. When exploring the arguments used in favor of or against marijuana legalization, it is not surprising that the issue is framed from two very different domains.

Proponents of marijuana legalization frame current marijuana policy as failed, thus placing decision-making in the loss domain. For those who seek to legalize marijuana, the current policy has resulted in an overburdened criminal justice system that suffers from reduced legitimacy. Furthermore, the racist origins of marijuana criminalization linger with the continuing racial disparities of drug sentencing. For these people, marijuana criminalization is a failed policy, one where the harms of the policy far outweigh the harms of using marijuana (Todd, 2018). They hope to convince voters to see the policy from this same loss perspective; as argued by prospect theory, those in a loss domain are more risk accepting. This translates into a greater willingness to change marijuana laws. The framing of legalization within the loss domain can be seen in the persuasion offered by proponents of legalizing marijuana. *The Columbian* editorial staff stated boldly:

> Prohibition of marijuana has failed as miserably as the prohibition of alcohol did back in the 1920s. It's time to recognize the obvious: The longer we fight the war against marijuana, the greater grows the defeat. (*Columbian*, 2012)

Another op-ed article from Colorado intended to persuade voters to favor marijuana legalization also explicitly frames marijuana policy as a failure. In addition, it specifically noted opponents' concerns about legalization and youth drug use.

> Marijuana prohibition has failed at all of its stated goals and young people should not be used as a smokescreen to continue these failed policies. (McAllister, 2012)

The campaign to overturn existing policy and legalize recreational marijuana frames the debate around the idea of current policy failure. By doing this, proponents of legalization place the voters' decision-making within the loss domain. Prospect theory research argues that this can be a successful campaign strategy. If proponents persuade voters that the existing policy is a failure, this increases the willingness of people to take risks and vote for policy change.

In contrast, opponents of legalization tend to emphasize the dangers associated with marijuana legalization, especially to the young. These arguments frame current policy as successfully protecting against youth drug use. By arguing that current policy is successful, the discussion about marijuana legalization is placed into a gain domain. According to prospect theory, people in a gain domain are more risk-averse. People who are in a gain domain would therefore be more reluctant to change policy by legalizing marijuana. It is not surprising that such concerns and aversion to change have typically been echoed in the comments voiced by opponents to marijuana legalization over the years. In an op-ed article in Colorado, two pediatricians argued:

> Amendment 64 will legalize marijuana for the general public. As pediatricians, we are concerned that increased marijuana access will lead to increased use by children and teens. . . . Don't forget to flip your ballot over and vote to keep Colorado kids healthy. Vote "no" to Amendment 64. (Baumer & MacLaurin, 2012)

In a newspaper article, a resident of DC spoke about marijuana legalization and noted "I'm worried about the message it will send to kids" (Dufton, 2015). These opponents of marijuana legalization, by framing current policy as protecting children, placed the debate within the gain domain. This would make an audience more risk-averse; highlighting the potential risks associated with a change in policy increases support for the status quo (continued marijuana prohibition).

The differing frames of the debate make sense in terms of persuasion strategies. But do the differing frames use claims and concerns of equal validity? With the passage of time, we now have an opportunity to assess whether or not marijuana legalization has had a negative impact on youth drug use. Were opponents of legalization correct? Has marijuana legalization led to increased youth drug use?

DATA AND METHODOLOGY

The government of the United States has multiple sources of information about illicit drug use in the United States. Among the most prominent are Drug Abuse Warning Network (DAWN),[1] Monitoring the Future (MTF)[2] surveys, National Drug Early Warning System (NDEWS),[3] NSDUH,[4] Treatment Episode Data Set (TEDS),[5] and the Youth Risk Behavior Surveillance System.[6] For our research, though, we cannot utilize all of the sources. For example, while MTF specifically focuses on youth drug use, it cannot be used to identify state-level trends due to its sampling process (Midgette & Reuter, 2019). Given our need for state-level data, we rely on the information gathered by the NSDUH.

While the sampling of NSDUH allows for state-level comparison, the ability to focus exclusively on youth drug use is more difficult when utilizing NSDUH. To understand the impact of marijuana legalization on underage minors, we need data on marijuana usage on people 20 years old and younger (legal use of marijuana—like alcohol—is restricted to those 21 and older). However, data from NSDUH is grouped into the following categories: all 12+; 12–17; all 18+; 18–25; and all 26+. No one category captures the 20 and lower group. For example, a majority within the 18–25 group is legally able to consume marijuana in states that have legalized it; thus, this is an inappropriate category to include. The group 12+ also includes a majority of people who are over the age of 21. Therefore, when exploring the data on youth drug use, we focus on the 12–17 category as the basis of comparison. Specifically, we examine how youth drug use among 12–17 years differed between 2008–2009 and 2018–2019.

The next part of the research design involves case and comparison selection. No state in the United States had legal recreational marijuana in

2008–2009. By 2018–2019, there were seven states that had enacted marijuana legalization and begun commercial sales: Alaska (2015); California (2018); Colorado (2014); Massachusetts (2018); Nevada (2017); Oregon (2015); and Washington (2013). One measure of the impact of legalization on youth drug use is to compare the data from those states from 2008/2009 and 2018/2019. Was there a statistically significant change in past year marijuana use for those between 12 and 17 years old following the introduction of commercial sales? However, this comparison alone is not really sufficient. What if youth drug use stayed the same in these states but everywhere else it went down? This might indicate that legalization did "increase" youth drug use by preventing it from lowering as observed elsewhere. Youth drug use in each state could also be compared to the national average. But again, this might not be as insightful as possible. What if the national average were driven by extreme changes in a small number of states? It is more constructive to examine youth drug use in states having legalized recreational use as compared to states without legal marijuana usage, as well as changes with legalized states and changes in the national average.

Which non-legalized states should be chosen for comparison? Comparative methodology (Munck & Synder, 2007) advises that we choose states that are most similar in all aspects except for that one element—legalized recreational marijuana. In this way, we minimize the variance of factors other than the policy. For this chapter, we use multiple measures to select "similar" states. To select "politically" similar states, we utilized Nate Silver's similarity score (Silver, 2008) and The Daily Kos state similarity index (Daily Kos, 2020). Economically similar states were chosen using state-level GDP per capita and state-level GINI. Finally, we consulted Elazar's categories of political culture to find additional states that were similar to those that had legalized marijuana (Elazar, 1966). Table 8.1 shows each state that has legalized marijuana and its non-legalized similar states.

As can be seen, the number of cases that each state gets compared to varies. Alaska has only three similar states. In contrast, California has 17 similar states. By comparing legalized states to themselves before legalization, the national average change between 2008–2009 and 2018–2011, and changes in similar states that have not legalized recreational marijuana, we believe we can have confidence in our findings.

THE EVIDENCE

The tables below show youth (12–17) marijuana use in 2008/2009 and 2018/2019 for each of the states that legalized marijuana and had commercial sales by 2018.

Table 8.1 States with Commercial Sale of Marijuana by 2018 and Their Comparable States

	Silver	*Daily Kos*	*Similar GDP*	*Similar GINI*	*Elazar Category*
Alaska	No non-legalized	Arizona	North Dakota	South Dakota	Alaska was not included
California	Illinois	New Jersey	Connecticut	Florida	Idaho, Iowa, Kansas, Maine, Michigan, Minnesota, Montana, New Hampshire, North Dakota, South Dakota, Utah, Vermont, Wisconsin
Colorado	Minnesota	Connecticut	Texas	North Dakota	Idaho, Iowa, Kansas, Maine, Michigan, Minnesota, Montana, New Hampshire, North Dakota, South Dakota, Utah, Vermont, Wisconsin
Massachusetts	Connecticut	Rhode Island	New York	Illinois	Connecticut, Delaware, Illinois, Indiana, Nebraska, Maryland, Missouri, New Jersey, New York, Ohio, Pennsylvania, Rhode Island, Wyoming
Nevada	No non-legalized	Texas	Indiana	Virginia	Connecticut, Delaware, Illinois, Indiana, Nebraska, Maryland, Missouri, New Jersey, New York, Ohio, Pennsylvania, Rhode Island, Wyoming
Oregon	Minnesota	Kansas	Ohio	Maine	Idaho, Iowa, Kansas, Maine, Michigan, Minnesota, Montana, New Hampshire, North Dakota, South Dakota, Utah, Vermont, Wisconsin
Washington	Minnesota	Connecticut	Wyoming	Maryland	Idaho, Iowa, Kansas, Maine, Michigan, Minnesota, Montana, New Hampshire, North Dakota, South Dakota, Utah, Vermont, Wisconsin

Source: Data extracted by authors from Elazar, 1966; Jarman, 2020; Silver, 2008; and Statistica.com.

Table 8.2 Marijuana Use in the Past Year, 12–17 Year Olds, 2008/2009 and 2018/2019 Legalized States

State	*2008–2009*	*2018–2019*	P *Value from Test of Differences*
Alaska	15.89	17.75	0.323
California	15.12	15.82	0.505
Colorado	18.55	17.6	0.643
Massachusetts	16.44	16.03	0.828
Nevada	16.45	16.76	0.868
Oregon	18.34	18.56	0.907
Washington	15.24	16.38	0.536

Source: SAMHSA, National Survey on Drug Use and Health: Comparison of 2008–2009 and 2018–2019 Population Percentages, 2020.

As the report from SAMHSA explains, the *p* value reflects the result of the test of the null hypothesis of no difference between 2008–2009 and 2018–2019 population percentages (SAMHSA, 2020). The test to estimate the Bayes significance level for the null hypothesis conducted on the data indicates that there was no statistically significant difference in states with commercial marijuana sales between 2008–2009 and 2018–2019 12–17 youth population percentages at either the 0.05 or the 0.10 level. Thus, the evidence shows that the legalization of marijuana in these states did not lead to any noticeable change in youth drug use.

However, what if marijuana use among youth decreased significantly in other states during that same period? A lack of change in legalized states would imply that legalization did have an impact on youth drug use by maintaining levels during an era of declining youth drug use. To investigate this possibility, we turn to youth drug use in comparable states as well as the national average and the regional average. Is there a hidden increase actually occurring?

Our first case is Alaska. It is located in SAMHSA's West region. As noted earlier, Alaska has few comparable states that have not legalized marijuana.

While SAMHSA found a statistically significant decrease in the percentage of youths who used marijuana in the past year between 2008–2009 and 2018–2019, that decline was not witnessed in the West region or in states comparable to Alaska.

Turning to our next legalized marijuana state, below is the data from California, the national average, the regional average, and comparable states. Like Alaska, SAMHSA places California in its West region.

As we found with Alaska, the decline in the national average of past year marijuana use was not seen in California, the region, nor most of the comparable states. Interestingly, two of the corresponding states sustained a statistically significant increase—not a decrease—in past year marijuana use among 12–17 year olds: Maine and Vermont.

Our next table provides the information for Colorado, a state that legalized recreational marijuana in 2014. In addition to the national average and the

Table 8.3 Marijuana Use in the Past Year, 12–17 Year Olds, 2008/2009 and 2018/2019 Alaska, National Average, Region, and Comparable States

State	*2008–2009*	*2018–2019*	P *Value*
Alaska	15.89	17.75	0.323
Total U.S.*	13.37	12.84	0.098
Region-West	15.26	15.5	0.725
Arizona	14.28	12.7	0.363
North Dakota	9.42	9.44	0.99
South Dakota	12.05	10.24	0.245

*Difference between the 2008–2009 and 2018–2019 population percentages is statistically significant at the 0.10 level.

Source: SAMHSA, National Survey on Drug Use and Health: Comparison of 2008–2009 and 2018–2019 Population Percentages, 2020.

Table 8.4 Marijuana Use in the Past Year, 12–17 Year Olds, 2008/2009 and 2018/2019 California, National Average, Region, and Comparable States

State	*2008–2009*	*2018–2019*	P *Value*
California	15.12	15.82	0.505
Total U.S.*	13.37	12.84	0.098
Region—West	15.26	15.5	0.725
Illinois	13.33	13.55	0.852
New Jersey	11.63	11.48	0.914
Connecticut	15.91	14.08	0.311
Florida	12.94	12.11	0.419
Idaho	13.44	12.04	0.376
Iowa	11.72	11.61	0.938
Kansas	12.12	11.61	0.734
Maine*	14.2	17.53	0.081
Michigan	14.21	13.38	0.461
Minnesota	11.29	12.59	0.41
Montana	15.5	15.98	0.785
New Hampshire	16.56	16.17	0.841
North Dakota	9.42	9.44	0.99
South Dakota	12.05	10.24	0.245
Utah	9.73	10.23	0.718
Vermont^	16.67	21.13	0.026
Wisconsin	13.71	12.01	0.278

^ Difference between the 2008–2009 and 2018–2019 population percentages is statistically significant at the 0.05 level.

* Difference between the 2008–2009 and 2018–2019 population percentages is statistically significant at the 0.10 level.

Source: SAMHSA, National Survey on Drug Use and Health: Comparison of 2008–2009 and 2018–2019 Population Percentages, 2020.

Table 8.5 Marijuana Use in the Past Year, 12–17 Year Olds, 2008/2009 and 2018/2019 Colorado, National Average, Region, and Comparable States

State	*2008–2009*	*2018–2019*	P *Value*
Colorado	18.55	17.6	0.643
Total U.S.*	13.37	12.84	0.098
Region—West	15.26	15.5	0.725
Minnesota	11.29	12.59	0.41
Connecticut	15.91	14.08	0.311
Texas	11.24	10.92	0.733
North Dakota	9.42	9.44	0.99
Idaho	13.44	12.04	0.376
Iowa	11.72	11.61	0.938
Kansas	12.12	11.61	0.734
Maine*	14.2	17.53	0.081
Michigan	14.21	13.38	0.461
Montana	15.5	15.98	0.785
New Hampshire	16.56	16.17	0.841
South Dakota	12.05	10.24	0.245
Utah	9.73	10.23	0.718
Vermont^	16.67	21.13	0.026
Wisconsin	13.71	12.01	0.278

^ Difference between the 2008–2009 and 2018–2019 population percentages is statistically significant at the 0.05 level.

* Difference between the 2008–2009 and 2018–2019 population percentages is statistically significant at the 0.10 level.

Source: SAMHSA, National Survey on Drug Use and Health: Comparison of 2008–2009 and 2018–2019 Population Percentages, 2020.

regional average, the table includes past year marijuana use for 12–17 year olds for comparable states.

The Colorado findings are the same as California. While California and Colorado share the same "political culture" similar states, the other "comparable" states differ. But nowhere—except for the national average—did youth drug use decline between 2008 and 2009 and 2018–2019 at a statistically significant level.

We now turn our attention to Massachusetts. This case is in a different SAMHSA region than our previous cases as well as different Elazar category.

In addition to the statistically significant decrease in the national average, one comparable state—New York—also experienced a decline in past year marijuana drug use among 12–17 year olds. There was also a statistically significant increase between 2008–2009 and 2018–2019 in youth drug use in the state of Nebraska. Given both the increase and decrease observed in comparable states, this suggests that no change is a reasonable expectation for Massachusetts regardless of the marijuana legalization.

Table 8.6 Marijuana Use in the Past Year, 12–17 Year Olds, 2008/2009 and 2018/2019 Massachusetts, National Average, Region, and Comparable States

State	*2008–2009*	*2018–2019*	P *Value*
Massachusetts	16.44	16.03	0.828
Total U.S.*	13.37	12.84	0.098
Region—Northeast	14.22	13.3	0.14
Connecticut	15.91	14.08	0.311
Rhode Island	16.31	16.21	0.955
New York*	14.87	13.09	0.093
Illinois	13.33	13.55	0.852
Delaware	15.53	14.43	0.531
Illinois	13.33	13.55	0.852
Indiana	12.9	12.42	0.753
Maryland	13.73	12.27	0.373
Missouri	11.54	11.35	0.897
Nebraska*	10.87	13.87	0.062
New Jersey	11.63	11.48	0.914
Ohio	12.97	11.88	0.283
Pennsylvania	12.87	12.01	0.436
Wyoming	14.19	12.44	0.304

* Difference between the 2008–2009 and 2018–2019 population percentages is statistically significant at the 0.10 level.

Source: SAMHSA, National Survey on Drug Use and Health: Comparison of 2008–2009 and 2018–2019 Population Percentages, 2020.

Our next case, Nevada, shares the same region as Alaska, California, and Colorado, while sharing the political culture category of Massachusetts. Nevada, though, has different politically and economically comparable states from all the other cases.

Yet again, neither the region nor most of the comparable states had a statistically significant decrease in past year marijuana use among 12–17 years. The national average did decline, as did past year marijuana use among 12–17 year olds in Virginia (significant at the 0.05 level) as well as in New York. Nebraska, another comparable state, experienced a statistically significant increase. So, of the 16 states in the comparison, two had decreases, one had an increase, and 13 were more or less unchanged between 2008–2009 and 2018–2019. Thus, Nevada was within the group's norm, despite legalization of marijuana.

Oregon began commercial sale of recreational marijuana in 2015. It is in SAMHSA's western region and shares the political culture of California and Colorado.

The data indicates that Oregon follows the pattern of Alaska, California, and Colorado. Although there was a decline in the national average of past year marijuana use there was not a corresponding decline in the state, the region, or most of the comparable states. As noted above, Maine and Vermont

Table 8.7 Marijuana Use in the Past Year, 12–17 Year Olds, 2008/2009 and 2018/2019 Nevada, National Average, Region, and Comparable States

State	*2008–2009*	*2018–2019*	P *Value*
Nevada	16.45	16.76	0.868
Total U.S.*	13.37	12.84	0.098
Region—West	15.26	15.5	0.725
Texas	11.24	10.92	0.733
Indiana	12.9	12.42	0.753
Virginia^	13.8	9.65	0.003
Connecticut	15.91	14.08	0.311
Delaware	15.53	14.43	0.531
Illinois	13.33	13.55	0.852
Maryland	13.73	12.27	0.373
Missouri	11.54	11.35	0.373
Nebraska*	10.87	13.87	0.062
New Jersey	11.63	11.48	0.914
New York*	14.87	13.09	0.093
Ohio	12.97	11.88	0.283
Pennsylvania	12.87	12.01	0.436
Rhode Island	16.31	16.21	0.955
Wyoming	14.19	12.44	0.304

^ Difference between the 2008–2009 and 2018–2019 population percentages is statistically significant at the 0.05 level.

* Difference between the 2008–2009 and 2018–2019 population percentages is statistically significant at the 0.10 level.

Source: SAMHSA, National Survey on Drug Use and Health: Comparison of 2008–2009 and 2018–2019 Population Percentages, 2020.

(similar states in terms of political culture) sustained a statistically significant increase in past year marijuana use among 12–17 year olds.

Our last case, Washington, has the longest experience with legalized marijuana since commercial sales were enacted in 2013 in the state. Perhaps this will have an impact on youth drug use of marijuana.

The data for Washington state and its comparable states again reveals a lack of statistically significant increase in past year marijuana use among 12–17 year olds. While there was a decline in the national average of past year marijuana use, this was not echoed in the region. And, as noted above, Maine and Vermont experienced increases, not decreases.

CONCLUSION

The evidence is conclusive. Marijuana legalization has not increased past year marijuana use among 12–17 year olds. And, the review above indicates, legalization of marijuana has not "prevented" a decrease in past year marijuana use; the majority of comparable non-legalized states experienced no change

Table 8.8 Marijuana Use in the Past Year, 12–17 Year Olds, 2008/2009 and 2018/2019 Oregon, National Average, Region, and Comparable States

State	*2008–2009*	*2018–2019*	P *Value*
Oregon	18.34	18.56	0.907
Total U.S.*	13.37	12.84	0.098
Region—West	15.26	15.5	0.725
Minnesota	11.29	12.59	0.41
Kansas	12.12	11.61	0.734
Ohio	12.97	11.88	0.283
Maine*	14.2	17.53	0.081
Idaho	13.44	12.04	0.376
Iowa	11.72	11.61	0.938
Michigan	14.21	13.38	0.461
Montana	15.5	15.98	0.785
New Hampshire	16.56	16.17	0.841
North Dakota	9.42	9.44	0.99
South Dakota	12.05	10.24	0.245
Utah	9.73	10.23	0.718
Vermont^	16.67	21.13	0.026
Wisconsin	13.71	12.01	0.278

^ Difference between the 2008–2009 and 2018–2019 population percentages is statistically significant at the 0.05 level.

* Difference between the 2008–2009 and 2018–2019 population percentages is statistically significant at the 0.10 level.

Source: SAMHSA, National Survey on Drug Use and Health: Comparison of 2008-2009 and 2018-2019 Population Percentages, 2020.

in past year marijuana use among 12–17 years. While two states (comparable to some of the cases) did have statistically significant decreases in past year use of marijuana (New York and Virginia), two other comparable states experienced a statistically significant increase in past year marijuana use.

Opponents of marijuana legalization might focus upon the decline in past year marijuana use among 12–17 year olds at the national level. Is the absence of this trend in legalized states not significant? However, as the above analysis revealed, most states and even regions did not experience any statistically significant decline in youth marijuana use. What, then, accounts for the national decline? It would seem that most of the decline occurred in the South region (from 12.06% to 11.19%—a decline that is statistically significant at the 0.10 level) and in some states such as New York and Virginia (SAMHSA, 2020). The evidence does not support an argument that youth drug use declined everywhere but in states with legalized marijuana.

Our findings are important. Youth drug use—as noted in the beginning of the chapter—has always been a crucial component of discussions about the legal state of marijuana. Such claims undoubtedly will continue to be central in future policy discussions. The data implies that arguments against

Table 8.9 Marijuana Use in the Past Year, 12–17 Year Olds, 2008/2009 and 2018/2019 Washington, National Average, Region, and Comparable States

State	*2008–2009*	*2018–2019*	P *Value*
Washington	15.24	16.38	0.536
Total U.S.*	13.37	12.84	0.098
Region—West	15.26	15.5	0.725
Minnesota	11.29	12.59	0.41
Connecticut	15.91	14.08	0.311
Wyoming	14.19	12.44	0.304
Maryland	13.73	12.27	0.373
Idaho	13.44	12.04	0.376
Iowa	11.72	11.61	0.938
Kansas	12.12	11.61	0.734
Maine*	14.2	17.53	0.081
Michigan	14.21	13.38	0.461
Minnesota	11.29	12.59	0.41
Montana	15.5	15.98	0.785
New Hampshire	16.56	16.17	0.841
North Dakota	9.42	9.44	0.99
South Dakota	12.05	10.24	0.245
Utah	9.73	10.23	0.718
Vermont^	16.67	21.13	0.026
Wisconsin	13.71	12.01	0.278

^ Difference between the 2008–2009 and 2018–2019 population percentages is statistically significant at the 0.05 level.

* Difference between the 2008–2009 and 2018–2019 population percentages is statistically significant at the 0.10 level.

Source: SAMHSA, National Survey on Drug Use and Health: Comparison of 2008–2009 and 2018–2019 Population Percentages, 2020.

legalization need to focus on different reasons if they wish to be accurate. While the fears of the impact of marijuana legalization on youth drug use continue to be voiced, evidence shows that these are exaggerated claims, not valid concerns.

NOTES

1. Drug Abuse Warning Network (DAWN) (2021). Site visited 05/04/2021. https://www.samhsa.gov/data/data-we-collect/dawn-drug-abuse-warning-network
2. Monitoring the Future (2021). Site visited 03/10/2021. https://www.drugabuse.gov/drug-topics/trends-statistics/monitoring-future
3. National Drug Early Warning System (2021). Site visited 05/01/2021. https://ndews.org/
4. National Survey on Drug Use and Health (2021). Site visited 05/01/2021. https://nsduhweb.rti.org/respweb/homepage.cfm

5. Treatment Episode Data Set (2021). Site visited 04/12/2021. https://wwwdasis.samhsa.gov/webt/information.htm

6. Youth Risk Behavior Surveillance System (2021). Sited visited 03/20/2021. https://www.cdc.gov/healthyyouth/data/yrbs/index.htm

REFERENCES

Baumer, S., & David M. (2012). Letters to the Editor. *Denver Post*, November 1, 2012.

Columbian. (2012). In Our View: Legalize and Tax Marijuana. *Columbian*, September 30, 2012.

Committee on Substance Abuse and Committee on Adolescence. (2004). Legalization of Marijuana: Potential Impact on Youth. *Pediatrics (Evanston)*, *113*(6), 1825–1826.

Dineen Wagner, K. (2019). More Reasons for Concern about Adolescent Cannabis Use. *Psychiatric Times*, *36*(9), 4–8.

Dougherty, D. M., Mathias, C. W., Dawes, M. A., Furr, R. M., Charles, N. E., Liguori, A., Shannon, E. E., & Acheson, A. (2013). Impulsivity, Attention, Memory, and Decision-making among Adolescent Marijuana Users. *Psychopharmacology*, *226*(2), 307–319. doi: 10.1007/s00213-012-2908-5

Dufton, E. (2015). Former Anti-drug Activists Reflect on Marijuana Legalization. *Washington Post*, April 17, 2015.

Dufton, E. (2017). *Grass Roots: The Rise and Fall and Rise of Marijuana in America*. Basic Books.

Edwards, K. D. (1996). Prospect Theory: A Literature Review. *International Review of Financial Analysis*, *5*(1), 19–38.

Elazar, D. J. (1966). *American Federalism: A View from the States*. New York: Crowell.

Hadland, S. E., & Harris, S. K. (2014). Youth Marijuana Use: State of the Science for the Practicing Clinician. *Current Opinion in Pediatrics*, *26*(4), 420–427. doi: 10.1097/MOP.0000000000000114

Hall, W., & Lynskey, M. (2016). Evaluating the Public Health Impacts of Legalizing Recreational Cannabis Use in the United States. *Addiction*, *111*(10), 1764–1773. doi: 10.1111/add.13428.

Jarman, D. (2020). How Similar Is Each State to Every Other? Daily Kos Elections' State Similarity Index Will Tell You. *Daily Kos*. https://fivethirtyeight.com/features/state-similarity-scores/

Jervis, R. (2004). The Implications of Prospect Theory for Human Nature and Values. *Political Psychology* *25*(2), 163–176.

Kahneman, D., and Amos T. (1979). Prospect Theory: An Analysis of Decision under Risk. *Econometrica* *47*(2), 263–291.

Larkin, P. L., Jr. (2018). Introduction to a Debate: "Marijuana: Legalize, Decriminalize, or Leave the Status Quo in Place?" *Berkeley Journal of Criminal Law* *23*(1), 73–83.

McAllister, S. (2012). The Real World Impact of Marijuana. *Daily Camera*, October 5, 2012.

McGinty, E. E., Hillary S., Sachini N. B., Brendan S., Marcus A. B., & Colleen L. B. (2016). The Emerging Public Discourse on State Legalization of Marijuana for Recreational Use in the U.S.: Analysis of News Media Coverage, 2010–2014. *Preventive Medicine 90*(September), 114–120.

Meier, M. H., Caspi, A., Ambler, A., Harrington, H., Houts, R., Keefe, R. S., McDonald, K., Ward, A., Poulton, R., & Moffitt, T. E. (2012). Persistent Cannabis Users Show Neuropsychological Decline from Childhood to Midlife. *PNAS, 109*(40), E2657–E2664. doi: 10.1073/pnas.1206820109

Midgette, G., & Peter R. (2020). Has Cannabis Use Among Youth Increased After Changes in Its Legal Status? A Commentary on Use of Monitoring the Future for Analyses of Changes in State Cannabis Laws. *Prevention Science: Official Journal of the Society for Prevention Research, 21*(1), 137.

Pew Research Center. (2015). *In Debate over Legalizing Marijuana, Disagreement Over Drug's Dangers*. www.pewresearch.org

SAMHSA (Substance Abuse and Mental Health Services Administration). *Comparison of 2008–2009 and 2018–2019 Population Percentages (50 States and the District of Columbia)*. https://www.samhsa.gov/data/report/comparison-2008-2009-and-2018-2019-nsduh-state-prevalence-estimates.

Silver, N. (2008). "State Similarity Scores." *FiveThirtyEight*. https://fivethirtyeight.com/features/state-similarity-scores/

Skalski, L. M., Towe, S. L., Sikkema, K. J., & Meade, C. S. (2018). Memory Impairment in HIV-Infected Individuals with Early and Late Initiation of Regular Marijuana Use. *AIDS and Behavior, 22*(5), 1596–1605. doi: 10.1007/s10461-017-1898-z

Todd, T. (2018). The Benefits of Marijuana Legalization and Regulation. *Berkeley Journal of Criminal Law, 23*(1), 99.

Tormohlen, K. N., Brooks-Russell, A., Ma, M., Schneider, K. E., Levinson, A. H., & Johnson, R. M. (2019). Modes of Marijuana Consumption Among Colorado High School Students Before and After the Initiation of Retail Marijuana Sales for Adults. *Journal of Studies on Alcohol and Drugs, 80*(1), 46–55. doi: 10.15288/jsad.2019.80.46

Tversky, A., & Daniel K. (1992). Advances in Prospect Theory: Cumulative Representation of Uncertainty. *Journal of Risk and Uncertainty, 5*(4), 297–323.

Wen, H., Hockenberry, J. M., & Cummings, J. R. (2015). The Effect of Medical Marijuana Laws on Adolescent and Adult Use of Marijuana, Alcohol, and Other Substances. *Journal of Health Economics, 42*, 64–80.

Yu, B., Chen, X., Chen, X., & Yan, H. (2020). Marijuana Legalization and Historical Trends in Marijuana Use among U.S. Residents Aged 12–25: Results from the 1979–2016 National Survey on Drug Use and Health. *BMC Public Health, 20*(156), 2–10. https://doi.org/10.1186/s12889-020-8253-4

Chapter 9

Using Administrative and Survey Data to Evaluate the Impact of Changing Marijuana Laws and Policies on Marijuana Use, Treatment Admissions for Marijuana, and Mortality Related to Marijuana and Other Drug Use*

Maggie Martin, Rebecca Ivester, Jesse Mishra, Maryam Salihu, Sonja Richard, and Ryan Kling

INTRODUCTION

Over the past decade, laws and policies relating to marijuana production and distribution have shifted significantly. This trend has correlated with an increase in consumption, as well as a more favorable public opinion regarding use. Currently, 16 states as well as the District of Columbia have legalized marijuana for both recreational and medical use, and an additional 19 states have legalized medical marijuana only (NORML, 2021). These laws are in various phases of implementation and continue to change. Although marijuana may be legal for medical and/or recreational use in many states, some research suggests its use can still have adverse effects, including dependency, mental health issues, accidents, and other health problems. As the landscape of marijuana law and policy in the United States change, it has become imperative to study the effects of the changes on a variety of public health outcomes.

Using secondary data from the Substance Abuse and Mental Health Services Administration's (SAMHSA) National Survey on Drug Use and Health (NSDUH) and Treatment Episode Data Set (TEDS), and the Centers for Disease Control and Prevention's (CDC) Wide-ranging Online Data for

Epidemiology Research (WONDER) Mortality dataset, this chapter examines the effects of legalization on reported use of marijuana, marijuana-related treatment admissions, and overall mortality, particularly in a time of the co-occurring opioid epidemic.

Marijuana Laws and the Debate around Legalization

Although laws intended to prevent and respond to illicit drug trafficking and abuse continually change, the basic framework for current federal laws and the infrastructure for their enforcement was established in the 1970s by Richard Nixon's declared "War on Drugs." The War on Drugs focused less on the public health consequences of substance use and more on the criminal element of drug trafficking and abuse (e.g., Dufton, 2012). The War on Drugs resulted in an increase in law-enforcement resources deployed to combat illicit drugs, an establishment of mandatory minimum sentences, and a relaxation of restrictions on police search and seizures. Marijuana was placed on the list of Schedule 1 drugs, the most restrictive and heavily penalized drug category, which is meant to be restricted to drugs that have no perceived medical application.

As marijuana use became more widespread, strict punishment of marijuana-related drug offenders was increasingly perceived as unjust. Public opinion has continued to shift toward an overall favorable view of marijuana legalization. According to a Gallup poll, as of November 2020, 68% of Americans support legalizing marijuana, compared with just 12% in 1969 (Brenan, 2020). Along with the public's perception of marijuana use, marijuana laws began to change at the state level, starting in 1996 with California's Compassionate Use Act (California Proposition 215, 1996). Today, 36 states and the District of Columbia have legalized marijuana for medical purposes, and 16 states plus DC have legalized it for recreational use, though it remains illegal at the federal level.[1]

Proponents of marijuana legalization argue that it could have significant societal benefits. One popular argument is that legalizing marijuana use, possession, and sales can reduce criminal justice system involvement (e.g., Chung et al., 2018; Franklin, 2020). In 2018, approximately 600,000 people were arrested for possessing marijuana (Federal Bureau of Investigation, 2019), and more than one-third of all drug possession arrests are for marijuana—even with possession of personal-use amounts decriminalized in many states. There is also the potential to reduce the significant racial and ethnic disparities in who becomes involved in the criminal justice system. Between 2010 and 2018, the arrest rate for marijuana possession was, on average, more than 3.6 times higher for black people than for white people (American Civil Liberties Union, 2020; Federal Bureau of Investigation, 2019).

Some advocates also point to considerable economic benefits, suggesting that legalization could result in budgetary savings from reduced spending on law enforcement in addition to revenue gains from taxation and licensing associated with legalizing marijuana (e.g., Perez et al., 2019; Popken, 2021). For example, the American Civil Liberties Union estimated in 2013 that the United States could save $3.6 billion by suspending the enforcement of marijuana laws. In addition, Ekins and Henchman (2016) estimate that a mature marijuana industry could generate up to $28 billion in tax revenues for federal, state, and local governments, including $7 billion in federal revenue, $5.5 billion from business taxes, and $1.5 billion from income and payroll taxes. States with legal industries are using revenue to fund other social programs. For instance, Washington State used state tax revenue from marijuana sales to fund Medicaid, and Colorado funded public education and school construction with revenue from the industry. Finally, some argue that the marijuana industry can create jobs through legal production, distribution, and sales (Zha, 2020). Barcott and colleagues (2021) estimate that over 320,000 people are currently employed in the cannabis industry, with nearly 80,000 jobs added in 2020.

Effects of Marijuana Legalization on Public Health Outcomes

Marijuana legalization may also have some health-related benefits. Marijuana has been demonstrated to relieve chronic pain, as well as reduce nausea for cancer patients undergoing chemotherapy (National Academies of Sciences, Engineering, and Medicine, 2017), and may also be helpful in treating mental health issues for some individuals, such as anxiety and post-traumatic stress disorder (e.g., LaFrance et al., 2020; Pawasarat et al., 2020; Walsh et al., 2017). Marijuana may also be used as an alternative to other riskier and more physiologically addictive substances, such as alcohol or opioids; some even argue that legalization of marijuana may reduce fatalities from opioid overdoses, possibly because people use marijuana more than opioids if it is available (Chan et al., 2020).

The research suggesting that some health benefits could be attributed to marijuana legalization is promising. However, legalization might also create some long-term negative public health consequences. Marijuana legalization might affect a wide range of health issues. In their evaluation of the public health impacts of legalizing recreational marijuana in the United States, Hall, and Lynskey (2016) identified several potential marijuana-related concerns, including increases in use and abuse, particularly among youth; increased numbers of emergency department visits, car accidents and fatalities related to marijuana intoxication; and prenatal and infant health problems.

One primary concern is that legalization may lead to increases in substance use disorder and addiction. Volkow and colleagues (2014) estimate that approximately 9% of marijuana users become psychologically dependent—most experts agree that cannabis is not a physiologically addictive substance like alcohol, opiates, and nicotine—with larger percentages among individuals who began using younger and those who use more frequently. Even with laws prohibiting minors from purchasing marijuana, legalization of the drug's use by others may make it easier for young people to obtain the substance. Paschall and colleagues (2021) found that in California adolescent use of marijuana has increased significantly since recreational use among adults was legalized in 2016. Adolescents are particularly vulnerable to marijuana abuse and dependence, as their brains are undergoing active development, making them more sensitive to the effects of tetrahydrocannabinol (THC), the primary active ingredient in marijuana (Volkow et al., 2014). Early or heavy use of products containing THC may also increase the likelihood of hospitalization for marijuana dependence or other related conditions.

While hospital admissions for marijuana treatment have generally declined in the United States since 2009, they spiked in Washington State soon after legal dispensaries opened. Treatment admissions for marijuana rose from approximately 6,200 in 2015 to 12,300 in 2016, and while they declined to about 8,000 the following year, they were still elevated over levels prior to legalization (SAMHSA, 2019). According to Cerdá et al. (2020), cannabis use disorder among young people aged 12 to 17 increased by approximately 25% after marijuana legalization. Hasin and colleagues (2017) find that the prevalence of cannabis use disorder increased at significantly higher rates in states that had passed medical marijuana laws than in states that had not. Other mental health issues associated with regular marijuana use include an increased risk of anxiety, depression, and psychosis, especially among new users.

As with alcohol, exposure to marijuana impairs a person's ability to drive, and marijuana is the illicit drug most frequently reported in connection with impaired driving and accidents (Volkow et al., 2014). People may be more likely to drive under the influence of marijuana after legalization because of increased availability, removal of penalties for possession, and lack of familiarity with the effects of newer and more diverse products. A study of marijuana-impaired drivers in Washington State found that THC levels had increased significantly from pre- to post-legalization (Couper & Peterson, 2014). Injuries and deaths due to marijuana intoxication via automobile collisions or other accidents (e.g., falls) may also be more likely as availability increases (Bergal, 2018). However, Aydelotte and colleagues (2017) found no differences in vehicle fatality rates in Washington and Colorado after marijuana legalization compared with in similar states without legalized marijuana. It is important to note that it is particularly challenging to measure the effects of marijuana on impaired driving because THC has differential effects based on an individual's size and tolerance, how recently the individual ingested the substance, ingestion with other substances such as alcohol, or even the strain of marijuana (National Institute on Drug Abuse, 2021).

Although most experts agree that there is minimal risk of dying from a marijuana overdose (Centers for Disease Control, n.d.), there is some anecdotal evidence that marijuana use can, in extremely rare cases, contribute to death. One review of cannabis-related deaths suggested the possibility that acute cannabis intoxication can lead to cardiovascular failure among young, otherwise healthy individuals (Drummer et al., 2019). There have also been a small number of dehydration-related deaths attributed to vomiting caused by chronic marijuana use in a very rare condition called cannabinoid hyperemesis syndrome (Nourbakhsh et al., 2019). Marijuana use is more likely to be related *indirectly* to fatalities. It is possible that impairment from the substance may contribute to fatal accidents, such as traffic fatalities, as discussed previously.

A burgeoning body of research suggests that legalization of marijuana may *reduce* fatalities attributed to other drugs, particularly opioids. As noted earlier, one line of thought argues that marijuana may serve as a replacement drug for more-addictive, more-deadly substances (Chan et al., 2020). Other research demonstrates that marijuana can be used to treat opioid use disorder (e.g., Wiese & Wilson-Poe, 2018). Finally, marijuana may be used to relieve symptoms of physical and mental health conditions that frequently cause individuals to turn to other drugs, including chronic pain, depression and anxiety, and post-traumatic stress disorder (e.g., LaFrance et al., 2020; Pawasarat et al., 2020; Walsh et al., 2017).

Existing research examining the effects of changing marijuana laws focuses primarily on public safety and criminal justice outcomes. This study helps to broaden the research base by examining the effect on public health outcomes. Clearly, the potential public health consequences of marijuana legalization are many and varied. This study seeks to quantify changes in these public outcomes related to changes in marijuana legislation across the United States. We investigate the relationship between legalization and

- reporting of marijuana use
- marijuana-related treatment admissions
- deaths attributable to one or more drugs

METHODS

Data

We used state/year-level administrative data from the NSDUH, TEDS-A, and WONDER Mortality Dataset. These datasets were used to estimate the effect of medical and recreational marijuana legalization on aggregate reported use of marijuana and other drugs, marijuana-related treatment admissions, and mortality.

NSDUH. NSDUH is a general population survey administered annually by SAMHSA. Note that NSDUH does not include institutionalized persons in its sample. We used three categories in these data: Marijuana Use in the Past Month, by State; Illicit Drug Use Other than Marijuana in the Past Month (through 2014); and Illicit Drug Use Other than Marijuana in the Past Month (2015 onward). The data are housed in the Substance Abuse and Mental Health Data Archive. Within that archive, data are aggregated into two-year segments such as 2002–2003, 2003–2004, and so on.

The two-year estimates are less precise than one-year estimates for locating the dates of medical or recreational legalization. Therefore, we ran all analyses with the NSDUH estimates assuming that legalization occurred in the second year of the estimate, and then, as a sensitivity test, re-ran the analyses assuming the legislation had changed in the first year. For Marijuana Use in the Past Month, by State, we have data from 2012 to 2018. For Illicit Drug Use Other than Marijuana in the Past Month, we combined the two datasets to collect data on years 2002–2014 and 2015–2018, but we are missing 2014–2015. Each dataset contains information on all U.S. states. We built five datasets, one for each category based on age groups offered by NSDUH (note that these age groups are not mutually exclusive): 12 or older, 12–17, 18 or older, 18–25, and 26 or older. All datasets received the same treatment.

TEDS-A. The Treatment Episode Data Set-Admissions (TEDS-A) is also produced by SAMHSA and consists of data on substance abuse treatment facility admissions. TEDS-A dates back to 1992 and contains demographic and substance abuse characteristics for individuals aged 12 years and older admitted to treatment facilities. Only treatment facilities that receive state or federal funds are required to report admissions data; therefore, these data represent just a sample of treatment facility admissions. Note that the data are unique at the admission level, not the person level.

From TEDS-A, we used the individual-level treatment admission data for 2000 through 2017. The data include both inpatient and outpatient admissions. Each observation in the data is one admission, and lists, among other things, the primary, secondary, and tertiary reasons for admission. Using this information, we generated variables that indicate whether marijuana was a patient's primary reason for admission, and, separately, whether marijuana was among a patient's top three reasons for admission. We then collapsed the data to the state/year level and produced variables that represent the total number of admissions where marijuana was the primary reason for admission and where it was among the top three reasons for admission.

In addition, we generated variables indicating whether medical marijuana legalization was implemented within a given state and year, and, separately, whether recreational marijuana legalization was implemented within a state and year. We transformed these counts to z-scores by standardizing these values within states and across years. Finally, we ran random effects models with either medical or recreational legalization as the primary predictor, and time and time-squared covariates.

CDC WONDER. Finally, we used the CDC WONDER Mortality (detailed) dataset to determine the number of deaths where a given drug type is listed as either the primary cause or one of "multiple" causes of death. The data, which capture the years 2010–2018, identify the primary and multiple causes of a person's death using the World Health Organization's International Classification of Diseases (ICD)-10 codes. We identified individuals who had at least one ICD-10 F code, which indicates mental or behavioral disorders due to psychoactive substance use, or ICD-10 T40 code, which indicates poisoning by, adverse effect of, or "underdosing" of narcotics and hallucinogens. Then, we generated variables indicating whether a specific drug type was mentioned in the decedent's primary death code or multiple causes of death code. Substance types include cannabis, cocaine, opioids, hallucinogens, inhalants, psychotherapeutics, and other stimulants.

Changes in marijuana laws. For our empirical analysis we looked to changes in state legislation for medical[2] marijuana use and possession as of 2019, and separately for recreational[3] use and possession.[4] While there is variation across states in the amount that is legal to possess and the acquisition method (for medical marijuana), we group them together, as the requirements are fairly similar. In addition, while the start date we choose for our analysis frequently occurs in the middle of a calendar year, changes in marijuana legislation are frequently anticipated by decreased social undesirability of marijuana use and law-enforcement activity, meaning we might expect effects of legislation to happen as soon as a law is passed, or even before then.

Analytic Plan

Given that it is impossible to conduct a natural experiment in this context, we employed a strong quasi-experimental design (difference-in-differences) to estimate the effect of marijuana legalization on public health outcomes. The difference-in-differences specification looks at trends within each state and attempts to isolate the effect of legalization. For example, if a group of states enacts legislation and observes an increase in marijuana use, another group of states that does not enact legislation is used to compare contemporaneous trends in marijuana use and "difference out" the effect of legalization. If used in the comparison states increased contemporaneously with use in the legalized states at roughly the same magnitude, then we would not attribute the change in legalization as a cause for an increase in marijuana use. We estimate the difference-in-differences model using state random effects, and conduct robustness checks to control for potential time-varying heterogeneity.

Model Specification

To estimate the effect of legalization of marijuana on public health outcomes, we analyzed the following regression:

TEXTBOX 9.1

$$Y_{ist} = \alpha + \beta^T X_{ist} + \sum \delta_s \left(state = s\right)_{is} + \gamma_1 \times time_t + \gamma_2 \times time_t^2 + \gamma_3 \times legal_{st} + \varepsilon_{is}$$

where:
i is individual, s is state, t is the year in each case, α is an intercept, and X is a vector of individual-varying covariates with parameters β. These covariates include race, age categories (12–17, 18–25, 26–34, 35–49, and 50-plus categories), gender, education, ethnicity, and race. δ_s is a set of dummy variables for each state, though in one model below they enter as a random effect. *time* is a variable that runs from 0 to 1 representing the year, where 0 represents the first year of the data, 1 represents the last, and the other years are uniformly distributed. γ_1 and γ_2 are the parameters on time and time squared. $legal_{st}$ is a dummy variable equal to 1 if the state was "legalized" at time t, 0 otherwise? γ_3 is the difference-in-differences parameter. ε_{is} is an error term clustered at the state level.

Below, we present results for each of our three primary datasets. For each dataset, we first report descriptive statistics relevant to our analysis. Each analysis dataset reports different covariates, so there is some variation in the covariate list. We then report results from the difference-in-differences analysis. For the NSDUH and WONDER analyses, we report only the parameter estimates associated with the change in legislation, while for the TEDS analysis we report all covariates. Complete regression results are available upon request.

RESULTS

Reported Use in the Past 30 Days (NSDUH)

Our first analysis checks the association between reported marijuana use and legalization of marijuana in a given state. As a falsification test, we also

Table 9.1 Mean Proportion of Reported Use in the Past 30 Days

Dependent Variable	*N*	*Mean*	*Std Dev*	*Min*	*Max*
Marijuana					
12–17 years	816	0.074	0.017	0.037	0.140
18–25 years	816	0.189	0.052	0.077	0.388
26 and older	816	0.055	0.026	0.019	0.181
Cocaine					
12–17 years	816	0.011	0.005	0.002	0.032
18–25 years	816	0.057	0.018	0.018	0.122
26 and older	816	0.015	0.005	0.005	0.052
All Drugs but Marijuana					
12–17 years	765	0.042	0.012	0.019	0.072
18–25 years	765	0.079	0.016	0.046	0.145
26 and older	765	0.027	0.005	0.011	0.055

Source: Data in this table come from the NSDUH dataset (2012–2018).

estimated the association of marijuana legalization with cocaine use and the use of all other drugs other than marijuana. We chose these drug types because SAMHSA had reported them for a long enough time series for our analysis. Table 9.1 reports summary statistics for this measure stratified by age group. We stratified the analysis only by age, since (a) statistics reported by state and year from SAMHSA are provided only one demographic variable at a time, and (b) the mean proportion of reported use differs the most across age groups. In general, young adults reported more drug use compared with minors and older adults. For the "all drugs but marijuana" category, SAMHSA did not report estimates by state and year for the year 2013.

We ran the difference-in-differences analysis for each of the drug categories and three age groups. As mentioned in the Methods section, since the NSDUH estimates are two-year estimates, we ran the models twice. The first model, presented here, assumed that the observations represented the second year of the two-year window. The second model assumed that the observations represented the first year of the window. In both cases we found similar statistically significant results, with the magnitudes roughly the same. We slightly prefer the model presented here, because even if marijuana legislation occurs in the first year of the two-year period, in many states there is a lag between legalization and commerce.

The regression models include the time parameters, state fixed effects, and indicators for the change in legislation. Table 9.2 reports the parameter estimates on the legalization indicator variable from each regression. The left-hand set of columns is for medical legalization, and the right-hand set of columns is for recreational legalization. The parameter estimates are interpreted as the change in the proportion of people reporting use after legalization.

Table 9.2 Regression Results for Reporting of Use in the Past 30 Days

	Medical			*Recreational*		
Dependent Variable	*Estimate*	*Std Error*	*z-score*	*Estimate*	*Std Error*	*z-score*
Marijuana						
12–17 years	0.0006	0.0020	0.31	0.0093**	0.0030	3.09
18–25 years	0.0040	0.0049	0.82	0.0363***	0.0080	4.51
26 and older	0.0033	0.0031	1.07	0.0337***	0.0042	8.06
Cocaine						
12–17 years	−5E-05	0.0005	−0.10	−5.1E-05	0.0004	−0.13
18–25 years	0.0047*	0.0020	2.38	0.0074	0.0040	1.85
26 and older	0.0007	0.0006	1.18	0.0028	0.0010	2.76
All Drugs but Marijuana						
12–17 years	0.0002	0.0011	0.19	0.0003	0.0010	0.35
18–25 years	0.0032	0.0024	1.30	0.0007	0.0029	0.22
26 and older	0.0017	0.0009	1.95	0.0017*	0.0008	2.11

NB: *p<0.05; **p<0.01; ***p<0.001
Source: Data in this table come from the NSDUH dataset (2012–2018).

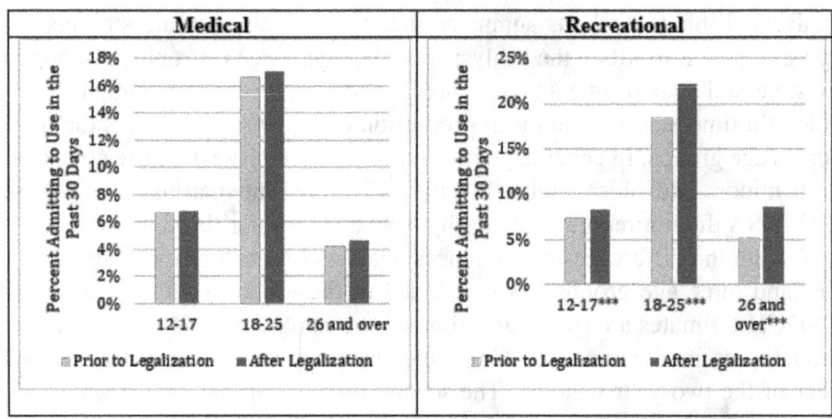

NB: *p<.05; **p<.01; ***p<.001

Figure 9.1 Estimated Change in Reporting of Use in Past 30 Days before to after Legalization. *Source: Data in this figure come from the NSDUH dataset (2012–2018).*

The findings demonstrate clear patterns of reported use associated with legalization. For marijuana, medical legalization is not statistically associated with reported use, while recreational legalization is strongly and positively associated with use. Figure 9.1 illustrates the change in reported marijuana use, using mean reported use prior to legalization in each state as the depiction of the "prior to legalization" category. For two associations related to other drugs—that between medical legalization and cocaine use for those

18–25 years old, and that between recreational legalization and use of all drugs but marijuana for those 26 and older—we find a statistically significant association between recreational legalization and use, though the estimated association is extremely small, at less than a fraction of a percentage point. However, given the relatively small percentage of users at baseline, even a very small percentage point increase may indicate a practically significant change in use.

Treatment Admissions Mentioning Marijuana as Primary Reason or One of Top Three Reasons for Admission (TEDS-A)

Our second analysis tests the association between marijuana legalization and treatment admissions where marijuana either is listed as the primary drug or is among the top three drugs listed. Table 9.3 reports summary statistics for variables in our regression models. Note the standardized number of admissions in the third and fifth rows of table 9.3. In our regression models, to combine states in the same model and have a sensible interpretation of model parameters, we converted total admissions to standardized admissions (i.e., z-scores), using the grand mean and standard deviation across all state-years.

Tables 9.4 and 9.5 report the regression results from our treatment admission difference-in-differences models, for admissions where marijuana is the primary reason for admission and admissions where marijuana is among the top three drugs mentioned, respectively. The left-hand columns are for medical legalization, and the right-hand columns are for recreational legalization. The parameter estimates are interpreted as the change in the z-scores of treatment admissions as a result of marijuana use after legalization.

Table 9.3 Means of Analysis Variables in TEDS-A Analysis

Variable	*N*	*Mean*	*Std Dev*	*Min*	*Max*
Number of admissions (MJ primary)	898	6,312	9,200	3	67,927
Standardized number of admissions (MJ primary)	898	0.000	0.972	−2.971	3.331
Number of admissions (MJ top three)	898	14,211	20,327	18	132,582
Standardized number of admissions (MJ top three)	898	0.000	0.972	−2.980	3.603
Recreational legalization indicator	898	0.023	0.151	0	1
Medical legalization indicator	898	0.295	0.456	0	1

Source: Data in this table come from the TEDS-A dataset (2000–2017).

Table 9.4 Regression Results for Primary Marijuana Admissions

	Medical			*Recreational*		
Variable	*Estimate*	*Std Error*	*z-score*	*Estimate*	*Std Error*	*z-score*
Type of legalization	−0.027	0.068	−0.40	0.492*	0.201	2.44
Time	4.722	0.369	12.80	4.806	0.369	13.01
Time-squared	−4.842	0.358	−13.52	−4.987	0.36	−13.86
Constant	−0.694	0.08	−8.66	−0.705	0.079	−8.89

NB: *$p<0.05$; **$p<0.01$; ***$p<0.001$
Source: Data in this table come from the TEDS-A dataset (2000–2017).

Table 9.5 Regression Results for Top Three Marijuana Admissions

	Medical			*Recreational*		
Variable	*Estimate*	*Std Error*	*z-score*	*Estimate*	*Std Error*	*z-score*
Type of legalization	0.011	0.07	0.16	0.676**	0.208	3.24
Time	3.761	0.383	9.82	3.875	0.382	10.14
Time-squared	−3.859	0.372	−10.38	−4.038	0.373	−10.84
Constant	−0.561	0.083	−6.74	−0.570	0.082	−6.94

NB: *$p<0.05$; **$p<0.01$; ***$p<0.001$
Source: Data in this table come from the TEDS-A dataset (2000–2017).

We find no statistically significant association between medical marijuana legalization and marijuana treatment admissions for marijuana as either the primary reason for admission or as one of the top three drugs listed, but we do find a positive and statistically significant difference with recreational legalization for both outcomes. We estimate just under one half of a standard deviation increase (0.492) in marijuana admissions where marijuana is the primary drug at admission, and an approximately two-thirds of one standard deviation increase (0.676) in admissions where marijuana is among the top three drugs at admission. This is difficult to interpret, so figures 9.2 and 9.3 convert the z-scores to treatment admissions. Each panel in both figures groups states into lower-admission states (fewer than 5,000 admissions) and higher-admission states (5,000 or more) and calculates the mean of admissions prior to legalization. We apply the parameter estimates to the difference for each group. When marijuana is the primary reason for treatment admissions (figure 9.2), for recreational marijuana, states with smaller numbers of admissions have an increase from 1,866 to 2,452 mean admissions per year. States with larger numbers of admissions have an increase from 12,645 to 18,354 mean admissions per year. When marijuana is among the top three

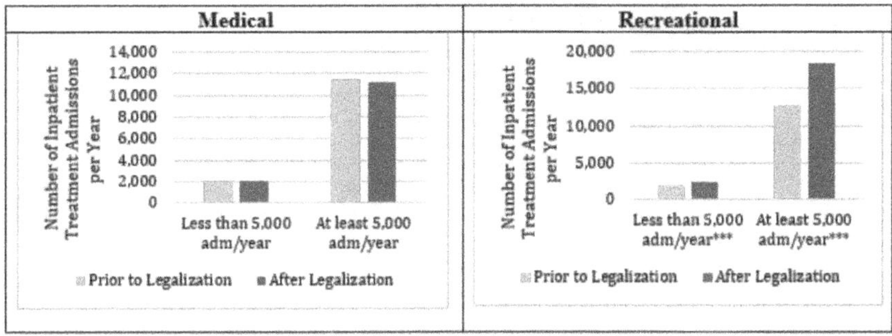

NB: *p<.05; **p<.01; ***p<.001

Figure 9.2 Change in Primary Marijuana Treatment Admissions. *Source: Data in this figure come from the TEDS-A dataset (2000–2017).*

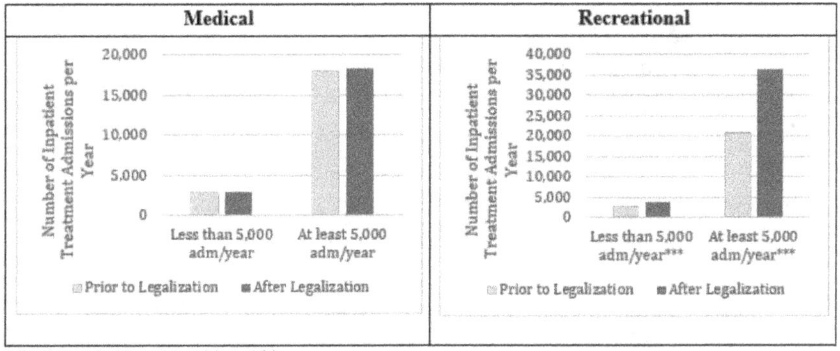

NB: *p<.05; **p<.01; ***p<.001

Figure 9.3 Change in Marijuana as One of Top Three Reasons for Treatment Admissions. *Source: Data in this figure come from the TEDS-A dataset (2000–2017).*

reasons for treatment admissions (figure 9.3), for recreational marijuana, states with smaller numbers of admissions have an increase from 2,897 to 3,668 mean admissions per year. States with larger numbers of admissions have an increase from 20,753 to 36,424 mean admissions per year.

Deaths Mentioning Drugs as a Cause (CDC WONDER)

Our third analysis checks the association between marijuana legalization laws and deaths where a given drug type was listed among the causes of death. We separately check for cannabis, cocaine, opioids, hallucinogens, inhalants, psychotherapeutics, and other stimulants. Outcomes identifying deaths where a drug other than cannabis was listed as a cause may act as falsification tests—that is, if we estimate no effect of marijuana

Table 9.6 Regression Results for Deaths with Drugs Mentioned as a Cause of Death

	Medical			*Recreational*		
Model	*Estimate*	*Std Dev*	*z-score*	*Estimate*	*Std Dev*	*z-score*
Marijuana	−0.009	0.160	−0.056	−0.057	0.125	−0.456
Cocaine	−0.067	0.047	−1.426	−0.091	0.063	−1.444
Opioids	0.033	0.088	0.375	−0.171*	0.070	−2.443
Hallucinogens	−0.122	0.286	−0.427	0.257	0.366	0.702
Inhalants	−0.235	0.196	−1.199	−0.282	0.156	−1.808
Psychotherapeutics	−0.038	0.066	−0.576	−0.088	0.064	−1.375
Other stimulants	0.235	0.166	1.416	−0.033	0.053	−0.623

NB: $*p<0.05$; $**p<0.01$; $***p<0.001$
Source: Data in this table come from the CDC WONDER dataset (2010–2018).

legalization on mortality due to other types of drugs, we have some evidence that marijuana legalization is not related to changes in mortality due to drugs. Unlike in the TEDS analysis, we estimated Poisson models for this outcome, since many state-year combinations report zero deaths for some of the drugs. To account for the variation in mean deaths across states, we included state fixed effects regressors. Table 9.6 reports the Poisson regression results from our difference-in-differences models, for each type of drug. The left-hand set of columns is for medical legalization, and the right-hand set of columns is for recreational legalization. Across all models for both medical and recreational legalization, we find no association with deaths attributed to marijuana, an unsurprising result, since, as referenced previously, death due to marijuana overdose is exceedingly rare. We do observe a significant decrease in the number of deaths attributed to opioid use after recreational use is legalized. We do not observe the same result for medical use, and with the number of models we have estimated to investigate deaths associated with marijuana legalization, we might expect to find a statistically significant result by chance. For other drug types, neither recreational nor medical marijuana legalization predicted a significant change in number of deaths.

DISCUSSION

This chapter provides evidence that medical and recreational marijuana legislation are differentially associated with the public health outcomes we measured. Whereas we found no effect for medical marijuana legalization, we found that recreational legalization was associated both with increased reported use and with treatment admissions, as well as with reductions in opioid-related deaths.

The effects were fairly strong, particularly for reported use and treatment admissions. These findings expand upon previous research by broadening analyses to all states that had legalized marijuana as of 2018 and using several secondary data sources to examine the effect of legalization on public health.

We estimate between a 3 and 4 percentage point increase in reported marijuana use for adults after recreational legalization, which is quite sizable relative to pre-legalization reported use. This result is expected given that marijuana legalization by definition lifts legal restrictions on use, and likely makes it easier to access for individuals who were apprehensive about using illicit channels to obtain the substance. We see significant increases in use for each age group, with the largest percentage increase (nearly 40%) observed among those 26 years and older. This cohort was the least likely to report using marijuana prior to legalization. It may be that those who report use post-legalization feel more permission to use marijuana now that it is legal, or they may feel more comfortable admitting to use in a survey. There is also a significant increase in reported use among 12- to 17-year-olds and 18- to 25-year-olds, which is of note given the concern surrounding young people's brain development, the possibility of getting addicted to marijuana, and the tendency for younger people to engage in risk-taking behavior while under the influence of drugs (Schauer et al., 2020), though marijuana use is not as commonly associated with risky behavior as use of other drugs, particularly alcohol (e.g., Perna et al., 2016).

We also found a small but statistically significant association between medical legalization and cocaine use among 18- to 25-year-olds, as well as one between recreational legalization and other types of drug use among those ages 26 years and older, but the effect for both associations is very small. These associations may be due to chance, or they may be small but real increases, possibly attributable to reduced disfavor and stigma around drug use that goes beyond marijuana use, particularly in states where public opinion has shifted enough to legalize recreational marijuana. In November 2020, Oregon passed a ballot initiative decriminalizing possession of small amounts of all drugs (e.g., Sutton, 2021), a move that might be a harbinger of changes in public opinion and perhaps even legislation in other states.

We also estimate that treatment admissions with marijuana as the primary reason for admission increased by approximately 900 admissions per year in smaller states with fewer treatment beds, and 4,500 more in larger states, though we see no increase in treatment admissions for substances other than marijuana. These findings are consistent with prior research (e.g., Mennis et al., 2021) and with the overall increase in marijuana use from before to after legalization. In other words, it is not surprising that the number of treatment beds related to marijuana use goes up when use itself increases. However, it does suggest a need to continue to better understand the consequences of marijuana use and the types of policies and practices that should be put in place or strengthened to support those with addiction or dependence.

Finally, we saw a statistically significant decrease in the number of deaths attributed to opioids in states. While this is consistent with other research (e.g., Chan, 2020; Hsu & Kovacs, 2021), we estimated a large number of models using the mortality data, and could have found a statistically significant result by chance. More research is needed on this association, but prior studies have suggested that marijuana may be used as a replacement for opioids for some conditions such as chronic pain and nausea (National Academies of Sciences, Engineering, and Medicine, 2017), and as a treatment for mental health conditions that individuals may otherwise self-medicate using opioids (e.g., LaFrance et al., 2020; Pawasarat et al., 2020; Walsh et al., 2017). Although marijuana carries a risk of psychological dependency and addiction (Volkow et al., 2014), individuals who use marijuana are less likely to become addicted than those who use opioids, and are far less likely to die as a result of marijuana use than opioid users (SAMHSA, 2020).

The results of this study suggest that marijuana does not have markedly negative public health consequences, although the increase in treatment admissions in particular does suggest some cause for caution and regulation. In fact, we see some support for the hypothesis that the availability of legal marijuana reduces opioid deaths by serving as a replacement substance, although more research is needed on this connection. It is important, however, to note several limitations of the current study.

Limitations

As alluded to above, the outcomes we looked at in this study are fairly broad indicators of public health issues, and it is challenging to draw any conclusions about causality based on significant findings, even with a strong quasi-experimental design. We might anticipate stronger associations between marijuana legalization and finer measures of public health consequences, such as DSM or ICD diagnoses of substance use disorder, or survey admissions to driving under the influence of or having an adverse reaction to marijuana (or other drugs). Future research is needed on such associations.

In addition, the data sources we used for our analyses are secondary data, and in the case of NSDUH, provided in the aggregate. We were not able to test individual years or different age group cuts. For instance, comparing use rates among individuals under 21 to rates among those 21 and older would be useful, given that most marijuana laws prohibit those under 21 from purchasing or using marijuana products. Similarly, the TEDS data are limited with respect to individual characteristics. We elected not to include them in the regression models since they are frequently missing.

In addition, CDC WONDER, in particular, has varying levels of quality and precision depending on states' data. For instance, states with data collection efforts that are funded by SAMHSA are likely to have better data on which drug(s) contributed to cause of death. The CDC WONDER data may also classify synthetic marijuana differently from traditional marijuana, so it is likely that any deaths attributable to synthetic marijuana were missed in our analysis.

It is also impossible to disentangle the effects of the opioid epidemic and attempts to address it from any effects that marijuana legalization may have. We used all of the states in the United States and controlling for as many potential confounders as possible to address any potential endogeneity problems (e.g., some marijuana laws may have been passed in part to reduce opioid misuse). While we have attempted to mitigate the endogeneity issue, we cannot be sure that the association we see between recreational marijuana legalization and reductions in opioid deaths is due to changes in marijuana laws themselves or to other, coincident, policy changes. Finally, given the recency of the passage and implementation of these laws, particularly recreational marijuana legislation, the timeframe of the study is relatively short, for recreational legalization especially. We may see more effects on public health outcomes as more states legalize marijuana and the timeframe for legalization is extended.

NOTES

* This project was supported by Award No. 2016-R2-CX-K001, awarded by the National Institute of Justice, Office of Justice Programs, U.S. Department of Justice. The opinions, findings, and conclusions or recommendations expressed in this publication are those of the authors and do not necessarily reflect those of the Department of Justice.

1. norml.org/laws
2. States that had passed medical marijuana laws at the time include California, Oregon, Alaska, Washington, Maine, Hawaii, Nevada, Colorado, Maryland, Vermont, Montana, Rhode Island, New Mexico, Michigan, New Jersey, Arizona, Delaware, Connecticut, Massachusetts, New Hampshire, Illinois, Utah, Minnesota, New York, Louisiana, Arkansas, Ohio, Pennsylvania, Florida, North Dakota, West Virginia, Missouri, and Georgia.
3. States that had passed recreational marijuana laws at the time include Colorado, Washington, Alaska, Oregon, California, Nevada, Maine, Massachusetts, Michigan, Vermont, and Illinois
4. Years of legalization were pulled from a variety of resources, including marijuana research and advocacy organizations (NORML, the Marijuana Policy Project, Weedmaps), as well as state policy and legislation websites.

REFERENCES

American Civil Liberties Union. (2020). *The war on marijuana in black and white: Billions of dollars wasted on racially biased arrests.* New York: American Civil Liberties Union.

Aydelotte, J. D., Brown, L. H., Luftman, K. M., Mardock, A. L., Teixeira, P. G. R., Coopwood, B., & Brown, C. V. R. (2017). Crash fatality rates after recreational marijuana legalization in Washington and Colorado. *American Journal of Public Health, 107*(8), 1329–1331.

Barcott, B., Whitney, V., & Bailey, J. (2021). *Leafly Jobs Report 2021.* Leafly.

Bergal, J. (2018). *Drugged driving deaths spike with spread of legal marijuana, opioid abuse.* Pew Charitable Trusts.

Brenan, M. (2020, November). *Support for legal marijuana inches up to new high of 68%.* Gallup.

California Proposition 215. (1996). Compassionate Use Act. Division 10, Chapter 6, Article 2, 11362.5. Retrieved from: https://leginfo.legislature.ca.gov/faces/codes_displaySection.xhtml?sectionNum=11362.5.&lawCode=HSC

Centers for Disease Control. (n.d.) *Marijuana and Public Health.* Retrieved from: https://www.cdc.gov/marijuana/index.htm

Cerdá, M., Mauro, C., Hamilton, A., Levy, N. S., Santaella-Tenorio, J., Hasin, D., Wall, M. M., Keyes, K. M., & Martins, S. S. (2020). Association between recreational marijuana legalization in the United States and changes in marijuana use and cannabis use disorder from 2008 to 2016. *JAMA Psychiatry, 77*(2), 165–171.

Chan, N. W., Burkhardt, J., & Flyr, M. (2020). The effects of recreational marijuana legalization and dispensing on opioid mortality. *Economic Inquiry*, *58*, 589–606.

Chung, E., Perez, M., & Hunter, L. (2018). Rethinking federal marijuana policy. *Center for American Progress.* Retrieved from: https://www.americanprogress.org/issues/criminal-justice/reports/2018/05/01/450201/rethinking-federal-marijuana-policy/

Couper, F. J., & Peterson, B. L. (2014). The prevalence of marijuana in suspected impaired driving cases in Washington State. *Journal of Analytical Toxicology, 38*(8), 569–574.

Drummer, O. H., Gerostamoulos, D., & Woodford, N. W. (2019). Cannabis as a cause of death: A review. *Forensic Science International*, *298*, 298–306.

Dufton, E. (2012, March 26). The war on drugs: How president nixon tied addiction to crime. *Atlantic.* Retrieved from: theatlantic.com/health/archive/2012/03/the-war-on-drugs-how-president-nixon-tied-addiction-to-crime/254319/

Ekins, G., & Henchman, J. (2016). *Marijuana legalization and taxes: Federal revenue impact.* Retrieved from: https://taxfoundation.org/marijuana-tax-legalization-federal-revenue/

Franklin, N. (2020, August 13). Legalization is the only way to improve the criminal justice system. *Newsweek Magazine.* Retrieved from: https://www.newsweek.com/legalization-only-way-improve-criminal-justice-system-opinion-1524746

Hall, W., & Lynskey, M. (2016). Evaluating the public health impacts of legalizing recreational cannabis use in the United States. *Addiction*, *111*(10), 1764–1773.

Hasin, D. S., Sarvet, A. L., Cerdá, M., Keyes, K. M., Stohl, M., Galea, S., & Wall, M. M. (2017). U.S. adult illicit cannabis use, cannabis use disorder, and medical marijuana laws: 1991–1992 to 2012–2013. *JAMA Psychiatry*, *74*(6), 579–588. doi: 10.1001/jamapsychiatry.2017.0724

Hsu, G., & Kovacs, B. (2021). Association between county level cannabis dispensary counts and opioid related mortality rates in the United States: Panel data study. *British Medical Journal*, *372*, 372–373.

LaFrance, E. M., Glodosky, N. C., Bonn-Miller, M., & Cuttler, C. (2020). Short and long-term effects of cannabis on symptoms of post-traumatic stress disorder. *Journal of Affective Disorders*, *274*, 298–304.

Mennis, J., Stahler, G. J., & Mason, M. J. (2021). Treatment admissions for opioids, cocaine, and methamphetamines among adolescents and emerging adults after legalization of recreational marijuana. *Journal of Substance Abuse Treatment*, *122*.

National Academies of Sciences, Engineering, and Medicine. (2017). *The health effects of cannabis and cannabinoids: The current state of evidence and recommendations for research.* Washington, DC.

National Institute on Drug Abuse. (2021, April 13). NIDA. 2021, April 13. *Does marijuana use affect driving?* Retrieved from: https://www.drugabuse.gov/publications/research-reports/marijuana/does-marijuana-use-affect-driving

NORML. (2021). *State laws.* Retrieved from: norml.org/laws

Nourbakhsh, M., Miller, A., Gofton, J., Jones, G., & Adeagbo, B. (2019). Cannabinoid hyperemesis syndrome: Reports of fatal cases. *Journal of Forensic Sciences*, *64*(1), 270–274.

Paschall, M. J., Garcia-Ramirez, G., & Grube, J. W. (2021). Recreational marijuana legalization and use among California adolescents: Findings from a statewide survey. *Journal of Studies on Alcohol and Drugs*, *82*(1), 103–111.

Pawasarat, I. M., Schultz, E. M., Frisby, J. C., Mehta, S., Angelo, M. A., Hardy, S. S., & Kim, T. W. B. (2020). The efficacy of medical marijuana in the treatment of cancer-related pain. *Journal of Palliative Medicine*, *23*(6), 809–816.

Perez, M., Olugbenga, A., & Chung, E. (2019). Using marijuana revenue to create jobs. *Center for American Progress.* Retrieved from: https://www.americanprogress.org/issues/criminal-justice/reports/2019/05/20/470031/using-marijuana-revenue-create-jobs/

Perna, E. B. D. F., Theunissen, E. L., Kuypers, K. P. C., Toennes, S. W., & Ramaekers, J. G. (2016). Subjective aggression during alcohol intoxication before and after aggression exposure. *Psychopharmacology (Berlin)*, *233*(18), 3331–3340.

Popken, B. (2021, March 31). N.Y. pot legalization could create $3.5 billion impact and 60,000 jobs. *NBC News.* Retrieved from: https://www.nbcnews.com/business/business-news/n-y-pot-legalization-could-create-3-5-billion-impact-n1262679

SAMHSA. (2019). *Key substance use and mental health indicators in the United States: Results from the 2018 National Survey on Drug Use and Health.* Retrieved from: https://www.samhsa.gov/data/sites/default/files/cbhsq-reports/NSDUHNationalFindingsReport2018/NSDUHNationalFindingsReport2018.pdf

SAMHSA. (2020). *Opioid overdose*. Retrieved from: https://www.samhsa.gov/medication-assisted-treatment/medications-counseling-related-conditions/opioid-overdose

Schauer, G. L., Clayton, H. B., Njai, R., & Grant, A. M. (2020). Adolescent marijuana use and related risk behaviors, national findings from 2015 to 2017. *American Journal of Preventive Medicine*, *59*(5), 714–724.

Sutton, E. (2021). Drug decriminalization in Orgegon officially begins today. *Drug Policy Alliance*. Retrieved from: https://drugpolicy.org/press-release/2021/02/drug-decriminalization-oregon-officially-begins-today

Volkow, N. D., Baler, R. D., Compton, W. M., & Weiss, S. R. (2014). Adverse health effects of marijuana use. *New England Journal of Medicine*, *370*(23), 2219–2227.

Walsh, Z., Gonzalez, R., Crosby, K., Thiessen, M. S., Carrol, C., & Bonn-Miller, M. O. (2017). Medical cannabis and mental health: A guided systemic review. *Clinical Psychology Review*, *51*, 15–29.

Wiese, B., & Wilson-Poe, A. R. (2018). Emerging evidence for cannabis' role in opioid use disorder. *Cannabis and Cannabinoid Research*, *3*(1), 179–189.

Zha, C. (2020, December). High economy: Impacts of marijuana legalization on the U.S. economy. *Economics Review at New York University*. Retrieved from: http://theeconreview.com/2020/12/18/high-economy-impacts-of-marijuana-legalization-on-the-us-economy/

Chapter 10

The Unintended Consequences of Marijuana Decriminalization on Illegal Commerce and the Opioid Crisis

Nikolay Anguelov, Michael P. McCarthy, and Thalia Valkanos

In the last two decades, two main drug policy issues have dominated national political attention: the decriminalization of marijuana and the opioid crisis. This chapter examines the link between them. Following up on the work of Anguelov (2018), analyzed is the impact of the proliferation of marijuana decriminalization on the opioid epidemic in the context of cultural normalization of drug use. A panel model analysis for all 50 states from 2000 to 2014, controlling for political ideology, type of marijuana decriminalization reform, and socioeconomic conditions, shows that drug-induced overdoses rose most as a function of increasing marijuana use, especially in states with large African American populations and conservative citizen ideology. The rates decrease slightly with the introduction of decriminalization of small amounts of marijuana possession but not with the legalization of medical marijuana use. The implication is that medical marijuana reform may be a de facto stimulant of illegal drug market activity while contributing to the cultural normalization of drug use and experimentation. The results support previous findings that link opioid abuse to habitual marijuana use.

INTRODUCTION

In the last two decades, two main drug policy issues have dominated national political attention: the decriminalization of marijuana and the opioid crisis. Marijuana legalization advocacy touts medical benefits. At the same time, opioid epidemic advocacy calls for understanding substance abuse as mental illness, not as a behavioral choice. It further calls for the removal of social stigmas against drug use and abuse, and even linking research emerges positing a connection between marijuana decriminalization and decreases in opioid overdose rates (Bachhuber et al., 2014; Livingston et al., 2017). Yet, research is inconclusive and more studies are emerging cautioning against the optimistic assumption that if people are given easier access to marijuana, they would opt to use it rather than more dangerous drugs (Shi, 2017; Shi & Liang, 2020). Specifically, Powell, Pacula, and Jacobson (2018) analyze the impact of medical marijuana legislation on overdose deaths from prescription opioids from 1999 to 2013, and with specific controls for population demographics and drug-overdose prevention laws, find that in states that have passed medical marijuana reform, its impact on overdoses was not significant.

The impact of medical marijuana laws (MMLs) is the focus in such works, with discussions on whether pain sufferers would opt for medical marijuana as opposed to stronger and, as the literature has established well, more dangerous and highly addictive opioids (Jones, Mack, & Paulozzi, 2013). Following up on the work of Anguelov (2018), this chapter examines the impact of the proliferation of marijuana decriminalization on the opioid epidemic in the context of the cultural normalization of drug use. A panel model analysis for all 50 states from 2000 to 2014, controlling for political ideology, type of marijuana decriminalization reform, and socioeconomic conditions, shows that drug-induced overdoses rose most as a function of increasing marijuana use, especially in states with large African American populations and conservative citizen ideologies. The rates decrease slightly with the introduction of decriminalization of small amounts of marijuana possession but not with the legalization of medical marijuana. The implication is that medical marijuana reform may stimulate illegal drug market activity, while contributing to the cultural normalization of drug use and experimentation. The results support previous findings that link opioid abuse to habitual marijuana use (Dupont, 2017; Fiellin et al., 2013; Osborne et al., 2017).

The findings here help elucidate on two previous studies that examine the interplay of marijuana reform and the opioid crisis: Jones, Mack, and Paulozzi (2013), who find that prescribed opioids drive the rise in overall deaths from drug overdoses, both alone and in combination with illicit drug-taking, including marijuana; and Powell, Pacula, and Jacobson (2018), who find that the introduction of MMLs does not significantly decrease deaths linked to overdoses from legally prescribed opioids. The problem is that, even in the context of a noted link between a rise in the prescription of opioid-based pain relievers, the opioid crisis is an outcome of a rise in illegal drug-taking (Deaton, 2017; Jones, 2013). Alexander, Kiang, and Barbieri (2018) breakdown mortality rates by race and type of opioid as a cause of death from 1979 to 2015, and specifically show that the "current wave," as the authors put it—2010–2015—is driven by heroin and fentanyl abuse, not by prescription-type substances.

This chapter puts at its core the interplay between legal and illegal drug markets, the commerce of marijuana in both, and the effect of legalization efforts on drug use and abuse. The findings raise many questions on the validity of measurement on drug use and abuse, the integrated relationship between the consumption of marijuana and other drugs, and the stimulus effect of marijuana decriminalization on illegal drug markets, which are the primary market for underage users. Evidence is emerging that youth consumption is stimulated by marijuana decriminalization reform (Alley, Kerr, & Bae, 2019; Cerdá et al., 2019; Koval, Kerr, & Bae, 2019) and there is a link between opioid abuse and marijuana use in young adults (Lankenau et al., 2012; Lord & Marsch, 2011; Madras et al., 2019).

THE OPIOID CRISIS AND MARIJUANA REFORM: INCENTIVIZING THE USE OF A "LESS-DANGEROUS" DRUG

Opioids are highly addictive narcotics that work on the Mu receptors in the brain, which are mainly located in the limbic region of the brain that controls the flight, fight, and freeze responses of the person, and triggers pleasure pathways by releasing the neurotransmitter dopamine (Chartoff & Connery, 2014; Johnson & North, 1992). The role of opioids in premature death has risen to such a level that the Food and Drug Administration (FDA) has begun requiring opioid manufacturers to provide training for doctors and creating patient education materials in an effort to lessen opioid abuse through patient negligence and over-prescription (Okie, 2010). To this point, in 2016, the Center for Disease Control (CDC) updated guidelines for prescribing opioids for chronic pain management, as efficacy for long-term use is lacking sufficient data to support the practice (Dowell, Haegerich, & Chou, 2016). This fact is especially important as addiction to opioids can happen in as little as five days of use.[1] When prescribed opioids are no longer available to patients, they experience withdrawal symptoms and are forced to find alternative opioid suppliers.

This interplay of promoting pain management while not acknowledging the promotion of "being high," is at the core of the literature on the opioid crisis. It evaluates the challenges of the advancement of pain management—legal, illegal, self-medication—as a social norm, that is, people in pain want and deserve to feel less of it, with the proliferation of a culture accepting of substance use. The thin line between substance use and abuse, while acknowledged, is seldom discussed as a function of a cultural change in attitudes toward drug prohibition. If anything, the literature calls for a collective action to end the stigma of drug usage in order to understand addiction better, enabling people struggling with addiction to seek help without social victimization.

In this scientific, academic, and social climate, the calls have emerged for employing marijuana as a tool to help steer at-risk-of-opioid-abuse segments of the population away from opioids. Its pain management benefits and non-addictive, at least in terms of physical dependence, nature, have driven the medical marijuana movement (Bradford & Bradford, 2017; Carillo, 2013; Hannah & Mallinson, 2018). The claim behind it is that marijuana has not been found to have any deleterious health effects. However, even if such claims are taken at face value, which they should not be, as even the literature offering support is cautioning that more research is needed (Boehnke, Litinas, & Clauw, 2016; Burgdorf, Kilmer, & Pacula, 2011; Wilkinson et al., 2016), the initial question of whether or not cannabis should be used medicinally is in doubt. Carr and Schatman (2019) argue that the phenotyping of new strains of marijuana has rendered earlier research on delta-9-tetrahydrocannabinol (THC) null and void. The authors show that modern-day high THC potency cannabis is linked to cardiovascular disease and pancreatitis. Burgdorf, Kilmer, and Pacula (2011) analyze marijuana's chemical composition, identifying the plant as having multiple cannabinoids, the most studied being THC. The authors argue that the other cannabinoids, such as cannabidivarin (CBD) oil, have received less research attention. This fact is of major importance as THC is the primary psychoactive substance and is thought to have multiple negative effects including anxiety, panic, and psychosis, while CBD is thought to possess the ability to lessen anxiety. Burgdorf, Kilmer, and Pacula (2011) focus on the lack of understanding of the effect on the user when the THC:CBD ratio is altered. The authors provide evidence that in a 12-year span from 1996–2008 THC concentration in marijuana seized in California rose from 4.56% to 11.76%, while CBD levels were not significantly changed. Since 2011 however, there has been increased interest in CBD, its properties, cultivating cannabis strains with higher CBD to THC ratios, and passing legislation to legalize the production and commerce of CBD compounds (Zeyl, Sawyer, & Wightman, 2020).

The gap in research lies in the lack of understanding how such increased THC potency impacts the feeling one has of "being high." As public attitudes toward drugs have shifted, the understanding of addiction and physical dependence on them have also changed. Within the last decade, the American Psychiatric Association (APA) has drawn a distinction between physical dependence on a substance and underlying mental health disorders, termed substance use disorder or SUD, that leads to heavy use and dependence. Reflecting this shift, the National Institute of Mental Health (NIMH) now proclaims boldly in the first sentence on its website landing page, defining substance use and mental health: "Did you know that addiction to drugs or alcohol is a mental illness?"[2]

If addiction is to be treated as mental illness, shouldn't researchers tackling the promotion of marijuana as an allegedly less-harmful option, examine if its use is linked to mental illness? Some research has started to breach that gap. Di Forti et al. (2015) find that regular users of high THC cannabis were three times more likely to develop psychosis than non-users or users of low-potency THC. Additionally, those using high-potency THC on a daily basis had a six to eight time larger chance of developing psychosis than others. The interpretation is that "marijuana psychosis" may be related to dopamine regulation (Di Forti et al., 2009), the same neurotransmitter affected by opioids. Kimbrel et al. (2015) find evidence of, as the authors put it "cannabis use disorder" and severity of PTSD incidents among veterans, including suicide attempts. Analyzing the academic works on psychotic behavior as a function of cannabis use, Berenson (2019) offers a most comprehensive narrative. The author presents multiple cases and studies where habitual marijuana usage is correlated with mental and physical illness. Whether such research presents compelling causals, evidence is unclear. The main issue is in tautology since it is recognized that SUD is a mental illness, it is important to account for the fact that people afflicted with SUD are more likely to have other mental health issues (Drake & Wallach, 1989; Szerman et al., 2018).

Yet, there is empirical evidence that supports substitution efforts, to put it cavalierly, to incentivize marijuana instead of opioid use. Livingston et al. (2017) received wide public attention when they offered estimates that Colorado's legalization of recreational use resulted in a decrease in opioid-related deaths. However, the results of that study show that the change was observed just for one year and the authors urge others to continue to examine the dynamic for long-term, lasting effects. Shi (2017) finds that from 1997 to 2014, opioid-related hospitalizations in states that legalized medical marijuana decreased by 23% and opioid-related deaths during such hospitalizations decreased by 17%. Yet, those metrics should not be conflated with overall overdose death rates as a function of opioid abuse, as many occur outside of hospitals (Ray et al., 2015; Vilke et al., 2003). This fact is also the major limitation in Boehnke, Litinas, and Clauw (2016), who survey 244 medical marijuana patients, finding that 64% of them decreased their opioid prescription use. Their population sample consists not only of medical record patients, that is, those under physician supervision for drug use, but also medical marijuana patients. It is important to remember that those are patients who have undertaken the high transaction costs of getting a medical card and are willing to pay the premiums at that particular marijuana dispensary. Overall in Colorado dispensary, premiums are 50% higher than illegal market sources (Davie et al., 2019). That could be why Subritzky, Pettigrew, and Lenton (2016) find that after legalization, over 40% of all marijuana commerce in Colorado remained in the black market.

Findings from studies that use dispensary data have external validity to like populations, meaning the segment of users that participate in legal dispensary option markets. This is why Powell, Pacula, and Jacobson (2018) find that medical marijuana reduced opioid mortality primarily through access to dispensaries. However, as the literature on the opioid crisis establishes, the crisis in overdose death rates is due to the high rate of illegal drug-taking of vulnerable populations (Jones, 2013). Those are citizens without adequate health coverage and resources, not those who willingly participate in the legal medical cannabis system. In related research, prone to similar limitations, Bachhuber et al. (2014) find that from 1999 to 2010, 13 states that had implemented medical cannabis laws experienced a mortal opioid overdose rate that was a mean 24.8% lower than states without medical cannabis laws. Although the work shows statistical significance, the authors acknowledge that more research needs to be done on the mechanism of medical cannabis law and an evaluation of state-to-state differences needs to be conducted before widespread implementation of any policy should occur. Hayes and Brown (2014) argue that the analysis of Bachhuber et al. (2014) has serious limitations in sample specificity and external validity because 60% of subjects had prescriptions for pain management. The question arises: If the other 40% are not being treated for pain, then what interaction with medical cannabis would they have? Related concerns are also voiced by Pacula and Smart (2017), who posit that research on achieving the intended benefits of cannabis reform is largely inconclusive despite the liberalizations of state-level marijuana laws over the past five decades. The authors suggest that inconclusive results are due to inconsistencies in populations of interest, timing of evaluations, and measures being studied. Simoni-Wastila and Palumbo (2013) state plainly that research simply has not been conducted on long-term health risks of rising THC concentrations or the reaction of State Medical Boards to decriminalization statutes. Yet, decriminalization promotion's social impetus goes on with powerful celebrity and political support, including from multiple Democratic presidential candidates in 2020 (Hughes, 2019).

MARIJUANA DECRIMINALIZATION RESEARCH

In the recent past, state-level efforts to reform marijuana laws have generated a large and evolving body of academic work. Much focus has been placed on the factors that shape the political will to implement a change (Bradford & Bradford, 2017; Cohen, 2009; Rubens, 2014), the expected fiscal benefits from taxing legal marijuana commerce (Caulkins et al., 2012; Khan, Thompson, & Tremblay, 2020), as well as costs (Elliott, Kersting, & Salyer, 2019) and the social justice goal to lower the disproportionately high rates of incarceration of minority citizens held on, what is often, minor marijuana convictions (Braun, 2018; Thompson, 2017). Such research is a function of the social acceptance of marijuana usage, yet not much discussion centers around why this social acceptance is at its all-time-high. From across disciplines, the main factors that emerge are social outcry against the injustice of the War on Drugs and the general lack of convincing scientific evidence that marijuana is any more harmful than alcohol, which is the most-often comparative analogy.

In the vast literature on marijuana use, estimates are ongoing as to what portion of the general public actually uses the drug and how often. The Department of Health and Human Services has tracked marijuana use since 1970 through the National Survey on Drug Use and Health, estimating usage rates, generally referred to as the SAMHSA rates.[3] Since 1970 they had remained relatively fixed until decriminalization gained impetus. A multi-author report by the National Academies of Sciences, Engineering, and Medicine shows that the SAMHSA rates barely varied until a noted growth trend emerges around 2007. Since then there has been a steady rise of people who report having used marijuana within the last month from 5.8% to 8.4% of the population, a 45% increase (NASEM, 2017).

Those usage rates are social signals that can be seen as a proxy for public opinion on marijuana use. With the onset of decriminalization and legalization of medical use laws, the usage rates started to marginally, yet steadily increase, especially in states that are known as leaders in not just decriminalization, but also a relatively more permissive reform in terms of possession, access, and oversight of marijuana use. Namely, in Vermont, Washington, California, Massachusetts, Oregon, and Colorado, from 2000 to 2014 the usage rates changed as:

Table 10.1 Self-reported, At-Least Monthly Marijuana Usage Rates among Voting-Age Adults from the National Survey on Drug Use and Health

State	*2000*	*2014*
Vermont	0.067[a]	0.132
Washington	0.051	0.127
California	0.050	0.091
Massachusetts	0.083	0.117
Oregon	0.061	0.124
Colorado	0.069	0.147

Source: Data from author study.
[a]Reported here to the third decimal in order to capture the fact that the rates' annual change is in fractions of a percent.

As a function of the large increases in these states, and also in others including Alaska, Arizona, Maine, and Montana, the average statewide usage rate rose from 0.043 in 2000 to 0.079 in 2014. Given the fact that the marginal increases are in fractions of a percent, it is not surprising that the longitudinal analysis in chapters 7 and 8 in Anguelov (2018) captures this variability and growth trajectory as the leading predictor of successfully passing marijuana decriminalization reform. Anguelov (2018) offers an analysis of the methodology of collecting the data with a focus on youth consumption, as it is among the most studied topics on the literature on drug use and abuse.

The youth usage national averages are reflected in the SAMHSA rates, as "anyone 15 and over" is part of the "geographic tracks," used to capture "percent of the population," yet these numbers would be under-represented because of the mere difficulties in capturing youth participation in such self-reported polls. Specific to high usage states such as California, underage citizens are not allowed to answer such questions without the formal consent of a legal guardian.

Since the decriminalization wave has started, much research is developing on "youth consumption," as is the emerging term. Specifically, Wen, Hockenberry, and Cummings (2015) examined ten states with MMLs from 2004 through 2012 on the experimentation, regular use, and dependence upon marijuana. The authors found an increased propensity in all three categories for users under the age of 21. At the same time, those states with MMLs did not have a corresponding increase in adolescents using alcohol. Similar results come from Hall and Lynskey (2016) who find that legalizing marijuana recreationally resulted in increased heavy use among current users and increase in the number of new users. Yu et al. (2020), using the SAMHSA usage rate as a dependent variable, also note a significant increase from 2006 to 2016 in self-reported use within the last month among young people in states that had legalized medical commerce, with higher rates for females. This fact is especially important given the work of Meier et al. (2012) who find that habitual use of cannabis during adolescence leads to a nonrecoverable loss of approximately six intelligence points compared to the population at large.

When it comes to youth consumption, the CDC has kept data on high-school students via the Youth Risk Behavior Survey (YRBS) since 1991. The trends in the averages on marijuana use are also increasing, indicating that from 2000 to 2014, around 40% of 9th to 12th graders had used marijuana at least once, 20% of them had in the last month, and 9% had tried it before the age of 13.[4] This is the main cannabis market demographic. It has been since the Vietnam War and will continue to be,[5] if historical trends continue.

Youth marijuana use, and specifically habitual consumption, has been studied at length for decades, and scholars have coined the term "adolescent cannabis use disorder" to describe a myriad of negative outcomes, including mental illness (Clark, Kirisci, & Moss, 1998; Crowley et al., 1998; Dennis et al., 2002; Martin et al., 2006; Stinson et al., 2006; Wittchen et al., 2007). Evaluating such research and adding more current empirical evidence, in their book chapter "Adolescent Cannabis Use Disorders" published in the second edition of *Adolescent Addiction Epidemiology, Assessment, and Treatment*, Leung, Hall, and Degenhardt (2020) explain that males are more apt to develop cannabis-use disorder, especially young men prone to "disruptive and antisocial behavior." The authors also explain the prevalence of dependence in adolescents diagnosed with anxiety and depression. In general, the authors conclude that "problem cannabis use" is associated with alcohol dependence and addiction to other drugs, academic failure, and imprisonment.

If one is to put adolescent marijuana consumption in the context of a cannabis market segment, it is not served by any legal option. Its "residual demand" function, which is the demand left in the general market that the main supplier cannot fill, is and will continue to be addressed by illegal commerce. This is also the main vulnerability population of interest in the literature examined in Anguelov (2018), chapter 5 on integrated drug abuse as mental illness. That research shows that drug addiction is multi-substance use and abuse reality, where experimentation with multiple substances occurs as a function of (a) early and habitual marijuana use, (b) availability, meaning the appearance of a new drugs such as crack in the 1990s and fentanyl today, (c) socioeconomic hardship and cultural marginalization, and (d) a defiant cultural attitude toward drug prohibition.

Based on such dynamics, this chapter explores the links among: (a) the cultural normalization of marijuana use, (b) the formal policy reforms of decriminalization, (c) the drug use and abuse as defined by the mental illness literature, and (d) habitual youth consumption of integrated opiates. The analysis tracks the findings of other studies on marijuana use, mental illness, and the connection to the opioid crisis, such as Kimbrel et al. (2017) and Di Forti et al. (2017), that connect marijuana use disorder with mental illness.[6]

Berenson (2019) offers an extensive analysis of clinical works of evidence that marijuana use may cause mental illness. Since extant research argues that the opioid crisis is an outcome of drug abuse as mental illness and it should be treated as such, it is logical to analyze the link between increasing marijuana use and the opioid epidemic. It is worth noting that among the emerging literature on marijuana decriminalization and its intended benefits, much attention is placed on passing MMLs as a remediation policy to lower opioid abuse. Studies find supporting evidence (Bachhuber et al., 2014; Boehnke, Litinas, & Clauw, 2016; Chan, Burkhardt, & Flyr, 2019; Livingston et al., 2017; Powell, Pacula, & Jacobson, 2018). The problem with such studies is that none of them control for marijuana usage rates. This is a very surprising fact and almost suggests bias.

DATA AND METHODS

The goal here is to see the connection, if any, between marijuana use and drug-related overdose deaths. The methodology uses the model of Anguelov (2018) and also includes an analysis of drug-related overdose deaths. Since 2007, drug-induced deaths have become more common than alcohol-induced or firearm-related deaths in the United States (Paulozzi, 2011). The majority of deaths are unintentional drug poisoning deaths, with suicidal drug poisoning, and drug poisoning of undetermined intent comprising the majority of the remainder. The variables are the following:

- CRUDE RATE—determined by the annual number of drug-induced overdoses per 100,000 people in each of the 50 states, from 2000 through 2014, as recorded in Center for Disease Control Morbidity and Mortality Weekly Report.[7] Drug-induced deaths are defined by the CDC as:

> Drug-induced deaths include all deaths for which drugs are the underlying cause, including deaths attributable to acute poisoning by drugs (drug overdoses) and deaths from medical conditions resulting from chronic drug use. A drug includes illicit or street drugs (e.g., heroin or cocaine), as well as legal prescription drugs and over-the-counter drugs; alcohol is not included. Adverse effects from drugs taken as directed and infections resulting from drug use are not included.

CRUDE RATE is analyzed in the context of the following variables:

- 1. Decriminalization of the possession of small amounts of marijuana
- 2. Legalization of medical marijuana commerce
- 3. Legalization of recreational marijuana adult use
- USAGE—determined as the percentage of the population 18 years or older who reported using marijuana in the past month from 2000 through 2014 (U.S. Census Bureau, SAMHSA)
- BALLOT——denoting the presence of a direct democracy measure
- CIT—the citizen ideology score of a state in a given year, as calculated by utilizing information on Congressional representatives, challengers to incumbents, and voting records of the citizens
- GOV—represents state government ideology, measured based on the make-up of state House and Senate members and party affiliation of the governor[8]

- SHARE AA—percent of the state population that is African America
- REAL GSP—a state's Gross State Product, otherwise known as GDP, employed as a control of both fiscal health and national economic importance
- GSP Government Sector—percent of state GDP from government contracting, which incorporates federal contracts, employed as a proxy for economic vulnerability to loss of such contracts in decriminalizing states
- Tax Revenue Change—percent change from two years to one year prior to the year of analysis to examine if states with legacies of decreasing (or relatively low increases) in public revenues would be more incentivized to innovate in hopes of increasing local tax bases

In light of the ongoing research efforts to better understand societal support for marijuana reform, the variables aim to capture social and socioeconomic factors as well as political tools that have led to state-level reforms.

FINDINGS AND ANALYSIS

In terms of type of reform, states have a choice. Table 10.2 below offers results of three models where type of reform is the dependent variable under three different assumptions. Model 1 treats all reform as a dichotomous outcome to measure the marginal impact of factors that have contributed to overall successful passing of state-level reform. Model 2 ranks reform type under an assumption of liberal progression to measure which factors have contributed to moving toward more liberal laws. Model 3 treats reform as a nominal state of choice.

It is important to offer this nuance in understanding factors that drive reform because of policy learning. Under four specifications of type of reform, coded as: 0—no reform, 1—decriminalization of possession of "small amounts," 2—legal medical marijuana use, and 3—legal recreational use, reform is a matter of policy choice. As more and more legislative options are evaluated at the state level, activists and politicians labor to understand the impacts of reform in terms of leading to beneficial outcomes.

To the public, the process is presented in phrases such as "legalizing marijuana," yet in all three types of reform, there's very little that makes its use actually legal. All three policies only impact citizens 21 years of age or older. It is subject to interpretation if the different types of reform are vested within each other and to what degree. It is impossible to have adult recreational use without allowing for small amount possession, yet it is possible to have MMLs without decriminalizing the possession of small amounts. In such a case, only citizens with medical marijuana "cards" are "allowed" to possess small amounts. Few states that passed MMLs did so without first having

Table 10.2 Model Results for Type of Marijuana Policy Reform, 2000–2014

	Model 1	*Model 2*	*Model 3[a] Multinomial General Structural Equation Model*		
	Logistic Regression: Reform Y/N	*Ordered Probit:*	*Option One: Decriminalization*	*Option Two: Medical*	*Option Three: Recreational*
Usage Rate	5.16***	5.76***	0.39***	6.22***	0.82**
	(1.2)	(1.02)	(0.05)	(0.68)	(0.24)
Citizen Ideology	0.02	0.03	0.01	0.003**	−0.08
	(0.04)	(0.02)	(0.01)	(0.001)	(0.09)
Government Ideology	0.02	−0.013	0.001	0.003	0.05
	(0.02)	(0.009)	(0.007)	(0.006)	(0.05)
Percent of Neighbors with Reform	0.31***	0.47***	−0.27*	0.30*	1.21
	(0.08)	(0.10)	(0.05)	(0.04)	(2.69)
African American Population	16.26	12.56	0.27*	2.41	22.60
	(13.75)	(11.12)	(0.12)	(1.93)	(26.85)
GSP Government Sector	7.72***	0.000067	−3.45e-06*	6.44e-06	1.32e-06*
	(2.21)	(0.000059)	(1.99e-06)	(0.00002)	(44.44e-07)
Tax Revenue Change	0.21*	1.32	−0.45	(0.20)	−5.50
	(0.11)	(1.99)	(2.23)	(1.52)	(4.76)
Real GSP	−4.71^	6.89e-07	5.42*	−7.85e-07	−0.00004
	(2.60)	(5.80e-06)	(2.22)	(2.64e-06)	(0.00003)
Ballot Initiative	0.22**	0.25**	0.13***	2.23***	21.82
	(0.07)	(0.08)	(0.04)	(0.31)	(450.11)
Number of Observations	750	750	750	750	750
Probability > Chi2	0.000	0.000	0.000	0.000	0.000
Wald Chi-2	92.61	34.23	LR Chi-2	574.65	
Pseudo R-squared	NA	NA		0.42	

Source: Data from author study.
[a]Evaluated against the hold-out option of not passing any marijuana decriminalization legislation
Predicted Probability Estimates dy/dx for Significant Variables
Non-converted Coefficients for Non-Significant Variables
Standard errors in parentheses
^*p*<0.1, * *p*<0.05, ** *p*<0.01, *** *p*<0.001

passed decriminalization reforms. In other words, few moved to a state coded as "2" from a state coded with "0."

Whichever way one chooses to code the decriminalization of cannabis, the models reveal that usage rates consistently emerge as the strongest predictor of successfully passing legislative change. The models indicate that the way marijuana reform is coded matters for estimating the marginal impact of public opinion, government and citizen ideology, the experience of neighboring states who have already passed cannabis reforms, or the economic health and dependence of a state on the government sector. Under all three assumptions usage rates, ballot initiative and the experience of neighboring states matter. The passage of MMLs is also a function of liberal citizen ideology. The economic conditions only show significance in the dichotomous model, revealing that states with fairly good tax bases and higher reliance on the government sector passed any one of the three types of decriminalization reform. This finding counters the rhetoric that state governments would be cautious to reform for fear of losing federal contract business, or that they would be more willing to legalize cannabis commerce if pressed for taxable income.

Regardless of coding options aiming to capture permissiveness levels of legal use, one factor remains consistent—a significant increase in self-reported marijuana usage rates leads to reform. These usage rates capture an important social dynamic in the national attitude toward marijuana use and also toward the state-level initiatives to reform. The facts that: (1) the rates were virtually unchanged until the onset of reforms, that (2) they are so low in terms of numeric value, ranging from about half a percent in 2000 to at the highest 15% in 2014, and (3) that they show such a steady increase since 2000, suggest that even under the very restrictive capture platform of estimating usage, Americans are either using more marijuana or are feeling more comfortable admitting that they did in the past month. Socially, this fact denotes a trend of acceptance of not just marijuana, but also of the defiance of legislating drug prohibition. It captures a cultural normalization of recreational drug use and federal government defiance. It is a legacy of the futility of the War on Drugs, which creates and promulgates a system of racial disparity of collateral damages.

The political culture to right such wrongs has been focused on promoting reform. The problem is that promoting reform and promoting marijuana use are hard to disentangle. Promoting reform is also done with a very pugilistic and ideological stance by scholars against the political branding of marijuana as the "gateway" drug, set forth by the Nixon and Reagan War on Drugs decades (Golub & Johnson, 2001, 2002; Mackesy-Amiti, Fendrich, & Goldstein, 1997; Morral, McCaffrey, & Paddock, 2002). Yet, there is research that finds supporting evidence of the "gateway" hypothesis (Clark, Kirisci, & Moss, 1998; DeSimone, 1998; Hall & Lynskey, 2005).

Even among scholars that question the strength of the relationship, namely in Golub and Johnson (1994), there is evidence of a gateway link, particularly for certain segments of the population that is generational. Although not explored in detail by the authors, there seems to be a cultural-attitude-toward-a-drug component, meaning a cultural approbation, if not outright celebration of cannabis and all it represents, as an emblem of social rebellion of youths. That link is better explored by Choo, Roh, and Robinson (2013), who find evidence of a gateway dynamic in high-school students with substance abuse history, that was unique to their individual environments and histories. More "at risk" or "marginalized" young people admitted to a stronger propensity to use harder drugs after using marijuana. In a related and similar in methodology study, Shukla (2013: 5) explains that when self-identified habitual marijuana users were asked about their experiences and thoughts on marijuana as a gateway drug, 45% expressed "mixed and conflicting" opinions, 19.6% "strongly supported the notion," while only 35% did not. Admittedly, in much of the above-mentioned *marijuana-as-the-gateway-drug* research, scholars posit that more research needs to be conducted and not enough data is available, or more precisely, were not available at the time, since most of these works are from a time before the opioid crisis came into social attention as a public health problem.

The literature on the opioid crisis indicates that it is a product of permissive attitude toward drug-taking, including self-medication, illegal drug-taking, drug-taking culture of experimentation with newly available substances such as fentanyl, and integrated, multiple-substance usage, which includes marijuana (Berridge, 2013; Rosenberg & Lundahl, 2019). Hall and Linskey (2005) explain that gateway links occur as a function of socialization into drug subcultures supportive of general illicit drug experimentation. Furthermore, evidence is emerging that marijuana decriminalization has a stimulus effect on illicit marijuana commerce (Fertig, 2019; Flaccus, 2019; Martin, 2019; Serna, 2018).

The stimulation of the black market for marijuana in, and around, states that have legalized adult recreational and/or medical marijuana markets is counter to the argument made by advocates of reform that opening a legal market would divert money away from criminal enterprises and drug cartels (McGinty et al., 2016). Indeed, reporting in states that have legalized recreational marijuana shows that, in some cases, the creation of a legal retail system has created additional opportunities for illegal growers, supplies, and dealers. For instance, the marijuana research firm BDS analytics, which tracks marijuana sales in states where adult consumption has been legalized, estimates that in 2019 more than three-quarters of all marijuana sales in California and Massachusetts, which both legalized recreational marijuana in 2016, were illegal (Martin, 2019).

Recent reporting from California and Massachusetts provides examples of how legal marijuana regimes are stimulating the black market, each in a distinct way. In California, long-running marijuana growing operations in California have little incentive to switch to the regulation-heavy recreational market. The sheriff of Mendocino County told the *New York Times* that, by April of 2019, deputies had seized more than $5 million worth of illegally produced cannabis oil concentrate, which is used in vaporizers (Fuller, 2019). Some of the long-time California growers cultivated for the medical marijuana system as "patient caretakers" and sold excess crop on the black market. The long history of illegal growing operations in California's rural northwest and the state's status as the oldest and most lax medical marijuana system in the country, means that growers have established methods for moving their product (Serna, 2018). As reported in the same article, marijuana from California "seeps out across the country illicitly, through the mail, express delivery services, private vehicles and small aircraft that ply trafficking routes that have existed for decades" (Ibid).

Similar issues exist in the Pacific Northwest. Oregon legalized marijuana in 2014 and has created a marketplace that is more open than other state. Low fees and regulatory barriers to entering the legal marijuana economy were intended to coax long-time illegal growing operations in the rural eastern counties out of the shadows (Slesky, 2019). As of 2020, Oregon has the most recreational marijuana retailers per capita (Bull, 2020). According the U.S. Attorney for the Oregon district, Billy Williams, this situation has allowed the black market to operate in plain sight. Following the bust of a trafficking ring in 2018, Williams said that "these cases provide clear evidence of what I have repeatedly raised concerns over: Oregon's marijuana industry is attracting organized criminal networks looking to capitalize on the state's relaxed regulatory environment" (Flaccus, 2019). Like California, Oregon's legal market has provided cover for black-market operations that move cannabis into neighboring states. For instance, in neighboring Idaho, state troopers reported a 665% increase in the amount of marijuana seized from 2016 to 2017, and in 2018 they reported over ton had been seized (Fertig, 2019).

A stricter regulatory system and a slow rollout of recreational marijuana laws appear to stimulate the black market as well. In Massachusetts, which legalized recreational marijuana the same year as California, the first retailers did not open until over two years later as legislators and regulators modified and promulgated over the ballot initiative language that lead to reform. Today, Massachusetts has 1 dispensary per 100,000 residents, compared to 16.5 in Oregon (Bull, 2020). According to reporting in the *Boston Globe*, this has led to an oligopoly, where little, if any, local competition keeps prices high and well above those in the black market (Martin, 2019). Users are further incentivized to seek alternatives to the legal recreational market due to long wait times at dispensaries, home grown laws that allow one household to produce more marijuana flower than any heavy user could reasonably consume in a year's time, and a sales-tax-free medical marijuana system with high limits on purchase amounts (Ibid). Importantly, in understanding the effect legalization has on the illicit cannabis market, we are still in uncharted territory. Data lag and regulatory differences between the states create complications for empirical research, as does the black market's tendency toward being difficult to document. Still, reporting on the legalization trend at the national and local level demonstrates that early adopters have not yet created a regulatory environment that delivers on the promise of diverting economic activity away from criminal enterprise and bring marijuana commerce into a taxable marketplace.

It is surprising that scholars are not examining a possible link between the social promotion of marijuana use, which de facto is the outcome of the political campaigning for decriminalization reform, and general "illicit drug experimentation," as Hall and Linskey (2005) put it. It is due to two main factors. One is that marijuana reform research is decidedly pro-reform, based on the assumption that the marijuana-as-the-gateway drug rhetoric is wrong and damaging to reform efforts. The other is the call to treat drug abuse as a mental illness, and that is a threatening position to pro-reform advocates, as evidence is emerging between the link of marijuana use and mental illness (Berenson, 2019; Di Forti et al., 2015; Kimbrel et al., 2017).

To address such a void in efforts, table 10.3 below shows the results of the impact of the diffusion and type of marijuana decriminalization state-level reform on state-level opioid-induced death rates.

The findings suggest that usage rates were the strongest predictor of a rise in that drug-induced death rate. The coefficient indicates a 1% increase in usage rates to have led to approximately 120% increase in the overdose death rate. The other significant predictors of change in the death rate all make much smaller marginal impacts. The second largest predictor is share of the population that is African American. In states with relatively large segments of the population, the overdose rate was on average 6% higher. Next are the marijuana decriminalization reforms for possession of small amount and recreational use. Passing those specific provisions led to a marginal decrease in the overdose rate of 3%. At the same time, legalizing medical use had no impact on overdose deaths, which directly challenges the findings in Chan, Burkhardt, and Flyr (2019), in particular. This fact could be a function timeframe differences, and Chan, Burkhard, and Flyr not controlling for usage rates. The last statistically significant variable is citizen ideology, indicating that each 1% increase in liberal legislation led to less than half of a percent decrease in the drug-induced death rate.

Interpreting these results needs to be put in the context of the magnitude and marginal change through the timeframe of the percent variables.

Table 10.3 Impact of Marijuana Decriminalization and Usage on Opioid-induced Death Rates,[a] 2000–2014

	2000–2014
Marijuana Usage Rate	119.55***[b]
	(18.09)
Citizen Ideology	−0.05*
	(0.02)
Government Ideology	0.004
	(0.01)
Type of Marijuana Reform	
Decriminalization of Small Amount Possession	−3.02***
	(0.27)
Medical Legal Commerce	−0.12
	(0.57)
Legal Recreation Use	−3.35*
	(1.54)
Ballot Initiative	−0.07
	(0.41)
Share of Population that is African American	5.72***
	(1.37)
Gross State Product	−3.53e-07
	(2.61e-07)
Constant	7.00***
	(1.43)
Model Details	
Probability > X^2	<0.0001
R-squared	0.19
Wald X^2	372.80
Observations	750

Source: Data from author study.
Dependent Variable: Drug-induced deaths—all deaths for which drugs are the underlying cause, including deaths attributable to acute poisoning by drugs (drug overdoses) and deaths from medical conditions resulting from chronic drug use. A "drug" includes illicit or street drugs (e.g., heroin or cocaine), as well as legal prescription drugs and over-the-counter drugs; alcohol is not included.
[a]The majority of deaths are unintentional drug poisoning deaths, with suicidal drug poisoning and drug poisoning of undetermined intent comprising the majority of the remainder. Adverse effects from drugs taken as directed and infections resulting from drug use are not included.
[b]Wald X^2 two-tailed tests, where NS = not significant, ^$p<0.10$, *$p<0.05$, **$p<0.01$, ***$p<0.001$
Clustered standard errors in parentheses

As already discussed, marijuana usage rates are fairly low. Their marginal changes, meaning from year to hear, are at a fraction of a percent. Yet, they show a steady trajectory of increase. The other independent variables show higher degree of variability, yet their impact on the opioid-related death rate, even for those that are statistically significant, is very small in comparison to the size of the coefficient of the marijuana usage rate. Interpreted literally, the results suggest that from 2000 to 2014, an average of a 1% annual increase in marijuana usage rates led to almost 120% increase in the opioid-related death rate. The fact that the independent variable with lowest unit of marginal change, that is, 0.01% has such a large elasticity impact on the dependent variable, while controls are included in the model, merits further investigation. Although the R-square is fairly low in the proposed model, meaning only about 19% of the change in the overdose death rate is explained by it, implying that more explanatory variables are needed, the significant relationships are not to be ignored. They capture a dynamic that is complicated and in need for much more analysis. The examination of the varied bodies of literature here on gateway links between marijuana use and experimentation with harder drugs, does not show conclusive evidence debunking the theory. Yet, the social and even academic tone on the hypothetical gateway relationship is very vocally questioned, simplified in policy prescription and political rhetoric. The academy is clearly promulgating a political stance toward reform, positing that should people be able to freely use marijuana, they would be less likely to choose harder and more dangerous drugs. Yet, there is not enough conclusive research to justify such a claim.

The results here, offering a very general and simple regression, would cast doubt on the previous approaches of employing marijuana usage rate data, as well as opioid-related death data, in longitudinal models. If scholars are to use these rates in causal analyses, they should be used as both causes and effect proxies, even at risk of endogeneity, because they are proxies that only can capture so much. The death rates are, unfortunately, the hard facts of the crisis. From works on preventative measures, to treatment and public health outreach, to education, to their dramatic spike in the recent past, the literature examined here shows that they are the outcome of gauging effectiveness in addressing the opioid crisis. Behind their drastic spike is the main fact of social behavior—defiance toward drug prohibition. That same fact is behind the recent rise in self-reported marijuana usage rates. The lurking variable that should give drug use and abuse analysts a pause is the time frame. Both of these sets of rates significantly rise in correlation with marijuana decriminalization reform.

That is a fact that is either purposefully ignored by the leading marijuana reform scholars, or at least, in the literature examined here, it was never mentioned or in any way acknowledged. It must be. The main reasons are that it is clear from examining the extent research that those most vulnerable to the opioid abuse are, as is the term "at-risk" segments of the population, lacking adequate economic opportunity, education, and health care. The evidence also outline the vulnerability in those with mental health issues who lack the necessary platforms and tools to learn, should there be such a thing, how to use drugs in ways to not endanger their lives. Is promoting marijuana as an alternative, safer or at least, less dangerous than opioids drug, the solution to address integrated, multi-substance drug abuse? Hardly. Especially for those who are prone to experimentation, unable and/or unwilling to participate in legal marijuana markets, or just socially defiant toward the "just-say-no" patronizing anti-drug campaigns of the past. What those campaigns failed to do is explain "why not." That is where reform, both political and scientific, needs to be refocused.

CONCLUSIONS AND IMPLICATIONS

Promoting marijuana reform is a political movement with definitive policy implications and nuances. Reform has started as a layered option that states chose that impacts marijuana market segments differently. It ranges from lowering criminal punitive measures for the possession to decriminalizing all adult recreational use. The problem is that at each state of reform, discretion of regulation and oversight is increased for authoritative administrative bodies, which is a legacy problem of the past that has resulted in racially-based inequality in criminal punishment.

The current system does little to address the foundations of this past system, because it does not take into account a core fact of marijuana consumption: it is driven by youth usage. All decriminalization efforts in America impact those age 21 and over. Yet, most marijuana consumption and law infraction is done by those under the age of 21, and more importantly and alarmingly, under the age of 18. According to the CDC, 40% of high-schoolers use marijuana regularly. In comparison, the "voting-age" usage rates for the general population are at their highest around 15% and only in certain states. Additionally, the analysis here shows that such youth consumption is well and competitively met by illegal marijuana suppliers that may be gaining competitive advantage over legal producers. Consequently, they are able to undercut legal production efforts.

The implications are political. If even legal market segments would opt for illegal supply options, due to better quality and price, the implication is that the extant deterrent measures are rendered moot in a culture of promoting the drug itself. Promoting its legalization is promoting its legality. If one is to use the rise of the self-reported usage rates as an indication of social manifestation of comfort in admitting habitual use, the spike would suggest a comfort in admitting defiance toward its prohibition at the federal level. The problem is that the social messaging is heard by all, and all includes the main marijuana consumer—the American teenager.

In the era when the opioid crisis is taking record number of young lives, marijuana potency is increasing, evidence is emerging of a link between marijuana potency and mental illness, criminalization efforts may be easing up, and a general attitude of drug experimentation continues, little incentives are offered for the young to abstain or learn more about marijuana abuse and/or integrated drug use. At the same time, political pro-reform rhetoric is strongly condemning any previously-posited links between marijuana and other drug abuse, as reflected by the "gateway" hypothesis. The findings here can directly challenge the wisdom of such a strategy.

By employing marijuana usage rates as a hypothetical cause in the drug-related mortality rates, we note that their marginal increase has had a strong impact on overdose death rates from 2000 to 2014. At the same time, decriminalization efforts have had a significant, but much lower positive impact and only in states that implement decriminalization reform that directly address illegal marijuana markets. The results indicate that overdose death rates decreased in states that passed reform lowering the punitive measures for the possession of small amounts of marijuana—a reform that impacts youth consumption and minority criminalization disproportionality, as well as in states that moved to the most permissive decriminalization options—legalizing adult recreational use. Meanwhile, legalizing medical commerce alone, referred to in the literature as passing MMLs, had no impact on the opioid-related overdose death rate at the state level.

NOTES

1. According to the Mayo Clinic, Mayo Foundation for Medical Education and Research (MFMER), https://www.mayoclinic.org/diseases-conditions/prescription-drug-abuse/in-depth/how-opioid-addiction-occurs/art-20360372
2. See: https://www.nimh.nih.gov/health/topics/substance-use-and-mental-health/index.shtml
3. https://www.samhsa.gov/data/data-we-collect/nsduh-national-survey-drug-use-and-health
4. Data available at: https://www.cdc.gov/healthyyouth/data/yrbs/pdf/trends/2017_us_drug_trend_yrbs.pdf
5. For details, see the discussion on the cultural normalization of marijuana use in Anguelov (2018) chapters 4, 8, and 9.
6. Literature on that argument tracked in Anguelov (2018), chapter 5.
7. Available at: https://www.cdc.gov/mmwr/mmwr_wk/wk_pvol.html
8. Utilizing the scores developed by: Berry, W. D., Ringquist, E. J., Fording, R. C., & Hanson, R. L. (1998). Measuring citizen and government ideology in the American states, 1960-93. *American Journal of Political Science*, 327–348.

REFERENCES

Alexander, M. J., Kiang, M. V., & Barbieri, M. (2018). Trends in black and white opioid mortality in the United States, 1979–2015. *Epidemiology*, *29*(5), 707–715.

Bachhuber, M. A., Saloner, B., Cunningham, C. O., & Barry, C. L. (2014). Medical cannabis laws and opioid analgesic overdose mortality in the United States, 1999–2010. *JAMA internal medicine*, *174*(10), 1668–1673.

Berenson, A. (2019). *Tell Your Children: The Truth about Marijuana, Mental Illness, and Violence*. New York: Simon and Schuster.

Berridge, V. (2013). *Demons: Our Changing Attitudes to Alcohol, Tobacco, and Drugs*. Oxford, UK: Oxford University Press.

Boehnke, K. F., Litinas, E., & Clauw, D. J. (2016). Medical cannabis use is associated with decreased opiate medication use in a retrospective cross-sectional survey of patients with chronic pain. *Journal of Pain*, *17*(6), 739–744.

Bradford, A. C., & David Bradford, W. (2017). Factors driving the diffusion of medical marijuana legalisation in the United States. *Drugs: Education, Prevention and Policy*, *24*(1), 75–84.

Braun, M. R. (2018). Re-assessing mass incarceration in light of the decriminalization of marijuana in Maryland. *University of Baltimore Law Forum*, *49*(1), 24–42.

Bull, B. (2020). *Report: Oregon Tops For Cannabis Dispensaries Per Capita*. KLCC, February 10, 2020.

Burgdorf, J. R., Kilmer, B., & Pacula, R. L. (2011). Heterogeneity in the composition of marijuana seized in California. *Drug and Alcohol Dependence*, *117*(1), 59–61.

Carr, D., & Schatman, M. (2019). Cannabis for chronic pain: not ready for prime time. *American Journal of Public Health*, *109*(1), 50–51.

Caulkins, J. P., Hawken, A., Kilmer, B., & Kleiman, M. A. (2012). High tax states: Options for gleaning revenue from legal cannabis. *Oregon Law Review*, *91*, 1041–1068.

Chartoff, E. H., & Connery, H. S. (2014). It's more exciting than mu: crosstalk between mu opioid receptors and glutamatergic transmission in the mesolimbic dopamine system. *Frontiers in Pharmacology*, *5*, 116. doi: 10.3389/fphar.2014.00116.

Choo, T., Roh, S., & Robinson, M. (2008). Assessing the "Gateway Hypothesis" among middle and high school students in Tennessee. *Journal of Drug Issues*, *38*(2), 467–492.

Clark, D. B., Kirisci, L., & Moss, H. B. (1998). Early adolescent gateway drug use in sons of fathers with substance use disorders. *Addictive Behaviors*, *23*(4), 561–566.

Cohen, P. J. (2009). Medical marijuana: the conflict between scientific evidence and political ideology. Part one of two. *Journal of Pain and Palliative Care Pharmacotherapy*, *23*(1), 4–25.

Crawford, S. (2013). The political economy of medical marijuana. Doctoral thesis disseration, Department of Sociology and the Graduate School of the University of Oregon.

Crowley, T. J., Macdonald, M. J., Whitmore, E. A., & Mikulich, S. K. (1998). Cannabis dependence, withdrawal, and reinforcing effects among adolescents with conduct symptoms and substance use disorders. *Drug and Alcohol Dependence*, *50*(1), 27–37.

Davie, A., Parco, J. E., Parco, H., Levy, D. A., Wheatley, M., & Van Wagoner, P. (2019). Chapter 16: Black, white, and green: The effect of legalization on Colorado's black market of cannabis. In McGettigan, T. (ed.), *The Politics of Marijuana: A New Paradigm.* (pp. 185–210). Bern, Switzerland: Peter Land Publishing.

Deaton, A. (2017). Economic aspects of the opioid crisis: testimony before the joint economic committee of the United States congress. In *Economic Aspects of the Opioid Crisis: Testimony before the Joint Economic Committee of the United States Congress.* Retrieved from: https://www.jec.senate.gov/public/_cache/files/37cbd2d6-da98-4d92-87bb-cb2a7ed7b91d/deaton-testimony-060817.pdf

Dennis, M., Babor, T. F., Roebuck, M. C., & Donaldson, J. (2002). Changing the focus: the case for recognizing and treating cannabis use disorders. *Addiction, 97*, 4–15.

DeSimone, J. (1998). Is marijuana a gateway drug? *Eastern Economic Journal, 24*(2), 149–164.

Di Forti, M., Morgan, C., Dazzan, P., Pariante, C., Mondelli, V., Marques, T. R., & Murray, R. M. (2009). High-potency cannabis and the risk of psychosis. *British Journal of Psychiatry: The Journal of Mental Science, 195*(6), 488–491. doi: 10.1192/bjp.bp.109.064220

Di Forti, M., Marconi, A., Carra, E., Fraietta, S., Trotta, A., Bonomo, M., & Stilo, S. A. (2015). Proportion of patients in south London with first-episode psychosis attributable to use of high potency cannabis: a case-control study. *Lancet Psychiatry, 2*(3), 233–238.

Dowell, D., Haegerich, T. M., & Chou, R. (2016). CDC guideline for prescribing opioids for chronic pain—United States, 2016. *JAMA, 315*(15), 1624–1645.

Drake, R. E., & Wallach, M. A. (1989). Substance abuse among the chronic mentally ill. *Psychiatric Services, 40*(10), 1041–1046

DuPont, R. L. (2018). The opioid epidemic is an historic opportunity to improve both prevention and treatment. *Brain Research Bulletin, 138*, 112–114.

Elliott, T. L., Kersting, L., & Salyer, R. (2019). The legalization of marijuana: Tax issues and costs to employers. *Journal of Management Policy and Practice, 20*(1), 15–25.

Fertig, N. (2019). How legal weed is killing America's most famous marijuana farmers. *POLITICO Magazine*, June 4, 2019.

Fiellin, L. E., Tetrault, J. M., Becker, W. C., Fiellin, D. A., & Hoff, R. A. (2013). Previous use of alcohol, cigarettes, and marijuana and subsequent abuse of prescription opioids in young adults. *Journal of Adolescent Health, 52*(2), 158–163.

Flaccus, Gillian. (2018). *Feds: 'Vast' Oregon Pot Trafficking Schemes Prompt 6 Arrests.* Associated Press.

Fuller, T (2019) "'Getting worse, not better': Illegal pot market booming in California despite legalization." *New York Times*, April 27, 2019.

Golub, A., & Johnson, B. D. (1994). Cohort differences in drug-use pathways to crack among current crack abusers in New York City. *Criminal Justice and Behavior, 21*(4), 403–422.

Golub, A., & Johnson, B. D. (2001). Variation in youthful risks of progression from alcohol and tobacco to marijuana and to hard drugs across generations. *American Journal of Public Health, 91*(2), 225.

Golub, A., & Johnson, B. D. (2002). The misuse of the "Gateway Theory" in U.S. policy on drug abuse control: A secondary analysis of the muddled deduction. *International Journal of Drug Policy, 13*(1), 5–19.

Hall, W. D., & Lynskey, M. (2005). Is cannabis a gateway drug? Testing hypotheses about the relationship between cannabis use and the use of other illicit drugs. *Drug and Alcohol Review, 24*(1), 39–48.

Hall, W., & Lynskey, M. (2016). Evaluating the public health impacts of legalizing recreational cannabis use in the United States. *Addiction, 111*(10), 1764–1773.

Hannah, A. L., & Mallinson, D. J. (2018). Defiant innovation: the adoption of medical marijuana laws in the American states. *Policy Studies Journal, 46*(2), 402–423.

Hayes, M. J., & Brown, M. S. (2014). Legalization of medical marijuana and incidence of opioid mortality. *JAMA Internal Medicine, 174*(10), 1673–1674.

Hughes, T. (2019). Where the 2020 Democratic candidates for president stand on marijuana legalization. *USA Today*, September 9, 2019. Retrieved from: https://www.usatoday.com/in-depth/news/nation/2019/09/07/2020-and-legal-weed-where-every-democratic-candidate-stands/2150503001/

Johnson, S. W., & North, R. A. (1992). Opioids excite dopamine neurons by hyperpolarization of local interneurons. *Journal of Neuroscience, 12*(2), 483–488.

Jones, C. M. (2013). Heroin use and heroin use risk behaviors among nonmedical users of prescription opioid pain relievers–United States, 2002–2004 and 2008–2010. *Drug and Alcohol Dependence, 132*(1–2), 95–100.

Jones, C. M., Mack, K. A., & Paulozzi, L. J. (2013). Pharmaceutical overdose deaths, United States, 2010. *JAMA, 309*(7), 657–659.

Khan, M. S., Thompson, P. N., & Tremblay, V. J. (2020). Marijuana tax incidence, stockpiling, and cross-border substitution. *International Tax and Public Finance, 27*(1), 103–127.

Kimbrel, N. A., Newins, A. R., Dedert, E. A., Van Voorhees, E. E., Elbogen, E. B., Naylor, J. C., & Calhoun, P. S. (2017). Cannabis use disorder and suicide attempts in Iraq/Afghanistan-era veterans. *Journal of Psychiatric Research, 89*, 1–5.

Lankenau, S. E., Teti, M., Silva, K., Bloom, J. J., Harocopos, A., & Treese, M. (2012). Initiation into prescription opioid misuse amongst young injection drug users. *International Journal of Drug Policy, 23*(1), 37–44.

Leung, J., Hall, W., & Degenhardt, L. (2020). Adolescent cannabis use disorders. In Essau, C. A. & Delfabbro, P. H. (eds.), *Adolescent Addiction Epidemiology, Assessment, and Treatment: A volume in Practical Resources for the Mental Health Professional.* Amsterdam: Elsevier, pp. 111–135.

Livingston, M. D., Barnett, T. E., Delcher, C., & Wagenaar, A. C. (2017). Recreational cannabis legalization and opioid-related deaths in Colorado, 2000–2015. *American Journal of Public Health, 107*(11), 1827–1829.

Lord, S., & Marsch, L. (2011). Emerging trends and innovations in the identification and management of drug use among adolescents and young adults. *Adolescent Medicine: State of the Art Reviews, 22*(3), 649.

Mackesy-Amiti, M. E., Fendrich, M., & Goldstein, P. J. (1997). Sequence of drug use among serious drug users: typical vs atypical progression. *Drug and Alcohol Dependence, 45*(3), 185–196.

Madras, B. K., Han, B., Compton, W. M., Jones, C. M., Lopez, E. I., & McCance-Katz, E. F. (2019). Associations of parental marijuana use with offspring marijuana, tobacco, and alcohol use and opioid misuse. *JAMA Network Open*, *2*(11), e1916015–e1916015.

Martin, C. S., Chung, T., Kirisci, L., & Langenbucher, J. W. (2006). Item response theory analysis of diagnostic criteria for alcohol and cannabis use disorders in adolescents: Implications for DSM-V. *Journal of Abnormal Psychology*, *115*(4), 807–814.

Martin, N. (2019). Why most mass. marijuana sales are on the black market, two years after legalization. *Boston Globe*, February 2, 2019.

McGinty E., Samples, H., Bandara, S. N., Saloner, B., Bachhuber, M. A., & Barry, C. L. (2016). The emerging public discourse on state legalization of marijuana for recreational use in the U.S.: Analysis of news media coverage, 2010–2014. *Preventive Medicine*, *90*, 114–120. doi: 10.1016/j.ypmed.2016.06.040

Meier, M. H., Caspi, A., Ambler, A., Harrington, H., Houts, R., Keefe, R. S., & Moffitt, T. E. (2012). Persistent cannabis users show neuropsychological decline from childhood to midlife. *Proceedings of the National Academy of Sciences*, *109*(40), E2657–E2664.

Morral, A. R., McCaffrey, D. F., & Paddock, S. M. (2002). *Using Marijuana May Not Raise the Risk of Using Harder Drugs*. Retrieved from: https://www.rand.org/pubs/research_briefs/RB6010.html

National Academies of Sciences, Engineering, and Medicine (NASEM). (2017). *The Health Effects Of Cannabis and Cannabinoids: The Current State of Evidence and Recommendations for Research*. Washington, DC: National Academies Press.

Okie, S. (2010). A flood of opioids, a rising tide of deaths. *New England Journal of Medicine*, *363*(21), 1981–1985.

Osborne, V., Serdarevic, M., Crooke, H., Striley, C., & Cottler, L. B. (2017). Non-medical opioid use in youth: Gender differences in risk factors and prevalence. *Addictive Behaviors*, *72*, 114–119.

Pacula, R. L., & Smart, R. (2017). Medical marijuana and marijuana legalization. *Annual Review of Clinical Psychology*, *13*, 397–419.

Powell, D., Pacula, R. L., & Jacobson, M. (2018). Do medical marijuana laws reduce addictions and deaths related to pain killers?. *Journal of Health Economics*, *58*, 29–42.

Ray, W. A., Chung, C. P., Murray, K. T., Cooper, W. O., Hall, K., & Stein, C. M. (2015). Out-of-hospital mortality among patients receiving methadone for noncancer pain. *JAMA Internal Medicine*, *175*(3), 420–427.

Rosenberg, D. R., & Lundahl, L. H. (2019). *Substance Abuse: An Issue of Pediatric Clinics of North America, Ebook* (Vol. 66, No. 6). Elsevier Health Sciences.

Rubens, M. (2014). Political and medical views on medical marijuana and its future. *Social Work in Public Health*, *29*(2), 121–131.

Serna, J. (2018) L.A. launches crackdown on unlicensed marijuana businesses; more than 500 people are charged. *LA Times*, September 7, 2018.

Shi, Y. (2017). Medical marijuana policies and hospitalizations related to marijuana and opioid pain reliever. *Drug and Alcohol Dependence*, *173*(1), 144–150.

Shi, Y., & Liang, D. (2020). The association between recreational cannabis commercialization and cannabis exposures reported to the U.S. National Poison Data System. *Addiction*. doi: 10.1111/add.15019.

Shukla, R. K. (2013). Inside the gate: Insiders' perspectives on Marijuana as a gateway drug. *Humboldt Journal of Social Relations*, *35*, 5–17.

Simoni-Wastila, L., & Palumbo, F. B. (2013). Medical marijuana legislation: what we know and don't. *Journal of Health Care Law and Policy*, *16*, 59–76.

Slesky, Andrew (2019). *Oregon, Awash in Marijuana, Takes Steps to Curb Production*. Associated Press.

Stinson, F. S., Ruan, W. J., Pickering, R., & Grant, B. F. (2006). Cannabis use disorders in the USA: Prevalence, correlates and co-morbidity. *Psychological Medicine*, *36*(10), 1447–1460.

Subritzky, T., Pettigrew, S., & Lenton, S. (2016). Issues in the implementation and evolution of the commercial recreational cannabis market in Colorado. *International Journal of Drug Policy*, *27*, 1–12.

Szerman, N., Parro-Torres, C., Didia-Attas, J., & El-Guebaly, N. (2018). Dual disorders: addiction and other mental disorders. Integrating mental health. In Javed, A. & Fountoulakis, K. (eds.), *Advances in Psychiatry* (pp. 109–126). Nuneaton, UK.

Thompson, B. Y. (2017). "Good moral characters": How drug felons are impacted under state marijuana legalization laws. *Contemporary Justice Review*, *20*(2), 211–226.

Vilke, G. M., Sloane, C., Smith, A. M., & Chan, T. C. (2003). Assessment for deaths in out-of-hospital heroin overdose patients treated with naloxone who refuse transport. *Academic Emergency Medicine*, *10*(8), 893–896.

Wen, H., Hockenberry, J. M., & Cummings, J. R. (2015). The effect of medical marijuana laws on adolescent and adult use of marijuana, alcohol, and other substances. *Journal of Health Economics*, *42*, 64–80.

Wilkinson, S. T., Yarnell, S., Radhakrishnan, R., Ball, S. A., & D'Souza, D. C. (2016). Marijuana legalization: impact on physicians and public health. *Annual Review of Medicine*, *67*, 453–466.

Wittchen, H. U., Fröhlich, C., Behrendt, S., Günther, A., Rehm, J., Zimmermann, P., & Perkonigg, A. (2007). Cannabis use and cannabis use disorders and their relationship to mental disorders: a 10-year prospective-longitudinal community study in adolescents. *Drug and Alcohol Dependence*, *88*, S60-S70.

Yu, B., Chen, X., Chen, X., & Yan, H. (2020). Marijuana legalization and historical trends in marijuana use among U.S. residents aged 12–25: Results from the 1979–2016 National Survey on Drug Use and Health. *BMC Public Health*, *20*(1), 156. doi: 10.1186/s12889-020-8253-4

Zeyl, V., Sawyer, K., & Wightman, R.S. (2020). What do you know about maryjane? A systematic review of the current data on the THC:CBD ratio. *Substance Use and Misuse*. *55*(8), 1223–1227. doi: 10.1080/10826084.2020.1731547

Index

adolescent cannabis use disorder, 151–52, 170, 194–95
American Civil Liberties Union (ACLU), 31–32, 85, 87
American National Election Study (ANES), 49–53, 59
American Psychiatric Association (APA), 190
American social power, 47

Black Lives Matter movement, 33–34, 43, 83
Bureau of Justice, 24, 27

cannabidivarin (CBD), 117, 132, 190
cannabinoid hyperemesis syndrome, 171
cannabinoids, 190
CDC WONDER dataset, 173, 179–80
Center for Disease Control (CDC), 167, 171, 189, 196
collateral consequences, 33
Compassionate Use Act of 1996, 133, 168
Controlled Substances Act of 1970, 132

Deferred Action for Childhood Arrivals (DACA), 70
defunding of police, 21–22, 25, 33–34, 36
delta-9-tetrahydrocannabinol (THC), 29, 117, 132–33, 170, 190–92
Department of Veterans Affairs, 133
difference-in-differences, 173–75, 177, 180

Eighteenth Amendment, 29–30

Federal Act on Narcotics and Psychotropic Substances in Switzerland, 109, 115
Federal Bureau of Investigation (FBI), 23–25
fentanyl, 189, 195, 200
Food and Drug Administration (FDA), 189

Gallup, 25, 28, 68–70, 168
gateway: drug, ix, 44, 199–200, 202, 204, 206; hypothesis, 199, 206

hedonic well-being, 134
HIV/Aids, 135, 145

immigrants, 61–79
International Classification of Diseases (ICD-10), 114, 173
intersectionality, 43, 45–49, 53–55

Japanese Traditional Medicine, 135

Latino(s), 61–64, 67, 69
LGBT+, 47

Marijuana Policy Project, 91
marijuana psychosis, 31, 170, 190–91
Marijuana Tax Act of 1937, 31, 62, 132
medical marijuana laws (MMLs), viii, 188, 194–95, 197, 199, 206
mental illness, 46, 191, 195, 202, 205
MeToo movement, 43
Mexican hypothesis, 62, 78
Mu receptors, 189
muscle relaxants, 138–39, 145

National Election Pool Poll, 67, 72–73
National Institute on Drug Abuse (NIDA), 29, 35
National Survey of Drug Use and Health (NSDUH), 152, 155, 167, 171–72, 174, 182
neurotransmitter, 189, 191
Nonsteroidal anti-inflammatory drug (NSAID), 139, 145

opioid use disorder, 171, 182

panel analysis, 187–88
Pearson correlation, 70
Pew Research Center, 13, 68–70, 72, 151
police: manpower, 23; misconduct, 21–22
political ideology, 187–88
post-traumatic stress disorder (PTSD), 135–36

QR Code, 136
Qualtrics, 136

regression: linear, 48–49, 59, 174–75, 177–78, 204; logistic, 9, 13, 50–51, 72–75; multinomial, 198; ordered probit, 198; Poisson, 180–83

SAMHSA, 152, 158–67, 172, 175, 182–83, 193–94
Schedule 1, 29, 44, 62, 132, 168
Shaleen Title, 90, 97
substance use disorder (SUD), 190–91
Supreme Court, 1–2, 70
SurveyMonkey, 136
Swissmedic, 114, 120

Temperance Movement, 30
transformative consumer research, 134
Treatment Episode Data Set (TEDS), 155, 167, 171–72, 174, 177–80, 182

Uniform Drug Narcotic Act, 31
United Nations Single Convention on Narcotic Drugs, 121

vertical integration, 131
victimless crime, 23–24
Volstead Act, 29

war on drugs, 2, 24, 27–28, 44, 46, 84, 98, 102, 113, 168, 199
Wickersham Prohibition Commission, 30

Youth Risk Behavior Survey (YRBS), 194

About the Editors

Nikolay Anguelov, PhD, is an associate professor of public policy at the University of Massachusetts, Dartmouth. He holds a PhD in policy studies with a specialization in regional economic development from Clemson University. Anguelov is the author of numerous academic articles and five books on political economy, notably *From Criminalizing to Decriminalizing Marijuana: The Politics of Social Control* (Lexington Books, 2018).

Jeffrey Moyer is visiting lecturer at Northeastern University, having earned his doctoral degree in public policy at the University of Massachusetts, Boston. His scholarly interests include drug policy, political diffusion, and democratic accountability in the face of technological and societal change.

About the Contributors

Paul Bacdayan, PhD, is an associate professor of management in the Charlton College of Business at the University of Massachusetts, Dartmouth. He earned his PhD in management at the University of Michigan, his MBA at Dartmouth College, and his BA at Yale College.

José Antonio Cisneros-Tirado, PhD, is a political scientist with a focus on democratic development and Latinx studies in the United States and Latin America. He graduated magna cum laude in international relations from UDLAP in Mexico, then pursued a master's degree and PhD in international development at the University of East Anglia in the United Kingdom. In 2016, he became a full-time professor at BUAP, Puebla, Mexico's fourth-largest public university, with more than 70,000 students. In 2021–2022, Cisneros Tirado was appointed Distinguished Visiting Professor in the Department of Government and Justice Studies at Appalachian State University.

Catherine M. Curran-Kelly, PhD, is the chair of the Department of Management and Marketing and associate professor of marketing in the Charlton College of Business at the University of Massachusetts, Dartmouth. She earned her PhD in marketing and her MBA at New Mexico State University, and her BA at Pennsylvania State University. Curran-Kelly is a Fulbright-Schuman Scholar.

Robert Hardaway is a professor of law at the University of Denver Sturm College of Law, and he has also taught evidence and procedure at George Washington Law School and the University of California (Hastings Law School). A former U.S. Navy JAG officer, county prosecutor, Colorado public defender, and private practice trial attorney, he is the author of dozens of law review articles, 24 books on law and public policy, including several treatises and casebooks, as well as hundreds of opinion articles in publications ranging from the *Los Angeles Times* to the *Chicago Tribune*. He has also appeared on a number of media outlets, including CNBC and CNN. His book *No Price too High: Victimless Crimes and the Ninth Amendment* (2003), with forewards by Gary Johnson and Federal Judge John L. Kane, addresses the lesson of prohibition in such areas as drugs, prostitution, and gambling.

Rebecca Ivester is a quantitative analyst at Abt Associates. Her background is in policy and policy analysis, and her primary work at Abt is focused on the processing and analysis of large data in criminal justice. Ivester's current projects include the National Corrections Reporting Program, the Statistical Support Program – Misdemeanors, and the Federal Justice Statistics Program.

Ryan Kling is a criminologist and statistician with more than 20 years of experience studying drug markets, drug use issues, and the federal justice system.

Maggie Martin, PhD, is an associate/scientist at Abt Associates, working primarily on criminal justice and behavioral health projects. At Abt, she directs an NIJ-funded project that assesses the association between marijuana legalization and changes in criminal justice processing, public health, and public safety outcomes. The NIJ study funded the work on Martin's book chapter. Martin holds a PhD in human development from Tufts University and an MA in psychology in education from Teachers College, Columbia University.

Céline Mavrot, PhD, is a postdoctoral fellow at the Yale University School of Public Health, New Haven, Connecticut, and the KPM Center for Public Management, University of Bern, Switzerland. She holds a doctorate in education from the University of Bern. Mavrot specializes in comparative policy analysis and policy evaluation. Her recent research focuses on public health controversies, for instance, tobacco control, published in *Public Policy and Administration*, and the COVID-19 crisis, published in *European Policy Analysis.*

Michael P. McCarthy, MPP, is the staff planner at the Planning Department in New Bedford, Massachusetts. He is a former senior policy analyst at the Public Policy Center, University of Massachusetts, Dartmouth. McCarthy is also a contributing author in *From Criminalizing to Decriminalizing Marijuana: The Politics of Social Control* (Lexington Books, 2018).

Marion McNabb, DrPH, MPH, is president of Cannabis Center of Excellence (CCOE), a 501c3 nonprofit organization that conducts citizen-science-focused population studies and programs in the areas of community engagement, medical cannabis, adult-use cannabis, and social justice in the cannabis industry. The CCOE serves as a virtual resource and network of cannabis industry professionals, academics, policymakers, healthcare providers, consumers, and patients who aim to break the stigma associated with cannabis and advance social justice. McNabb has more than 15 years of global public health experience working in the areas of digital health, HIV/AIDS, maternal and child health, and family planning, working primarily in Africa and Haiti. She earned her DrPH at the Boston University School of Public Health and her MPH at the Johns Hopkins University School of Public Health.

Melissa R. Michelson (PhD, Yale University) is dean of arts and sciences and professor of political science at Menlo College. She is a nationally recognized expert on Latinx politics, voter mobilization experiments, and LGBTQ rights, and past president of the LGBT Caucus and the Latino Caucus of the American Political Science Association. She is the award-winning author of seven books, notably *Mobilizing Inclusion: Transforming the Electorate through Get-Out-the-Vote Campaigns* (2012) and, most recently, *LGBTQ Life in America* (2021). Michelson's work also appears in a variety of top-rated academic journals and such popular outlets as the *Washington Post's* Monkey Cage blog.

Jesse Mishra is an associate analyst at Abt Associates. He provides research and evaluation support for projects related to criminal justice and health policy.

Paul Musgrave, PhD, is an assistant professor of political science at the University of Massachusetts, Amherst. He studies political parties and U.S. foreign policy, international relations theory, and how oil and politics mix. His research has appeared in *International Organization*, *International Studies Quarterly*, *Security Studies*, *Presidential Studies Quarterly*, and *Comparative Political Studies*, and he has written for the *Washington Post*, *Foreign Policy*, and other leading media outlets. He holds a PhD in government with a focus on international relations from Georgetown University.

Sonja Richard is a versatile health researcher with nine-plus years of experience, including numerous studies and initiatives for federal health agencies. She is highly skilled at data gathering and analysis, assessment development, project management, report writing, and technical assistance.

Maryam Salihu is a PhD student in the public policy program at the University of Massachusetts Boston. Her areas of interest include social and economic policy, as well as inter-country relations to reduce poverty. Before joining the doctoral program at the University of Massachusetts, Salihu worked as an analyst at Abt Associates, where she worked on criminal justice policy and international development.

Renee Scherlen is professor of political science at Appalachian State University. She holds a PhD in political science from the University of Texas. Her areas of teaching and research focus on U.S. foreign policy and Latin American politics. She is coauthor of *Lies, Damned Lies, and Drug War Statistics* (2014).

Joe R. Tafoya, PhD, is an assistant professor at DePaul University, Chicago. His research is focused on raising Latino political engagement, understanding evolving views toward immigrants, and advancing integration of recent arrivals to the United States. Tafoya is first generation in higher education and teaches courses in Latino politics, public opinion, and computational statistics.

Thalia Valkanos, MPP, is an environmental engineer with a strong interest in public policy. Her portfolio included environmental, energy, and judiciary issues. Valkanos works as the environmental, health, and safety supervisor at the Aspen Aerogels manufacturing facility in East Providence, Rhode Island.

Steven White, PhD, DBA, is a professor of marketing and international business in the Charlton College of Business, University of Massachusetts, Dartmouth. He earned his DBA in marketing and information systems and his MBA in international marketing at Cleveland State University, and his MA in interpersonal and public communication and BSBA in selling and sales management at Bowling Green State University.

Geoffrey Whitebread, PhD, is an assistant professor in the School of Civic Leadership, Business, and Social Change at Gallaudet University. His research uses a variety of methodological tools to advance the understanding of social equity in the public sector, including the intersectionality framework.

Clyde Wilcox, PhD, is a professor of government at Georgetown University and interim dean of Georgetown University in Qatar. He writes on religion and politics, gender politics, the politics of social issues, interest groups, campaign finance, and science fiction and politics. He has lectured in more than 40 countries and consulted for the syndicate *Mini Page*.

www.ingramcontent.com/pod-product-compliance
Lightning Source LLC
Chambersburg PA
CBHW050645280326
41932CB00015B/2787

* 9 7 8 1 7 9 3 6 5 1 5 4 9 *